ENGAGE IN PUBLIC SCHOLARSHIP!

Engage in Public Scholarship!
A Guidebook on Feminist and
Accessible Communication

Alex D. Ketchum

Concordia University Press
Montreal

Copyright Alex D. Ketchum 2022. CC BY-NC-ND.

Every reasonable effort has been made to acquire permission for copyright material used in this publication, and to acknowledge all such indebtedness accurately. Any errors and omissions called to the publisher's attention will be corrected in future printings.

Design and typesetting: LOKI
Proof reading: Saelan Twerdy
Index: Jess Klaassen-Wright

Printed and bound in Canada by Imprimerie Gauvin, Gatineau, QC

This book is printed on Forest Stewardship Council certified paper and meets the permanence of paper requirements of ANSI/NISO Z39.48-1992.

Engage in Public Scholarship! is set in Bitter by Sol Matas. Bitter's large x-heights are accentuated by thick stroke square serifs for increased print legibility and screen accessibility. Sans serif elements are set in the high-contrast Domaine Sans from Klim type.

Concordia University Press's books are available for free on several digital platforms. Visit www.concordia.ca/press

First English edition published in 2022
10 9 8 7 6 5 4 3 2 1

978-1-988111-35-3 Paper
978-1-988111-36-0 E-book

Library and Archives Canada Cataloguing in Publication

Title: Engage in public scholarship! : a guidebook on feminist and accessible communication / Alex D. Ketchum.
Names: Ketchum, Alex D., author.
Description: Includes bibliographical references and index.
Identifiers: Canadiana (print) 20210389508 | Canadiana (ebook) 20210389613 | ISBN 9781988111353 (softcover) | ISBN 9781988111360 (HTML)
Subjects: LCSH: Communication in the social sciences. | LCSH: Communication in the humanities. | LCSH: Communication in learning and scholarship. | LCSH: Feminism. | LCSH: Universities and colleges—Public services.
Classification: LCC H61.8 .K48 2022 | DDC 378.1/03—dc23

CONCORDIA   Concordia University Press
UNIVERSITY   1455 de Maisonneuve Blvd. W.
PRESS   Montreal, Quebec H3G 1M8

Concordia University Press gratefully acknowledges the generous support of the Birks Family Foundation, the Estate of Linda Kay, and the Estate of Tanneke De Zwart.

This book has been published with the help of a grant from the Federation for the Humanities and Social Sciences, through the Awards to Scholarly Publications Program, using funds provided by the Social Sciences and Humanities Research Council of Canada.

CONTENTS

	Part 1	**Challenges of Access and Accessibility**
3	Chapter 1	Introduction
22	Chapter 2	Benefits
35	Chapter 3	"Access" for the Audience and the Public
62	Chapter 4	"Access" for the Scholar
82	Chapter 5	Open Access
119	Chapter 6	Open Data and Open Source
	Part 2	**Toolkits**
137	Chapter 7	Proprietary Platforms, Corporate Influence, and Social Media
161	Chapter 8	Self-produced Digital Public Scholarship
196	Chapter 9	Self-produced Physical Forms of Public Scholarship
217	Chapter 10	Sustainability and Maintenance
243	Chapter 11	Events
279	Chapter 12	Working with Journalists and Writing Op-Eds
310	Chapter 13	Conclusion
315	Acknowledgements	
323	Bibliography	
342	Index	

PART 1
Challenges of Access and Accessibility

CHAPTER 1
Introduction

The form our creativity takes is often a class issue.
Audre Lorde

1 What Is Feminist and Accessible Scholarship?

Activist and writer Audre Lorde said of poetry: "Yet even the form our creativity takes is often a class issue. Of all the art forms, poetry is the most economical."[1] The form and genre of a publication reflects the position and conditions of the creator as much as the intended audience. This book addresses the challenges of creating feminist and accessible scholarship. While advocating for scholars to undertake public-facing work, this book confronts the oversimplified narratives surrounding this endeavour. Guided by Lorde's words, this volume takes seriously the class, gender, racial, sexual orientation, and disability of scholars as writers and creators, but does not stop there. The kind of work produced

---

1   Lorde, "Age, Race, Class, and Sex," p. 18.

by the scholar also impacts the kind of audience that is able to have access to it. In this way, this book examines the power dynamics that impact who gets to create certain kinds of academic work and for whom these outputs are accessible. The environmental, social, and economic conditions in which scholars are presently working, marked by digital technologies and climate change, matter.

Two initial questions guide this book: what is "feminist" scholarship? and what is "accessible" scholarship? This text does not focus on all feminist scholarship, but rather is interested in a feminist perspective on public-facing scholarship that aims to be accessible. These questions are further complicated by the challenge of sustainability.

1.1   What Is Accessible Scholarship?

What is "accessible" scholarship? For readers, researchers, and the public, barriers to accessing information range from paywalls for journal articles,[2] to hard-to-read texts, to images without alternative text descriptions that pose difficulties for people with visual impairments.[3] Even when texts are made freely available online, they require access to the internet, which is not universal.[4]

---

2   Suber, "Removing the Barriers to Research."

3   Shawn Newman, "Publishing Disability/Access," lecture, Disrupting Disruptions: The Feminist and Accessible Publishing, Communications, and Technologies Speaker and Workshop Series, McGill University, Montreal, Canada, February 25, 2019.

4   Porter and Donthu, "Using the Technology Acceptance Model to Explain How Attitudes Determine Internet Usage."

Introduction

Barriers to accessing information and audiences are not new phenomena. Issues over who could get published and who could connect with audiences plagued book publishing and bookstores in the second half of the twentieth century, as chronicled by librarian Kristen Hogan in *The Feminist Bookstore Movement: Lesbian Antiracism and Feminist Accountability*. These difficulties have been met with resistance. Hogan chronicles how lesbian feminists created presses, bookstores, and distribution networks. Other scholars have shown how marginalized communities have created periodicals, zines, and other forms of media when they have been unable to find traditional publishers.[5] More recent examples of resistance include changing pre-existing interfaces. Disability technology activist Chancey Fleet and editor Shawn Newman show that it is possible for journals and communications devices to be designed in a way that can be more effectively utilized by people with visual impairments.[6] Today, the most commonly proffered solutions to address the challenges of inaccessible publishing practices and barriers to knowledge dissemination rest with the internet and the promise of technological innovations. However, the technologies required for knowledge dissemination are not neutral but are, in fact, subject to bias. In addition, these technologies must be built and maintained—processes that raise questions of sustainability.

---

5   Kempson, "My Version of Feminism."
6   Chancey Fleet (guest) and Sareeta Amrute (host), "Dark Patterns in Accessibility Tech," *Databites* (podcast), episode 121, June 5, 2019, *Data and Society*, https://datasociety.net/library/dark-patterns-in-accessibility-tech/.

Engage in Public Scholarship!

In its current form, the internet does not solve the problem of inaccessible publishing practices. Although the internet theoretically levels the playing field and offers the promise of democratic access to knowledge and the ability to spread it, the reality is quite different.[7] In *Algorithms of Oppression*, information studies scholar Safiya Umoja Noble shows that, while we may assume that search engines such as Google offer an equal playing field to all ideas, identities, and activities, the combination of private interests and near-monopoly status of a small number of search engines leads to biases against women and people of colour down to the level of algorithms.[8] Similarly, in *Weapons of Math Destruction: How Big Data Increases Inequality and Threatens Democracy*, Cathy O'Neil shows that the algorithms—or mathematical models—being used today are unregulated and uncontested, and, importantly, reinforce discrimination. Technological developments rely both on who is creating the code and on the available data sets. Artist-researcher Mimi Onuoha's project Missing Datasets shows holes in data collection, particularly concerning women, people of colour, and LGBTQ communities.[9] Likewise, Lauren Klein and Catherine D'Ignazio's *Data Feminism* argues, "in a world in which data is power, and that power is wielded unequally, data feminism can help us understand how it can be challenged and changed."[10] These concerns are reflected

---

7   Morozov, *The Net Delusion.*
8   Noble, *Algorithms of Oppression.*
9   Onuoha, "On Missing Datasets."
10   Lauren Klein, "Data Feminism: Community, Allyship, and Action in the Digital Humanities," lecture, Disrupting Disruptions: The Feminist and Accessible Publishing, Communications, and Technologies Speaker and Workshop Series, McGill University, Montreal, Canada, October 25, 2019. Refer also to D'Ignazio and Klein, *Data Feminism.*

Introduction

in the AI Now Institute's 2018 Report, which states, "As the pervasiveness, complexity, and scale of these systems grow, this lack of meaningful accountability and oversight —including basic safeguards of responsibility, liability, and due process—is an increasingly urgent concern."[11] Cait McKinney, who writes on activist information management and interface design, shows that with thoughtful intent, digital technologies can be used to overcome, rather than reinforce, inequality.[12] It is this kind of thoughtful engagement with communications technologies and publishing that this project hopes to elicit.

The first part of this book focuses on the present challenges of feminist accessible scholarship and considers the above discussed complexities of access, including, but not limited to: paywalls, cost, valuation, technological barriers, and skill sets. This definition is expanded in chapter three. "Accessibility," then, becomes an objective rather than a definition.

1.2 What about Feminism?

Feminism provides useful tools for complicating the discussion around accessibility and public-facing scholarship. It is especially useful for thinking about the ethics of care, labour, and intersecting identities of producers and consumers of knowledge. Feminist

---

11 Whittaker et al., *AI Now 2018 Report,* p. 7.
12 McKinney, "Finding the Lines to My People."

theories bring to light the intertwined hierarchies embedded in doing this work. Feminist activists and scholars have extensively considered the role of power dynamics in communications strategies.

Feminists have long taken seriously the role of work and who is doing that work. Feminists have challenged workplace inequity since the 1960s (and as part of labour movements since the late nineteenth century). Philosopher and activist Silvia Federici's analysis of unpaid reproductive labour and its effects on the sexual division of labour, the globalization of care work, and the development of affective labour, particularly guides this book's analysis of the undervalued labour of public-facing scholarship, which is often relegated to the most marginalized scholars in the academy.[13] Public-facing work involves emotional labour, both in the sense of sociologist Arlie Hochschild's definition of the work that is required by certain professions of managing one's own emotions and in the way that subsequent writers, such as Gemma Hartley, have expanded this definition to include the unpaid, invisible work we do to keep those around us comfortable and happy.[14] This analysis envelops other terms associated with care-based labour such as emotion work, the mental load, mental burden, domestic management, clerical labour, and invisible labour. Important topics this book addresses include, Who will do this work of public scholarship? And who benefits from this work?

---

13   Federici, *Revolution at Point Zero.*
14   Hochschild, "Emotion Work, Feeling Rules, and Social Structure"; Hartley, *Fed Up.*

Introduction   9

Feminist theory can thus open up conversations around accessible, public scholarship in a radical way because it upturns the deeply oppressive norms around who does or who does not get to occupy spaces and produce the kinds of scholarly work that the academy values. As scholar of publishing Hannah McGregor argues, "there is a different feminist praxis in saying, 'I'm going to do this work such that people that have been deliberately excluded from it, it will be there for them vs I'm going to do this extra emotional labour for you because you have some extra right to my time and energy.'"[15] She shows that while both concepts fall under the word "accessible," one form can further marginalize and oppress when it requires constantly being available to people who think that they deserve your time and energy. A form of accessibility that includes boundaries and acknowledges labour politics has the potential to be liberatory. Feminist theory provides a useful analytical framework to understand the power dynamics that operate here.

There are many types of feminism. I am not interested in imposing a single prescriptive definition of feminism when discussing public-facing, accessible scholarship. The feminism of this text is, in the broadest sense, about the social, political, and economic equity of all sexes and genders. The feminist framework of this text seeks to create a socially just world and combats the forces of sexism, heterosexism, transphobia, racism, classism, ableism, and

---

15   Hannah McGregor (host), "Emoji Faces Feminist Friendship with Erin Wunker," *Secret Feminist Agenda* (podcast), September 8, 2017, https://secretfeministagenda.com/2017/09/08/episode-1-9-emoji-faces-feminist-friendship-with-erin-wunker/.

Engage in Public Scholarship! 10

colonialism, while taking environmental concerns seriously. Feminism is not static; rather, feminism is an ideal that one is striving towards. It is a process.

1.3 Sustainability

A focus on sustainability addresses one of the major challenges raised by this project. The AI Now Institute's 2019 report demonstrated that the "climate impact of AI development has become a particular area of concern, as recent research demonstrated that creating just one AI model for natural-language processing can emit as much as 600,000 pounds of carbon dioxide."[16] Servers storing large data sets, artificial intelligence and machine-learning computing processes, and increasing global internet usage all account for an ever-growing percentage of the world's energy consumption. Experts such as Jessica McLean estimate that this consumption will continue to grow.[17] In addition, while the climate impact of our technology is a pressing issue, this book also addresses a second meaning of sustainability: the challenge of maintenance, repair, and retention. In order to create truly feminist and accessible scholarship, sustainability, maintenance, and the right to repair are vital and increasingly important as our technological dependence deepens.

16 Whittaker and Crawford, *AI Now 2019 Report*, p. 13.
17 Jessica McLean, "For a Greener Future, We Must Accept There's Nothing Inherently Sustainable about Going Digital," *The Conversation,* December 16, 2019.

2 Context

This book is not the first call for scholars to create accessible, public-facing scholarship. We have witnessed an increased interest in circulating the results of research in the social sciences and humanities more broadly throughout society. This push for accessibility and public communications has been especially evident when considering publicly funded research. The Social Science and Humanities Research Council of Canada includes a mandate of public dissemination of findings in their funding applications. In the United States, the Andrew W. Mellon Foundation has committed itself to numerous endeavours to make research available. These projects range from digitization efforts, open-access projects, and funding experimental publications. With funding committees placing a greater emphasis on public scholarship, scholars in the humanities and social sciences need resources on how to actually *do* public-facing work. Simultaneously, this call comes at a time when social media and forums like blogs and podcasts have proliferated.[18] The Pew Center reports that more than 65 percent of adults use some form of social media.[19] At the moment there is a dearth of materials that address how to make one's work

---

18   Westerman, Spence, and Van Der Heide, "Social Media as Information Source."

19   Perrin, "Social Media Usage."

Engage in Public Scholarship!

accessible.[20] While the dissemination of research sounds inherently good, we need to think more thoroughly about what this actually means, and what public communications truly look like.

What this text does is bring together discussions of data bias, publishing practices, and labour rights within a feminist and accessibility discourse. While humanities and social science scholars will critique "traditional" academic publishing and communications strategies for being inaccessible, sexist, classist, and racially biased, the kinds of solutions proffered—such as open access and "innovative new technologies," which frequently involve machine learning and artificial intelligence (AI) in order to operate—often romanticize and fetishize technological

---

20 Most resources are relegated to posts on websites such as *Inside Higher Ed* (Joseph Stanhope Cialdella, "Connecting Public Scholarship and Professional Development," August 27, 2018; Nathan Jurgenson, "Making Our Ideas More Accessible," May 11, 2012) and *The Chronicle of Higher Education* (Julie Ellison, "Public Scholarship Deserves Standing," October 18, 2011). There are academic articles detailing why scholars must do academic work published in journals such as the *Journal of Higher Education Outreach and Engagement* (Barker, "The Scholarship of Engagement"; Bridger and Alter, "The Engaged University, Community Development, and Public Scholarship"), yet these fail to engage with most of the topics that this book will cover. The majority of texts focus on theory over praxis. Mira Sucharov's book, *Public Influence: A Guide to Op-Ed Writing and Social Media Engagement*, does offer useful tips, yet it is limited to only one aspect of public scholarship and does not discuss the complexities of the technologies that scholars will have to reckon with in the digital age. Likewise, Katharyne Mitchell's edited collection, *Practising Public Scholarship*, was published over a decade ago and while a useful resource, it does not include a thorough discussion of technology. Hannah McGregor's peer-reviewed podcast *Secret Feminist Agenda* speaks to the issues of public scholarship, feminism, and accessibility, yet barely touches the topic of technology.

Introduction

13

alternatives. These proposals do not look at how inequity can be perpetuated or only shifted—especially at the level of algorithms and data sets. The technologies behind open-access scholarship, self-publishing, website design, and other communicative technologies that humanities and social science scholars use as alternatives to traditional academic publishing are not neutral but are in fact subject to bias. As data journalist Meredith Broussard argues in *Artificial Unintelligence*, we must not fall into the trap of "technochauvinism" or assume that a technological solution is always better. Although this project is not merely about AI, it situates the ethical challenges of AI and data within larger discussions of technology, communications, and access. It is vital that humanities and social science scholars engage with these topics if we seek to truly expand accessibility and create ways of communicating our scholarship in a socially just manner.

3 What Is Included and for Whom

Public-facing scholarship can take a variety of forms. This book considers public-facing work done by scholars on social media; in refereed and non-refereed journals, magazines, and newspapers (whether or not they are open access); in books published both by university presses and trade presses; podcasts; blogs; project websites; digital humanities websites; videos and live streams. This book also discusses physical exhibits, public readings and performances, events, and conducting interviews with journalists as productive forms of translating one's research to the public.

This book provides scholars with practical solutions for public scholarship. Furthermore, it is useful for publishers, editors, computer scientists, and activists who want to think creatively and ethically about their communications strategies. Readers will not require previous knowledge about computer science, feminist theory, or labour rights, yet people with training in these topics will still find the discussions provoking.

This book is primarily directed at humanities and social science scholars. Federal funding bodies for scientific and medical research, such as the Natural Sciences and Engineering Research Council (NSERC) and the Canadian Institutes of Health Research (CIHR) in Canada, also require open-access publications (and did so before SSHRC). While certain science and medical research projects do contain data sets that must be kept private, components of the work and research can and should be explained publicly. Furthermore, this book does not negate the importance for natural scientists to communicate their research with the public. The importance of this task is underlined when thinking about global warming. Despite consensus among the scientific community regarding climate change, 39 percent of Canadians do not believe that climate change

Introduction

is driven by human activity.[21] The Yale Program on Climate Change Communication found that only 13 percent of Americans correctly identified that over 90 percent of all climate scientists have concluded that human-caused global warming is occurring.[22] These percentages show a gap between scientific evidence and public understanding of this vital issue. The co-founder of Communication Partnership for Science and the Sea (COMPASS), Jane Lubchenco, argues that "scientists have a tremendous amount to contribute to solving society's most pressing problems and many are eager to engage with society, but they often need help in learning how to be effective."[23] Looking at ways scientists and environmentalists have historically tried to communicate with the public will aid in current efforts to improve their methods for imparting scientific knowledge to non-scientists. Groups such as COMPASS have sought to do this work. While the natural sciences must contend with questions of how to communicate their work to the public and may find the discussions and strategies provided in this book beneficial, a deep engagement with the natural sciences is outside of the scope of this book.

---

21 Mildenberger et al., "The Distribution of Climate Change Public Opinion in Canada."
22 The Yale Program on Climate Change Communication, "Yale Climate Opinions Maps," January 1, 2014, https://climatecommunication.yale.edu/about/projects/yale-climate-opinion-maps/.
23 COMPASS, "About," 2017, https://www.compassscicomm.org/.

4   Organization

This project began with a series of questions: What are effective strategies for scholars to disseminate their research, especially beyond the academy? How can scholars accountably communicate their work with the public and not perpetuate problematic dynamics? What does it mean for publishing to be accessible and feminist? What forms of knowledge dissemination are most socially just? How are different forms of knowledge dissemination valued? What is the historical context of these discussions? This project seeks to address these questions and more.

This book looks at the various methods available for knowledge dissemination. It is guided by the principles of what art historian Jon Bath describes as a "public first scholarship," in which work is made initially with the public in mind, rather than creating "traditional" research outputs within a university context and then making it public later.[24] Although this book will present a number of challenges, the goal is not to dissuade but rather encourage and promote accessible scholarship. It is through recognizing these barriers and difficulties that this book hopes to open possibilities for publicly accessible scholarship. Rather than offer empty rhetoric, this book puts material conditions at the forefront.

The book is divided into two parts. It begins by examining the benefits of public scholarship for the researcher, for the public,

24   Bath, "Artistic Research Creation for Publicly Engaged Scholarship."

Introduction

for the university, and for the world at large. This conversation is framed within a discourse that acknowledges the threat of the post-truth era, and understands the importance of an informed public within the framework of digital citizenship to counter disinformation campaigns.[25] By focusing on the benefits and challenges of publicly accessible scholarship, this book delves into the inherent neoliberal paradoxes in this subject: the university wants engagement with the larger community, but does not like activism; the university wants more public resonance, but does not value this labour as much as specialized, inaccessible scholarship; the university wants instructors to publish more scholarship, but overburdens them with an overwhelming teaching load. This book does not argue against specialization or the benefits of framing conversations at times for a small group of peers; however, this book challenges the systematic preferencing of a specific kind of publication/dissemination as having preeminence.

The third and fourth chapters delve into the question and complexity of accessibility. This section will make clear that the forms of access being discussed are wide ranging. By highlighting that accessibility includes issues of disability, class, education, linguistics, region, technology, and training, we will have a more specific understanding of what we mean when we discuss "the public" in public scholarship. Issues of accessibility go beyond readership/users. There are barriers that can limit who is able to do public scholarship.

---

25   Mutale Nkonde (guest), "Episode 96: Intersection of Race and Technology," *Sunday Civics* (podcast), 2020, https://www.sundaycivics.org/episodes/episode96.

Engage in Public Scholarship! 18

The costs of public scholarship are greater for scholars from marginalized identities within the academy. Not enough attention has been given to the gender, racial, and class identities of the researchers who are able to do this kind of work. This section shows the labour issues involved in public scholarship. A further discussion of the conditions of academic in/justice pertaining to the hiring power of certain academic positions is flushed out in the appendix.

Chapters five and six discuss issues with the concept of "openness," as it relates to open access, open source, and open data. It concludes with the idea that openness is not a goal in and of itself, but the result of a just, feminist framework. These chapters also address the question: Open for whom? Making more information available is not the solution for every context. As always, questions of remuneration are at the forefront. Critiques of techno-utopianism and technochauvinism inform this conversation. As will be explored in the next section, technology is not invariably the solution—there are problems that come with technologies.

The second part of the book consists of toolkits. Chapters seven, eight, and nine offer practical strategies for engaging in public scholarship. This section begins by exploring the ways to determine the digital and physical forms for your public scholarship. Does it make the most sense for you to create zines? To build websites, to start a podcast, to engage audiences through social media, and/or more? These chapters also address the problems with the technologies that enable public scholarship, and as a result, this section complicates and challenges much of the existing literature

Introduction 19

on public scholarship. By looking at the issues behind the technologies often touted as the solutions for public scholarship, this section will push scholars to think critically about the tools they use for their work. Pivotal to this discussion is the understanding that tech is not neutral. In order to demonstrate these challenges, I discuss corporate control of "new media" and web platforms, algorithmic bias, and Big Data. Since electronic products still tie the digital to physical landscapes, I also address mining, e-waste, and how environmental burdens of the supply chain are disproportionately borne by people in the Global South. The next chapter addresses the topic of sustainability.

Chapter ten addresses challenges facing scholars creating public scholarship including labour, remuneration, and environmental degradation. Questions surrounding the sunsetting of projects, digital humanities projects' maintenance, the "right to repair," and the risk of the "digital dark ages" contribute to these dynamics. As this book does not want to dwell only on problems, this chapter also offers solutions to the issues raised.

Chapters eleven and twelve proffer more advice on distribution. The first looks at what it means to create and curate accessible events as a form of public scholarship, and the following chapter takes seriously the intellectual work of collaboration with journalists.

While this book provides an overview of conversations relating to accessibility, this text does not include an in-depth discussion of the barriers that determine who enters the

Engage in Public Scholarship!

academy, what kinds of knowledges are valued, and critiques of peer review. For more information about these debates, see the work of Patricia Hill Collins,[26] Alison Jaggar,[27]and Karen Potts and Leslie Brown.[28]

5 A Note on Citational Practices

Inspired by the work of Rigoberto Lara Guzmán, Sareeta Amrute, and Alexandra Mateescu's zine, *How to Cite Like a Badass Tech Feminist Scholar of Color*, this book employs citational practices that re-centre the voices of women, queer folks, and people of colour whose work is often overlooked in traditional academic texts, even when these scholars are the ones doing the on-the-ground work.[29] Citational practices are political and can uphold oppressive hierarchies of what kinds of knowledge are considered legitimate.[30] As this project seeks to destabilize academic hierarchies that determine what counts as legitimate scholarship, the book follows in the path of scholars such as Therí Pickens who (in texts such as *Black Madness :: Mad Blackness*) have used citational practices to move "beyond the strictures of traditional academic

---

26 Collins, *Black Feminist Thought.*
27 Jaggar, *Just Methods.*
28 Potts and Brown, "Becoming an Anti-oppressive Researcher."
29 Refer to Chakravartty et al., "#CommunicationSoWhite."
30 Liboiron et al., "Equity in Author Order."

Introduction 21

or institutional structures."[31] Amongst peer-reviewed academic articles and monographs, this book cites podcasts, films, zines, radio interviews, social media posts, public appearances, and poetry.

6   TL;DR

To summarize this section and avoid the issue of "too long; didn't read," this text serves as an introduction to the key challenges to feminist and accessible public scholarship. It is a survey focused on making readers aware of debates and offering solutions. As a result, this book is more expository than argumentative. This book demonstrates that public scholarship is necessary and needed, that there are often unrecognized challenges, and that there are solutions to move forward and make public scholarship a more accessible endeavour for readers/users and writers/creators alike. Therefore, the key scholarly contribution this text makes is bringing these topics together in a single volume and showing how integral the oft-overlooked components of labour rights and technology are when considering what it means to create public-facing scholarship. This project provides the framework to rethink credentials and conventions, and to establish adjudicative criteria for the success of newer forms of media, all while remaining acutely aware of the risks that marginalized scholars experience when undertaking public engagement.

---

31   Pickens, *Black Madness :: Mad Blackness*, p. x.

CHAPTER 2

Benefits

While this book will discuss the numerous challenges that exist for scholars interested in feminist and accessible publishing practices, this book will not function as merely a critique. Public-facing, feminist, and accessible scholarship is important and worthwhile. There are benefits to doing this work for individual scholars, for their institutions, and for society at large. This chapter will expand on the big-picture benefits for these groups. The following chapters will then detail more specific benefits for these communities.

1 Digital Citizenship and the Post-truth Era

Feminist and accessible publishing is particularly relevant in the recent political climate. In 2016, the Oxford English

Benefits

Dictionary's word of the year was "post-truth," which was defined as "relating to or denoting circumstances in which objective facts are less influential in shaping public opinion than appeals to emotion and personal belief." Since then, more attention has been given to the role of scholars in combating misinformation. As Elizabeth Davis and Megan Boler argue in their book, *Affective Politics of Digital Media*, there is a need for robust interdisciplinary scholarship on the relationship between modern information economies, digitally mediated sociality and emotionality, the resurgence of Western fascisms, and the rise of grassroots justice (and injustice) movements in the age of "post truth." Now more than ever it is necessary that scholars effectively communicate with the public to solidify trust in scholarship. The practices described in this book lead to more robust scholarship and invite public participation during the post-truth era, in which there is a circuitous slippage between facts and alt-facts, knowledge, opinion, belief, and truth. Building on her prior book, *The People's Platform: Taking Back Power in the Digital Age*, writer and activist Astra Taylor's *Democracy May Not Exist, But We Will Miss It When It Is Gone* argues that this work is vital in order to protect democratic institutions. Feminist and accessible publishing fosters literacy in the post-truth era, while drawing attention to the labour and material conditions behind this pursuit.

Employing feminist and accessible publishing and technological communications strategies is vital to helping the public understand online disinformation and its impact on society, ultimately reinforcing democratic and citizen resilience. As sociologist Jessie Daniels and librarian Polly Thistlethwaite argue in *Being a Scholar in the Digital Era*, the "proliferation of digital technologies is changing what it means to be a scholar now in ways that are at once exciting, foreboding, and puzzling."[1] Similarly, educational technologist Martin Weller shows that the internet, in particular, shifts many scholarly practices.[2] By being accountable to different audiences, scholars who apply feminist and accessible publishing and communications technologies help combat online disinformation of the post-truth era. Such work promotes greater media literacy.

The creation of effective tools for scholars to communicate their research to the public further benefits the public by giving them greater access to expert research. In 2019, the University of Minnesota Press released a statement on the value of university presses. The piece noted that

> the primary responsibility of a scholarly press is to publish verified knowledge and informed, fact-based debate. And yes, that is more critical now than ever. In the two decades since the original "Values" statement, we've all witnessed the rise of clickbait media, the hollowing out of news and opinion sources under profit-driven corporate ownership, and the suppression of knowledge and open debate by political interests … At a time when facts are literally under siege, we demonstrate the importance of verified knowledge and

---

1   Daniels and Thistlethwaite, *Being a Scholar in the Digital Era*, p. 1.
2   Weller, *The Digital Scholar.*

Benefits

the university research mission. Universities and our society at large don't always realize it, but they need us.[3]

It is not solely the responsibility of university presses to do this work. The Federation for the Humanities and Social Sciences of Canada promotes research and teaching for the advancement of an inclusive, democratic, and prosperous society. The Federation endeavours "to strengthen, promote, and, where necessary, defend the contributions of the humanities and the arts to human flourishing and to the well-being of diverse and democratic societies."[4] Scholars have a responsibility to do this work in both refereed and non-refereed publications. However, while interest exists in doing this kind of work due to the vital role it has in protecting our democratic institutions, few resources advise scholars how to proceed.

2   Academic Institutions and Public Accountability

The increased interest in circulating the results of research more broadly throughout society stems from financial imperatives in addition to political motivations. When

---

3   University of Minnesota Board of Directors, "Value of University Presses," University of Minnesota Press website, 2019, https://www.upress.umn.edu/about-us/the-value-of-university-presses.

4   Federation for the Humanities and Social Sciences of Canada, "About," 2019, https://www.ideas-idees.ca/about/about-the-federation.

Engage in Public Scholarship! 26

research is publicly funded through state, provincial, or federal funding bodies, it is necessary to justify how tax dollars are spent. Further, when research is cloistered behind paywalls, written in inaccessible jargon, and undertaken without explanation of why the project matters, public support and money for institutions fades. However, when research funding bodies and universities show how the work is a public good it is easier to justify expenses, especially during an age of austerity.

Employees at governmental and non-governmental policy-making institutions often do not have access to academic articles behind paywalls. As a result, even if a scholar's research would be useful to inform policy making, the piece cannot fulfil its potential impact when employees and researchers outside of the academy cannot access research results. In order to address these concerns, the Social Science and Humanities Research Council of Canada includes a mandate for the public dissemination of findings in its funding applications and publishes a list of projects it has funded. The parallel federal funding bodies for science and medical research include similar requirements. However, these laudable requirements only apply to the work funded by these bodies. Chapters five and six will speak to the limitations of these measures in more detail, but the impetus for justifying the use of public funds remains.

The mandate of public dissemination is not made to stifle specialized publication practices in which experts can communicate with one another. Instead, it acknowledges that when research languishes behind paywalls, it is difficult

Benefits

27

for this work to benefit the public at large and influence public policy. Later sections of this book will detail how to create different versions of one's research and how to communicate various results. One of those methods is the opinion editorial, henceforth referred to as the op-ed. Describing the role of academics' ability to influence public policy through op-ed writing, Bob Sommer and John Maycroft show that "for academics who are experts in their field and want to have a more direct impact upon public policy debate, publishing an op-ed is vital—both for gaining attention and to enhance credibility with policy makers. A successful op-ed shows that an academic knows what policy makers need and understands that policy making is messier in the capitol than it is in academia."[5] They continue to discuss the ways that op-eds enable academics to extend their expertise beyond the reach of scholarly circles and into civic conversation, as "the op-ed page also provides a forum in which academics, policy makers, and the public can debate the meaning and practical implications of scholarly knowledge ... bringing interest to ideas that might otherwise remain limited to academic journals."[6] So often academic research is not applied to policy, or able to be taken up by community organizations when it could be. The authors show that "not including the citation of government reports, just more than one-quarter of the op-eds (27 percent) did mention academic or institutional study results."[7] While Sommer and Maycroft show that academics can use op-eds

---

5   Sommer and Maycroft, "Influencing Public Policy," p. 588.
6   Sommer and Maycroft, "Influencing Public Policy," p. 590.
7   Sommer and Maycroft, "Influencing Public Policy," p. 595.

as mechanisms for change or setting a political agenda, creating other forms of accessible scholarship has this benefit as well.

Creating scholarship that can be considered by government officials, policy makers, and even community groups bolsters democratic principles. Encouraging the general public to participate in scholarly discussions can lead to more informed participation in civic life. As psychologists Amy Chapman and Christine Greenhow argue, "in the era of 'fake news,' the distribution and discussion of accurate and timely research is critical, and citizen-scholars, through open, public, and social scholarship, can play a significant role in promoting an informed citizenry."[8] They are particularly interested in how scholars use social media platforms to disseminate their work, a practice they call "social scholarship." Chapman and Greenhow show that "social scholarship integrates the use of these social media tools throughout the research and publication process in ways that promote wider access, openness, transparency, and collaboration."[9] This approach differs from Sommer and Maycroft's as it relies on social media rather than the older media techniques of op-eds, and as a result, allows scholars to reach different publics and thus be responsible to different publics. Readers of newspaper op-eds may not be the same audiences that one can address with social media. Social media can be particularly useful in addressing smaller, or more specific, publics.

8   Chapman and Greenhow, "Citizen-Scholars," p. 7.
9   Chapman and Greenhow, "Citizen-Scholars," p. 5.

3 Social Media and Scholarship: Smaller Communities

Misinformation can circulate rapidly on social media platforms; however, this does not negate the important role of social media as part of the feminist and accessible publishing and communications technologies toolkit. Social media platforms enable academics to respond and attend to communities outside of formal academic structures in ways that peer-reviewed articles cannot. Technology scholars Stefania Manca and Maria Ranieri show that research on "scholars' use of social media suggests that these sites are increasingly being used to enhance scholarly communication by strengthening relationships, facilitating collaboration among peers, publishing and sharing research products, and discussing research topics in open and public formats."[10] These digital spaces are not limited to formal constraints for research communication. Amy Chapman and Christine Greenhow argue further that "in addition to ... using Twitter to promote wider access, openness, transparency, and collaboration through social scholarship, other social media such as Facebook and the academic social network sites (ResearchGate and Academia. edu) also have the potential to influence open, social scholarly

---

10 Manca and Ranieri, "Networked Scholarship and Motivations for Social Media Use in Scholarly Communication," p. 123.

Engage in Public Scholarship! 30

practices."[11] Manca and Ranieri contend that "generic social media sites such as blogs or Twitter may stretch social boundaries, enabling more powerful mechanisms of serendipity, hybridization, and cross-fertilization than those generated by specialized academic social media sites."[12] Choice of platform shapes the effectiveness of the discourse and especially influences the kinds of communities that the researcher engages.

Social media can be particularly useful for communicating with and amongst certain subcultures and marginalized communities. Media scholar André Brock's research on the role of Black Twitter[13] is particularly pertinent. He states that "Twitter's combination of brevity, multi-platform access, and feedback mechanisms has enabled it to gain mindshare far out of proportion to its actual user base, including an extraordinary number of Black users."[14] Communications scholar Sherri Williams adds that "Black feminists' use of hashtag activism is a unique fusion of social justice, technology, and citizen journalism ... It should serve as a fertile ground for emerging news for journalists, a point of connection for white feminists, and a ripe area of study for academics."[15] Outside of Black Twitter, social media platforms have been useful for scholars to communicate

---

11   Chapman and Greenhow, "Citizen-Scholars," p. 5.

12   Manca and Ranieri, "Networked Scholarship and Motivations for Social Media Use in Scholarly Communication," p. 134.

13   The phrase "Black Twitter" comes from Choire Sicha's article, "What Were Black People Talking About on Twitter Last Night?" *The Awl*, November 11, 2009.

14   Brock Jr., "From the Blackhand Side," p. 529.

15   Williams, "Digital Defense," p. 343.

Benefits 31

with colleagues and potential audiences outside of the academy. This work, which will be expanded upon in chapter seven, ranges from sharing already produced research to building new ways of articulating inquiries and results, to these platforms being sites of academic inquiry in and of themselves. The use of social media by scholars further expands the potential audience for academic research, and calls into question how audiences are created and what work is available to them. As will be discussed more in chapters five and six, being allegedly "open" or accessible is not the same as being "findable" or "found."

4 Accountability to Different Audiences Aids Individual Scholars

Although the material and practical challenges that doing public-facing research poses to scholars will be discussed later in this book, there are numerous benefits for scholars as individuals. Having to explain how your research impacts society benefits your work. New audiences raise new questions and approaches that an individual researcher may not have considered before. As science communicator Rackeb Tesfaye explained when discussing her podcast *Broad Science*, in which children ask scientists to explain their research, the kinds of questions kids ask actually help researchers think about

Engage in Public Scholarship!   32

their projects differently.[16] Speaking about one's research at bookstores, being interviewed by journalists, tweeting, or writing a blog post, yields different questions and insights from the various audience members. These lines of inquiry serve to inspire and challenge. By making research accountable to different audiences, the work itself is strengthened.

5   Beyond Doing Research "On": Doing Research "With"

Feminist and accessible publishing and communications practices ask scholars to move beyond doing research "on" and instead do research "with." Philosopher Lorraine Code shows how "a society legitimates presumptions of credibility and trust that attach differently according to how speakers and interpreters are positioned within them."[17] Feminist and accessible publishing and communications practices allow us to think critically about whose knowledge is valued. Building on the work of other feminist researchers, such as sociologist Patricia

---

16   Rackeb Tesfay, "Broad Science and Intersectional Approaches," lecture, Disrupting Disruptions: The Feminist and Accessible Publishing, Communications, and Technologies Speaker and Workshop Series, March 15, 2020, YouTube video, 1:09:02, https://www.youtube.com/watch?v=M-WLbaFzcPg& feature=emb logo.

17   Code, "Incredulity, Experientialism and the Politics of Knowledge," p. 291.

Benefits 33

Hill Collins and historian Joan W. Scott,[18] we can move beyond a hierarchical research dynamic in which positivist approaches maintain preeminence. Rather, we can look to other ways of knowing, be they from the point of emotion or experience.

Public-facing scholarship does not wholly disrupt the power dynamics between researcher and subject. However, there is the potential to build new kinds of research relationships when research includes a framework that social workers Karen Potts and Leslie Brown call "becoming an anti-oppressive researcher." They write, "being an anti-oppressive researcher means that there is political purpose and action to your research work ... It means making a commitment to the people you are working with personally and professionally in order to mutually foster conditions for social justice and research. It is about paying attention to, and shifting, how power relations work in and through the processes of doing research."[19] Accessible methods of distribution are key to anti-oppressive research; part of this work means that the people you work with should be able to access research outputs. Giving a PDF of an article is not enough. Rather, the researcher must communicate with the community in ways that are useful to it. To write "about" a community without having a means of distributing findings to that group is irresponsible scholarship.

---

18 Collins, "Learning from the Outsider Within"; Scott, "Experience."
19 Potts and Brown, "Becoming an Anti-oppressive Researcher," p. 255.

6 Conclusion

While there are multiple barriers to doing publicly accessible scholarship, there are also benefits. Publicly accessible work is rarely paid. It requires learning new skill sets. It is barely taken into account in academic job applications and tenure files. It makes researchers vulnerable to doxxing and racist and sexist online attacks. Most of these barriers are institutional, yet they are felt by individuals. It is particularly important that those with the most power—and not only those who are most vulnerable—embrace strategies of public scholarship. Through modelling other forms of scholarship, the most privileged individuals within an institution can set new standards by which others can be judged. Through lowering risk and expanding who can participate in public scholarship, researchers, universities, and society will benefit. New audiences allow scholars to hear fresh perspectives on their work that can enable further insight and collaboration. Writing in new genres and distributing findings on non-traditional platforms can spark creativity and even be pleasurable. More diverse communities will be able to access research and divisions between academic institutions and those outside of them will decrease.

CHAPTER 3

"Access" for the Audience and the Public

1 Accessible Scholarship Is Accessible for Whom?

This chapter thinks critically about the question, for whom is accessible scholarship actually accessible? Who is the imagined audience for public-facing scholarship? In addition, who or what is the public? What barriers prevent potential audiences or publics from accessing this scholarship? As scholars, what can we do to reduce or mitigate these problems? The chapter begins by proffering a definition of the "public" in public scholarship. Next, the chapter engages with disability studies discourses and offers design justice as a framework from which to approach questions of accessibility. This chapter continues to discuss multiple barriers for audiences, such as language, visual and auditory access, and access to technology. Although the discussion of planning accessible events is reserved for chapter eleven, this chapter provides grounding and context for why certain measures are necessary. Awareness of these barriers is the first step to empower scholars to mitigate them.

1.1   Public

The concept of accessible scholarship imagines an audience, usually referred to as "the public." Who actually is the public? Are scholars part of the public? Are we referring to audiences outside of the academy? The Merriam-Webster definition of "public" includes "affecting all the people or the whole area of a nation or state," "being in the service of the community or nation," "accessible to or shared by all members of the community," and "of or relating to business or community interests as opposed to private affairs." These definitions are insufficient for the purposes of this project. They either refer to the confines of the nation state, to which this project is not bound; or they speak of a division from private business and are thus divorced from the context of this book; or they refer to the idea of "community"—a concept that raises new questions such as "who or what is the community?" Works referring to the "public" rarely define "the public" and the notion is thus then taken for granted and risks misunderstanding.

For the purposes of this book, "the public" refers to an audience comprised of people who are not directly involved in academic institutions. This definition does not mean that this audience has never taken part in the academy, but rather that forms of scholarly communications such as

"Access" for the Audience and the Public

peer-reviewed journals, monographs, and academic conferences are not their primary methods of communicating and gathering information. Therefore, scholars can exist both as part of the academy and also as part of the public for different aspects of their lives. This conceptualization of the public becomes useful when imagining an audience for scholarly outputs, whether traditional or non-traditional.

The public is heterogeneous. As a result, knowing your intended audience is key to knowing which public you are trying to address and for whom you are attempting to make your work accessible. The risk of imagining one's audiences is that one's own biases may prevent a scholar from thinking about whom could be included or excluded from accessing their work. Able-bodied privilege is one form of privilege that may make many barriers to access less obvious. You might not be aware that the only entry to a building has stairs if you do not have mobility issues. If you are not hard of hearing, you might not prioritize creating transcripts for your podcast or circulating text versions of a talk in advance. This chapter will draw attention to different barriers that may prevent potential audiences from accessing public scholarship, with the goal that you will keep these considerations in mind when you create your public communications.

1.2 How Can Something Be Accessible for All Publics?

How can scholarly dissemination be accessible for all publics? In short: it cannot. There will always be limitations

Engage in Public Scholarship! 38

to the reach of scholarly outputs. As disability justice advocate Lydia X.Z. Brown remarked, "we're never going to find a setup that works for literally everybody."[1] In other work, Brown builds upon this concept, noting "there is no one size fits all."[2] Evidenced below, there are always limitations to scholarly publications and communications strategies. It is important to understand the limitations of one's output to find the appropriate form the publication should take. In some cases, it might mean producing more than one kind of output.

Disability justice scholars and activists provide helpful frameworks through which to approach the work of creating feminist and accessible public scholarship and communications.[3] From a disability studies perspective, we need to think of the kind of barriers that prevent people from being able to actually access the materials that we produce. We also need to think of the social contexts that prevent someone from being able to actually interact with our work. In addition, there is the matter of the hurdles that exist in the work itself. One in five people in the United States

---

1   Patty Berne, Lydia X.Z. Brown, Leah Lakshmi Piepzna-Samarasinha, and Allegra Heath-Stout, "Podcast Episode 61: Organizing in a Pandemic: Disability Justice Wisdom," *Irresistible* (podcast), April 14, 2020, https://irresistible.org/podcast/61.

2   Matt Mullenweg (host) and Lydia X.Z. Brown (guest), "Episode 13: Attorney Lydia X.Z. Brown on Making Work More Accessible," *The Distributed Podcast* (podcast), October 31, 2019, https://distributed.blog/2019/10/31/episode-13-attorney-lydia-x-z-brown-on-making-work-more-accessible/.

3   Simplican, "Feminist Disability Studies as Methodology."

"Access" for the Audience and the Public   39

lives with a disability.[4] Around 6.2 million Canadians live
with a disability, or roughly 1 in 6 people,[5] and 13.9 million
people in the United Kingdom are living with a disability
—approximately 1 in 4.7 people).[6] As disability justice advocate
Alice Wong makes clear in her book *Disability Visibility*, while
some disabilities are visible and others are less apparent,
all are underrepresented in media and popular culture. It
is because of this lack of representation we must listen to
and re-centre the perspectives of people with disabilities,[7]
especially when we think about making public scholarship
inclusive and accessible. Influenced by the work of disability
studies advocates such as Alison Kafer, who fuses feminist
theory, queer theory, and disability studies,[8] and Leah Lakshmi
Piepzna-Samarasinha, who encourages us to not think
of collective access as a chore but instead as a collective
responsibility and pleasure—in our communities and political
movements,[9] this book complicates the conceptualization
of accessible public scholarship. The writing of each chapter
of this book was guided by asking, who is the audience for

4   CDC Newsroom, "CDC: 53 Million Adults in the US Live with a Disability,"
    July 30, 2015, https://www.cdc.gov/media/releases/2015/p0730-US-
    disability.html.
5   Stuart Morris, Gail Fawcett, Linden R. Timoney, and Jeffrey Hughes,
    "The Dynamics of Disability: Progressive, Recurrent or Fluctuating
    Limitations," *Canadian Survey on Disability Reports,* December 2, 2019,
    https://www150.statcan.gc.ca/n1/pub/89-654-x/89-654-x2019002-eng.
    htm.
6   Department for Work and Pensions, "Family Resources Survey 2016/17,"
    Gov.uk, March 22, 2018, https://assets.publishing.service.gov.uk/
    government/uploads/system/uploads/attachment_data/file/692771/
    family-resources-survey-2016-17.pdf.
7   Sins Invalid Collective, "Mission and Vision," 2020, https://www.
    sinsinvalid.org/mission.
8   Kafer, *Feminist, Queer, Crip.*
9   Piepzna-Samarasinha, *Care Work.*

whom we are trying to make our work accessible and what more can be done to increase access?

Prioritizing accessibility not only benefits individuals with visible or known physical, psychological, or cognitive disabilities. While frameworks such as universal design (UD) at first appear to offer the tools necessary to do this work, Aimi Hamraie shows that while "often taken for granted as synonymous with the best, most inclusive, forms of disability access, the values, methodologies, and epistemologies that underlie UD require closer scrutiny."[10] As Sasha Costanza-Chock likewise argues, universal design emphasizes that

> we should try to design for everybody and that by including those who are often excluded from design considerations, we can make objects, places, and systems that ultimately function better for all people. [However], disability justice shares that goal, but also acknowledges both that some people are always advantaged and others disadvantaged by any given design, and that this distribution is influenced by intersecting structures of race, class, gender, and disability.[11]

Instead, Costanza-Chock and the Design Justice Network offer the framework of design justice.

---

10 Hamraie, "Designing Collective Access."
11 Costanza-Chock, "Design Justice, AI, and Escape from the Matrix of Domination," p. 53.

"Access" for the Audience and the Public 41

A design justice framework works to ensure that all participants, including individuals with obvious and non-obvious disabilities and/or chronic health conditions, people of all ages and body types, individuals across the gender spectrum and of all sexual orientations, from all class, racial, and ethnic backgrounds are able to engage in and with the work. According to Costanza-Chock, "design justice, in other words, requires that we specify, consider, and intentionally decide how to best allocate both benefits and harms of the objects and systems we design, with attention to their use context." She clarifies that "it doesn't mean the lowest common-denominator design. Quite the opposite: it means highly specific, intentional, custom design that takes multiple standpoints into account. It is not about eliminating the benefits of excellent design unless everyone can access them; instead, it is about more fairly allocating those benefits."[12] Rather than focus on making "accommodations," which shifts the burden to the individual participants and acts as a retroactive patch to overcome barriers in an environment or system, accessibility from a design justice standpoint means that you will design your work to be inclusive for the communities that you aim to reach from the start. The goal is that the publication will not require adaptation or modification to remove barriers to participate. Design justice is not about "limit[ing] ourselves to a minimal set of supposedly universal design choices, but rather as a prism through which to generate a far wider rainbow of possible choices, each better tailored to reflect the needs

---

12 Costanza-Chock, "Design Justice, AI, and Escape from the Matrix of Domination," p. 230.

Engage in Public Scholarship! 42

of a specific group of people."[13] However, as noted by Lydia X.Z. Brown, this may mean that you produce multiple forms of the same material, intended for different audiences.[14]

While design justice provides a useful approach for thinking about public scholarship and communications, it is not without its limitations. Sociologist Ruha Benjamin worries that an over-reliance on design thinking means that in an unequal society, some humans will be prioritized over others in human-centred design. Further, Benjamin wonders if "in enrolling so many issues and experiences as design-related ... it could also sanitize and make palatable deep-seated injustices, contained within the innovative practices of design."[15] Remaining cognizant of Benjamin's push back against design, this book acknowledges that while design justice is not the only framework available, it is useful for guiding how scholars approach and design the form their scholarly outputs for the public will take.

2   Language and Jargon

Language, in multiple senses, poses barriers to accessibility. Even when an audience can actually access a publication,

---

13   Costanza-Chock, "Design Justice, AI, and Escape from the Matrix of Domination," p. 230.
14   Berne, Brown, Piepzna-Samarasinha, and Heath-Stout, "Podcast Episode 61: Organizing in a Pandemic: Disability Justice Wisdom."
15   Benjamin, *Race After Technology*, p. 176.

"Access" for the Audience and the Public

the content itself might not actually be accessible depending on the intended audience. Barriers include the choice of language, literacy, and choices surrounding vocabulary.

Every scholar makes decisions around the language of their publications. Take this book, for example. It is written in English. This means that the book is not readily accessible for people who cannot read English. That does not mean that the book is completely inaccessible. The book may later be translated by professional translators. Translation applications such as Google Translate or DeepL might provide readers with some understanding. Due to the audience this book aims to target, publishing this text in English makes sense, but that does not make it completely accessible. Language limits access.

Not everyone can read, whether sighted or not. According to the National Centre for Education Statistics, one in five US adults (21 percent) have "insufficient" English literacy skills.[16] In Canada, as of 2012, only 51.5 percent had level 3 literacy, which is defined as the ability to read and navigate dense, lengthy, or complex texts.[17] People who are Blind or have difficulty seeing may be unable to read your words. Technologies such as screen readers or text-to-speech apps

---

16 Statistics Canada, "Literacy in the Information Age: Final Report of the International Adult Literacy Survey," *Organisation for Economic Co-Operation and Development*, 2020, http://www.oecd.org/education/skills-beyond-school/41529765.pdf.

17 Statistics Canada, "Table 37-10-0049-01 Literacy, Numeracy—Average scores and distribution of proficiency levels, by labour force status, highest level of education and age group," https://doi.org/10.25318/3710004901-eng.

Engage in Public Scholarship! 44

can help mitigate these barriers, but documents must be formatted in ways that allow them to work, as explained in more detail below.

Jargon, vocabulary, complex grammatical constructions, and idioms can pose additional barriers for audiences. Special words or expressions that are used by a particular profession or group can be useful when a text is written for a small group of experts. However, when a text is written for larger audiences, jargon excludes readers. Abbreviations can likewise act as shorthand, yet they can confuse readers who are less aware of the topic. As abbreviations differ between languages, audiences who are interacting with your materials in a second language may feel confused. Consider spelling out the entire phrase. If abbreviations are necessary to reduce repetition, consider including a glossary explaining the abbreviations. Since idioms typically present a figurative, non-literal meaning attached to the phrase that depends on language, diaspora, and geography, they can reinforce cultural barriers.

Language choices will include or exclude audiences; when writing about a specific group, especially one that you have done research with, it is particularly important to use language and a form that makes that work accessible to that group. As social workers Karen Potts and Leslie Brown note, "formal written report form is commonplace and although useful, it is almost inherently classist, exclusionary, and appropriative in that it requires translating marginal

"Access" for the Audience and the Public 45

knowledges into the language of the elite."[18] They, like Moya Bailey, Nathaniel Jurgensen, Leslie Allison Brown, and Susan Strega, argue that if you do research with a group of people, that group should be able to access that information—otherwise you are merely extracting resources from that community.[19] In some cases, literacy barriers or professional requirements may mean that a scholar will need to produce two or more outputs to disseminate their research findings. Producing multiple forms of dissemination is a viable solution for public scholarship. These considerations over language suggest that, beyond public-facing scholarship, language can enable what Hannah McGregor calls "community oriented scholarship."[20] Words are tools. Do the tools you use help you communicate an idea better or prevent understanding?

3 Disability, Assistive Tech, and Accessible Technologies

Visual culture and the written word dominate scholarship, including public scholarship. However, this format of

---

18 Potts and Brown, "Becoming an Anti-oppressive Researcher," p. 276.
19 Bailey, "#transform(ing) DH Writing and Research"; Nathan Jurgenson, "Making Our Ideas More Accessible," *Inside Higher Ed,* May 11, 2012; Brown and Strega, *Research as Resistance.*
20 Hannah McGregor (host), "Secret Feminist Agenda Bonus Episode: Fireside Chat with Alex Ketchum," *Secret Feminist Agenda* (podcast), March 24, 2020, https://secretfeministagenda.com/2020/03/24/bonus-episodefireside-chat-with-alex-ketchum/.

dissemination is inaccessible to people who are Blind, Deaf-Blind, or have limited vision. Other forms of research dissemination such as podcasts, events, and films are inaccessible to people who are Deaf, hard of hearing, and/or have other disabilities. Assistive technologies can enable the 15 percent of the global population that has a disability to access public-facing scholarship.[21] The forms in which we choose to publish should not limit those technological aids. It is important to publish our writing in formats compatible with screen readers (an assistive technology that renders text and image content as speech or Braille output), which are useful for people who are Blind, Deaf-Blind, or have limited vision. One strategy has also included changing pre-existing interfaces. Editor Shawn Newman shows that it is possible for artistic journals to be designed in a way that can be more effectively utilized by people with visual impairments, such as providing alt-image text and utilizing formats that are compatible with screen readers.[22] Technologies and the internet can increase inclusion of disabled people in society.[23] For example, "making internet accessible for one type of disability can help make [it] accessible for another (e.g. making navigation possible through keyboards helps both blind users and users with

---

21   United Nations, "Factsheet on Persons with Disabilities," 2020, https://www.un.org/development/desa/disabilities/resources/factsheet-on-persons-with-disabilities.html.

22   Shawn Newman, "Publishing Disability/Access," lecture, Disrupting Disruptions: The Feminist and Accessible Publishing, Communications, and Technologies Speaker and Workshop Series, McGill University, Montreal, Canada, February 25, 2019.

23   Terven, Salas, and Raducanu, "New Opportunities for Computer Vision-Based Assistive Technology Systems for the Visually Impaired."

"Access" for the Audience and the Public   47

motor impairments)."[24] Assistive technologies can be useful tools in our work of making public scholarship and communications more accessible, and it is important that our forms of dissemination are formatted so that these aids can work. However, assistive technologies are not a complete solution.

In some cases, technology makes matters worse. For example, "technology often creates 'new dimensions of disability' in that what is seen as an 'obvious disability' shifts (e.g. dyslexia in online forums, forced to disclose disability vs. wheelchair user, who can now chose to disclose) but norms remain."[25] Assistive technology coordinator Chancey Fleet describes "the state of non-visual access to everyday digital interactions" as an area which deeply needs and deserves more attention and exploration by those working in tech. She argues that such "encoded inhospitality" is not intended to cause harm. Rather, most of these "dark patterns" within our everyday technology are developed and designed without insight from the Blind community.[26] The needs of disabled people should be centred in the creation of assistive technologies. Disability rights activists have, in response, used the slogan "Nothing About Us Without Us" in order to reflect the idea that no policy or technology should be decided

---

24 Lazar and Jaeger, "Reducing Barriers to Online Access for People with Disabilities," p. 69.
25 Foley and Ferri, "Technology for People, Not Disabilities," p. 193.
26 Chancey Fleet (guest) and Sareeta Amrute (host), "Dark Patterns in Accessibility Tech," *Databites* (podcast), episode 121, June 5, 2019, *Data and Society*, https://datasociety.net/library/dark-patterns-in-accessibility-tech/.

Engage in Public Scholarship! 48

by or created by any representative without the full and direct participation of members of the group(s) affected by that policy and technology.[27] This book supports this movement and centres the voices of the people affected by the technologies and dissemination formats discussed. In addition, this book presents both the benefits and the limitations of technologies and dissemination formats.

Able-bodiedness is often assumed when making decisions about the dissemination of public scholarship. Instead, centring disability in our decision making can open up new possibilities for communication. As argued by Sethuraman Panchanathan and Troy McDaniel, it is vital that computing solutions are person-centred.[28] Alan Foley and Beth A. Ferri echo this sentiment and add that there is an assumption that tech provides disabled people access to the resources available to able-bodied people. They argue for a shift from this binary of access and no-access to focus on tech-centred disparities. Tech can also create social disparities as it is often designed with able bodies in mind. By making normative assumptions about bodies, tech "privileges particular ways of being, which are grounded in normative, social, cultural and economic practices, further reified in the design, manufacture, marketing and implementation of technology."[29] Technology built in this way, therefore, forces people with disabilities to assimilate to one standard

---

27 Charlton, *Nothing About Us Without Us*.
28 Panchanathan and McDaniel, "Person-Centered Accessible Technologies and Computing Solutions through Interdisciplinary and Integrated Perspectives from Disability Research."
29 Foley and Ferri, "Technology for People, Not Disabilities," p. 193.

"Access" for the Audience and the Public

rather than embracing all people, enforcing what Robert McRuer calls "compulsory ablebodieness."[30] Foley and Ferri encourage us to think instead of "accessible technology," as opposed to assistive technology.[31] This challenges the idea that tech for disabled people has to be specialized, rather than the idea that all tech should be inclusive.

As a result, this book will proffer tips for centring accessibility, which may include technologies; however, it is not techno-utopic. It is important to discuss these tools, as "technology has always been a part of the construction of disability, and of the nature of disabled lives. Consequently, disability studies has long-considered questions of technology, and continues to do so."[32] An integration of technology, justice, and power is necessary, especially when thinking about feminist and accessible public scholarship. Disability is not the only barrier to access.

4   Class Access, Paywalls, and Tools

Financial barriers limit dissemination of public scholarship. Paywalls, a lack of tools, a lack of training, and a lack of internet affect access. Journal articles behind

---

30   McRuer, *Crip Theory*.
31   Foley and Ferri, "Technology for People, Not Disabilities."
32   Bennett and Keyes, "What Is the Point of Fairness?" p. 1.

Engage in Public Scholarship! 50

paywalls are inaccessible for people without a subscription or a university affiliation. Levels of access to tools and technologies influence accessibility as a whole, including tools that enable access for people with disabilities.[33]

When data journalist Meredith Broussard conducted a study of the Philadelphia school system regarding the relation between academic success and computer access, she found that the root of the issue had nothing to do with computers; instead, the problem was that students and school districts had insufficient numbers of books.[34] Not everyone has access to computers or training. Racial, class, age, and gender discrepancies between who has access to these tools, technologies, and skill sets create barriers to accessibility. However, digital dissemination of scholarship is not always the right solution. Accessible public scholarship does not necessarily equate to digital or virtual scholarship—it can mean books, newspaper articles, zines, or events. At other times, a digital copy is the most cost-efficient and effective form to share scholarship with various audiences. Thinking of target audiences can guide the form of dissemination.

There is an environmental and social cost of producing the tools for dissemination. The costs of material production of the physical versus the digital will be discussed in more detail in chapter ten. However, it is important to note that the cyber or virtual world does not actually exist in the cloud—there are material ramifications. As evidenced

---

33   Wilson-Hinds, "Affordability and Disability Access Technology."
34   Broussard, *Artificial Unintelligence.*

"Access" for the Audience and the Public 51

by Kate Crawford and Vladan Joler in AI Now Institute's report, "Anatomy of an AI System," the deleterious effects of producing much of our technology has an impact on the physical world. Cutting trees to print on paper or mining materials to create a computer also affect different communities. This is not to say that scholars are wholly responsible for the workplace conditions in computer factories, the environmental impact of server farms, and the polluted waters from mining practices. Instead, it is important to highlight that there is nothing inherently sustainable about going digital.[35] Furthermore, disseminating knowledge in digital formats often relies upon the internet, a form of technological infrastructure to which not everyone has equal access.

5 Internet Accessibility and Technology as Infrastructure

In the digital age internet access appears ubiquitous. The reality is different. A digital divide separates those with reliable, fast internet access from those without. As so much information (and service delivery) is now online,

---

35 Jessica McLean, "For a Greener Future, We Must Accept There's Nothing Inherently Sustainable about Going Digital," *The Conversation*, December 16, 2019.

Engage in Public Scholarship!

this division is considered a human rights issue.[36] The lack of digital infrastructure may prevent audiences from accessing your scholarship. Furthermore, even among those who have access to the internet, cyber spaces are not equally welcoming for all users. In addition, internet access is not a guarantee for all communities in the future. Thinking critically about internet access is crucial when deciding forms for disseminating public scholarship.

5.1 Geography, Rural and Urban Digital Divide

Many forms of scholarly dissemination, from traditional ones such as journal articles to nontraditional publications, require access to the internet. In fact, there is a digital divide not only in terms of access to the internet but also in terms of speed. Between 2000 and 2003, the divide in internet access shifted to a divide in high-speed access.[37] Mediocre broadband access is not equally distributed. In the United States, "more than 42 million Americans lack access to any type of broadband, and millions more can't afford it thanks to a lack of competition and apathetic revolving door regulators."[38] People who are younger, more educated, and live in urban areas are more likely to have broadband in their homes. As Steven A. Rains shows, when people have access to broadband, they are more likely to use the internet

---

36 Taylor, "From Zero to Hero."
37 Whitacre and Mills, "A Need for Speed?"
38 Karl Bode, "Why North Dakota Has the Best Internet in the United States," *Vice*, May 6, 2020.

"Access" for the Audience and the Public

for research.[39] While his study looks at research for health-related inquiries or communication, this finding can be extended to searching for other kinds of information. Rains argues that in order to help bridge the gap, it is important that everyone not only have access to the internet but that they also have a high-quality connection. These kinds of divides are evident outside of the United States as well.

General internet access is related to individual characteristics such as education, age, and race; household characteristics; place-based characteristics; and the availability of infrastructure. Higher levels of income and education increase the probability of high-speed access and decrease the probability of depending on dial-up. Black and Latinx households are less likely to have internet access and less likely to have high-speed access.[40] The situation is even worse for Indigenous people; issues of access are compounded particularly for rural and remote Indigenous communities in the United States and Canada.[41] When surrounded by others with high-speed access, individual households are more likely to have high-speed access (local access rates are significant).[42] However, it is not just having a connection that matters. As Brian E. Whitacre and Bradford F. Mills show, the rural-urban gap in dial-up internet access was closed by 2003 in the United States,

---

39 Rains, "Health at High Speed."
40 Whitacre and Mills, "A Need for Speed?"
41 Mark Buell, "Connecting Indigenous Communities," *Internet Society*, September 22, 2017, https://www.internetsociety.org/blog/2017/09/connecting-indigenous-communities/.
42 Whitacre and Mills, "A Need for Speed?"

Engage in Public Scholarship! 54

however, in the same year access rates to a high-speed internet connection were 14 points higher in urban areas than rural areas.[43] Since urban areas have greater economies and the concentration of demand decreases the price, urban areas have better access to broadband. Without broadband, rural communities must depend on dial-up or satellite internet, which is less stable. Rural dial-up lines are becoming overloaded, dial-up can no longer handle many modern internet technologies,[44] and satellite internet can be affected by the weather. Rural location, age, education, sex, and market size are the greatest indicators of broadband access.[45] As a result, these discrepancies affect who can access certain forms of public scholarship.

Climate change and political instability impacts internet accessibility. Chipo Dendere, a professor of African studies at Wellesley College, shows the role political leaders play in internet shutdowns.[46] Dendere and others agree that the climate crisis will both exacerbate this political instability and impact internet access.[47] The internet is a utility that will be very affected by environmental factors such as, but not limited to, rising sea levels.

---

43   Whitacre and Mills, "A Need for Speed?"
44   Galloway, "Can Broadband Access Rescue the Rural Economy?"
45   Prieger, "The Supply Side of the Digital Divide."
46   Rose Eveleth (host), "Power: Mother Against Digital Danger," *Flash Forward Podcast* (ft. Chipo Dendere), December 10, 2019, https://www.flashforwardpod.com/2019/12/10/power-mothers-against-digital-danger/.
47   Kevin Lozano, "Can the Internet Survive Climate Change? How a Warming World Is Sparking Calls for a Greener Web," *New Republic*, December 18, 2019.

"Access" for the Audience and the Public 55

All of these factors support the conclusion that not every community has equal access to the internet. Geographic, racial, and class divisions impact access to broadband. This limited internet access affects one's audience's abilities to access the internet, particularly resources that require higher broadband use such as video streaming. While the American and Canadian governments have spoken about ameliorating these discrepancies,[48] at the moment they continue to exist.[49] When making decisions about the form our public scholarship will take, broadband use should be taken into consideration.

5.2 Trolls and Violence Online

Even if everyone had access to the internet, dissemination barriers would remain. While early dreams of the internet imagined a utopic paradise and the democratization of all knowledge, the reality is different.[50] Apart from the disparity between who receives technological training,[51] online violence experienced by girls, women, non-binary folks, and people of colour is well documented.[52] The internet is not a welcoming place for everyone—it can

---

48 Prieger, "The Supply Side of the Digital Divide."
49 Adam Jacobson, "'Internet Is the Only Lifeline They Have': Canada Needs to Confront 'Digital Divide' amid COVID-19 Crisis," *CBC Radio*, March 27, 2020.
50 Taylor, *The People's Platform.*
51 Girls Who Code, "The Gender Gap in Computing Is Getting Worse," 2020, https://girlswhocode.com/about-us.
52 Mantilla, "Gendertrolling."

Engage in Public Scholarship! 56

be a hostile or violent space.[53] In order to address this, the Feminist Internet Project created a set of feminist principles for the internet. The project advocates access to the internet as a human right. This idea

> was first proposed at the United Nations by Special Rapporteur on the Promotion and Protection of the Right to Freedom of Opinion and Expression in 2011. However, debates around the standards of internet access continue among the technical community, private sector, governments, and civil society, with varying and often competing interests in connecting the remaining 4 billion (60 percent of the global population) to the internet. Amidst these debates, women in developing countries are often instrumentalized as a vulnerable target group (as often happens in global development debates) rather than a stakeholder group with a crucial say in the kind of internet access that guarantees rights rather than restricts them.

They state that "our feminist principle on access emphasizes the kind of internet we want: affordable, equal, and universal, and is especially significant when we look at the current digital gender gap affecting internet users today where 200 million less women than men are connected."[54]

---

53 Sobieraj, *Credible Threat.*
54 Feminist Internet, "Feminist Principles of the Internet," 2020, https://feministinternet.org/en/principle/access.

"Access" for the Audience and the Public

The questions of internet safety will be addressed in more detail in the next chapter.

6 Web Accessibility

In addition to the lack of high-speed internet connections and having enough bandwidth, web design impacts who can actually use materials that are put online.[55] We must remember that "as ever more education, employment, communication, entertainment, civic participation, and government functions move primarily or exclusively online, the high levels of inaccessibility on the Web and in internet-enabled mobile technologies threaten to make people with disabilities into the second-class citizens of the information society."[56] Kerry Dobransky and Eszter Hargittai draw attention to the disability divide in internet access,[57] while Chris Hofstader urges us to consider internet accessibility beyond accessibility.[58] The so-called "Bible of Internet Design" by Steve Krug encourages an approach to design in its title, *Don't Make Me Think*, but as Sasha Costanza-Chock points out, his book fails to consider race, class, gender, and multilingual barriers to internet

---

55   Carter and Markel, "Web Accessibility for People with Disabilities."
56   Lazar and Jaeger, "Reducing Barriers to Online Access for People with Disabilities," p. 69.
57   Dobransky and Hargittai, "The Disability Divide in Internet Access and Use."
58   Hofstader, "Internet Accessibility."

Engage in Public Scholarship! **58**

design.[59] Sarah Horton and Whitney Quesenbery further discuss the importance of designing accessible user experiences to create a web for everyone.[60] In doing public scholarship, there are principles of web design that can increase accessibility.

Multiple organizations seek to make internet resources more accessible. The World Wide Web Consortium (W3C) is one of these organizations. They produce updated guidelines, such as "How Persons with Disabilities Use the Web"[61] and the "Web Content Accessibility Guidelines (WCAG) 2.0."[62] They are not alone in this work.[63] Lourdes Moreno, Paloma Martínez, and Belén Ruiz-Mezcua have written "Disability Standards for Multimedia on the Web"[64] and Erin Perfect, Atul Jaiswal, and T. Claire Davies have written about the effectiveness of assistive technology to enable internet access for individuals with deaf-blindness.[65] These sources recommend using high contrast display and using a tool to allow users to switch from dark text on a light

59 Costanza-Chock, "Design Justice, AI, and Escape from the Matrix of Domination."
60 Horton and Quesenbery, *A Web for Everyone.*
61 Shadi Abou Zahra, "How People with Disabilities Use the Web," *W3C,* May 15, 2017, https://www.w3.org/ WAI/people-use-web/.
62 Ben Caldwell, Michael Cooper, Loretta Guarino Reid, and Gregg Vanderheiden, "Web Content Accessibility Guidelines WCAG 2.0," *W3C,* December 11, 2008, https://www. w3.org/TR/WCAG20/.
63 UK Home Office, "Designing Accessible Services," 2019, https:// ukhomeoffice.github.io/accessibility-posters/?fbclid=IwAR0sV9gdcby8f CB8Y9rKUi OUHOzhOFLc5wQIh-4AlBtdXwR9kFR-Ew0Fga.
64 Moreno, Martínez, and Ruiz-Mezcua, "Disability Standards for Multimedia on the Web."
65 Perfect, Jaiswal, and Davies, "Systematic Review."

"Access" for the Audience and the Public   59

background to light text on a dark background. They also recommend:

- avoiding flashing animations;
- enabling alt-text (the written copy that appears in place of an image on a website if the image fails to load on a user's screen. This text helps screen-reading tools describe images to visually impaired readers);
- not using images to present text information;
- using skip navigation (a "skip navigation" link is implemented by placing a named anchor at the point on the page where the main content begins);
- offering a magnifying tool;
- captioning and/or transcribing video and audio content;
- and using descriptive link text ("find pictures of cute animals here" rather than "here"), as screen-reader users may jump through links and need to know where they lead.

W3C Director and an inventor of the World Wide Web Tim Berners-Lee argues that "the power of the Web is in its universality. Access by everyone regardless of disability is an essential aspect."[66] Alan Foley and Beth A. Ferri add that increasing accessibility is beneficial for everyone, as "many of the so-called accommodations

---

66 Abou-Zahra, Shadi, Andrew Arch, James Green, Alan Chuter, Sylvie Duchateau, Jack Welsh, William Loughborough, Catherine Roy, Sharon Rush, and Yeliz Yesilada. "Accessibility," WC3, 2018, https://www.w3.org/standards/webdesign/accessibility/.

Engage in Public Scholarship! 60

that make the web more accessible for disabled users enhance its use for all users."[67]

In the words of the *New York Times Magazine*, "So the internet didn't turn out the way we hoped ... The internet hasn't lived up to all of our dreams for it ... The internet is unequal—and becoming more so."[68] Ultimately, we need to encourage using technologies that centre human behaviour, needs, and societal/cultural differences to increase usability.[69] Media law and public policy researcher Kira Allmann and feminist scholar Anasuya Sengupta echo this sentiment that "most debates around the internet and human rights focus on narrowing the digital divide and facilitating freedom of expression. But a human rights-based approach to the internet must look beyond issues of access toward questions of online knowledge equality and equity."[70] Relying on digital methods of dissemination for public scholarship requires attentiveness to: the kinds of digital divides; the proliferation of tools, assistive technologies, and accessible tech; the language within the publication itself; as well as a reflection on whether digital distribution is the most effective form.

---

67 Foley and Ferri, "Technology for People, Not Disabilities."
68 Bill Wasik, "The Internet Dream Became a Nightmare," *New York Times*, November 13, 2019.
69 Panchanathan and McDaniel, "Person-Centered Accessible Technologies and Computing Solutions through Interdisciplinary and Integrated Perspectives from Disability Research."
70 Kira Allmann and Anasuya Sengupta, "Beyond Internet Access: Seeking Knowledge Justice Online," *Open Global Rights*, January 22, 2019.

7 Conclusion

This chapter complicated our understanding of accessibility. It made clear that the forms of access being discussed are wide ranging. By highlighting that accessibility includes issues of disability, class, education, language, technology, and training, we will have a more specific understanding of what we mean when we discuss "the public" of public scholarship. This framework will be discussed and complicated throughout the entire book. This book does not assume the identity of able-bodiedness of its readers. Chapter four will discuss barriers for scholars themselves.

CHAPTER 4

"Access" for the Scholar

1 Barriers for the Researcher

Issues of accessibility extend beyond the experience of the public. There are barriers that limit who is able to do public scholarship. The risks involved in this work vary greatly for scholars, depending on their position within the university (whether they are a graduate student, adjunct, tenure track, or tenured) and the oppression that they face due to their race, gender, sexual orientation, class, religion, able-bodiedness, ethnicity, and age. How a scholar's institution regards public-facing work compounds these difficulties.

Public scholarship is not valued the same as other forms of scholarship. While individual universities, such as Syracuse, have begun to consider changes to the

"Access" for the Scholar

university's tenure and promotion policies that make it possible to assess the many forms of publicly engaged research, scholarship, and creative activity,[1] this is not the dominant trend. As Hannah McGregor has discussed in numerous episodes of her podcast *Secret Feminist Agenda*,[2] public work is usually framed as additive or as something extra that a scholar may engage with after their research, teaching, and service work. This framing affects who participates in public-facing work.

Public scholarship is a labour issue. The costs of public scholarship are greater for the scholars already marginalized within the academy. This section centres on two questions. Who benefits and who suffers most when engaging with audiences outside of academy? How do these experiences affect the kinds of materials that are made available?

2   Tenure File

The tenure process emphasizes peer-reviewed publications; as a result, tenure-track scholars are not incentivized to do public-facing work. While institutions may vary in their criteria, tenure is primarily decided on the basis of scholarship and research, then teaching, and then

---

1   Julie Ellison, "Public Scholarship Deserves Standing," *The Chronicle of Higher Education,* October 18, 2011.

2   McGregor, *Secret Feminist Agenda*, 2019, https://secretfeministagenda. com.

service—in that order.[3] Non-refereed scholarship such as books, blogs, podcasts, zines, websites, exhibitions, and articles hold little weight in a tenure file. As the Imagining America: Artists and Scholars in Public Life Tenure Team Initiative on Public Scholarship found, "many faculty members experience a frustrating clash between their intellectual goals, which include pursuing community-based scholarship and art-making, and institutional tenure policies."[4] The consequence of these policies is that public scholarship is less likely to be prioritized for tenure-track professors facing this competitive process.

The emphasis on traditional routes of scholarly publications, such as journal articles and monographs, is amplified in the current environment of the datafication of scholarly publishing. With an increased ease of accessing data, hiring and grant committees have been shown to link a scholar's significance more closely with bibliometrics such as: the h-index, which measures the productivity and impact of an author (the scholar has an index of h when she has published h papers, each of which has been cited at least h times); the journal impact factor, which measures the relative importance of a journal in a given field; and the citation count, which measures the impact of a paper in a given field. Communications scholar Corina MacDonald argues that current bibliometrics have the effect of not only measuring

---

3   Whicker, Kronenfeld, and Strickland, *Getting Tenure.*
4   Ellison and Eatman, "Scholarship in Public," p. iii.

"Access" for the Scholar

impact but also producing impact.[5] MacDonald builds on the work of sociologist David Beer who writes that these kinds of productivity measures "are also responsible for producing as well as tracking the social. They shape behaviours. As people are subject to these forms of measurement, they will produce different responses and outcomes, knowing, as they often will, what is coming and the way that their performance will become viable."[6] As hiring committees, tenure-granting bodies, and grants boards consider these bibliometric factors in decision making, the scholars who share their scholarship within traditional publication routes gain stronger footing within the academy. Such behavioural reinforcement thus packs the academy with scholars who emphasize a particular kind of scholarly engagement and pushes out or marginalizes scholars who may engage in other forms. In addition, bibliometric factors and citation tracking are vulnerable to a lack of transparency within the algorithms. Only citations in particular publications are counted. Citation practices have long been noted to have gender bias across fields.[7] These challenging factors compound the gender bias in the process of peer review to even get an article published.[8] Therefore, tenure-track scholars from marginalized communities, including but not limited to women and non-binary scholars,

---

5 Corina MacDonald, "Datafication in Scholarly Publishing," lecture for Disrupting Disruptions: The Feminist and Accessible Publishing, Communications, and Technologies Speaker and Workshop Series, February 5, 2020, YouTube video, 42:30, https://www.youtube.com/watch?v=jAkCg8gn o&feature=emblogo.
6 Beer, "Productive Measures," p. 10.
7 Copenheaver, Goldbeck, and Cherubini, "Lack of Gender Bias in Citation Rates of Publications by Dendrochronologists."
8 Tregenza, "Gender Bias in the Refereeing Process?"

Engage in Public Scholarship!

are judged by flawed bibliometrics that prioritize publishing records that rely on methods of dissemination known to exhibit gender bias.

Alternative metrics (called altmetrics to distinguish them from bibliometrics) offer another option for assessing the societal impact of research. These web-based metrics offer new ways to measure public engagement with research output by including the impact of publications and other scholarly material, using data from social media platforms such as Twitter or Mendeley. However, these metrics also have disadvantages including bias, lack of measurement standards, and replication.[9] At present, traditional scholarship retains prominence in hiring and tenure processes and bibliometric data reifies this positioning.

Tenure-track scholars may still choose to engage in public scholarship, yet this decision often comes at a cost. Time spent on non-refereed publications and projects is time taken away from work that can "be counted." Such conditions force untenured scholars to calculate the risk of participating in the kind of public-facing scholarship that funding bodies and universities claim to value. Non-tenure-track scholars must participate in this kind of calculus as well, as will be discussed in the next section in more detail.

The work of "knowledge translation" that is required of scholars becomes more necessary during a period in which the journalistic network that would once help convey

---

9   Bornmann, "Do Altmetrics Point to the Broader Impact of Research?"

"Access" for the Scholar 67

scholarly thought to a public audience has been undercut. As newspapers and media outlets across Canada and the United States have drastically cut those media roles, social media has become a recourse. Now, however, the labour is done by the scholars, rather than someone else. Here, too, the double-edged sword of neoliberalism and austerity function to increase the unpaid labour of individuals in order to supply the public with the information to support an informed democratic voting body.

The irony is that participating in public-facing scholarship is a component of responsible scholarship, especially when scholars are conducting community-engaged scholarship. For scholars dedicated to making their research accessible, especially scholars working with communities that cannot read journal articles behind paywalls, doing public scholarship is not actually optional, but necessary. Scholars have a responsibility to both their research communities and the public. Treating the public component of research as only additive does not just dissuade scholars from engaging in ethical research and publishing practices, it punishes them. Within university bureaucratic processes and hierarchies, enacting these forms of anti-oppressive praxis can be detrimental to a scholar's career. There is nothing inherent in this dynamic, however—change is possible.

Failure to recognize the scholarly impact of public-facing work hurts researchers, the university, and society. By not connecting with the public, research does not have the

Engage in Public Scholarship!

social impact that it otherwise could.[10] This is especially pertinent in the post-truth age. Journal articles behind paywalls can languish with fewer than five views, whereas a blog post or an op-ed may be read by thousands or hundreds of thousands. Isolating the research happening in the university from the rest of society creates further divisions that can influence how the public views educational institutions and may impact future funding decisions. To be clear, this is not an argument against peer-reviewed articles, but rather an endorsement of creating multiple versions of one's work that speak to different audiences.

Besides revising the tenure process, peer review can be applied in new ways. The aforementioned podcast, *Secret Feminist Agenda*, is undergoing an experimental peer review with Wilfrid Laurier University Press.[11] Lauren Klein and Catherine D'Ignazio's book, *Data Feminism*, underwent open review with MIT Press in order to acknowledge "a foundational principle of this project: that all knowledge is incomplete, and that the best knowledge is gained by bringing together multiple partial perspectives." The authors explain,

> As we describe more fully in our values statement, we recognize that the people who are most directly affected by specific topics and issues are the ones who know the most about them. In our book, we have

---

10   Rouse and Woolnough, "Engaged or Activist Scholarship?"
11   Siobhan McMenemy, "Scholarly Podcasting Open Peer Review," 2019, https:// wlupress.wlu.ca/Scholarly-Podcasting-Open-Peer-Review.

"Access" for the Scholar

attempted to elevate their voices, and amplify their ideas. In our attempt to do so, we have also likely made mistakes. We strive to be reflexive and accountable in our work, and we hope to learn from you about places where we've gotten things wrong, and about how we can do better.[12]

While the two examples above are not definitive in revising how an academic committee would review post-publication public-facing work, rethinking peer review can make public scholarship more palatable to tenure and promotion committees. It is not the only solution, but a working solution.

Having tenured scholars who have the privilege of experimenting with their publication techniques and review processes sets new precedents that may enable emerging scholars more opportunities to validate their public scholarship within review committees—a validation that comes with economic ramifications. As Wendy Chun, a well-established scholar and Canada 150 Research Chair of New Media, remarked during her public lecture "My Mother Was a Keypunch Operator" at Concordia University on February 5, 2019, it is up to established scholars to start taking risks and changing norms. In her experimental approach, she aims to "weave together the personal, theoretical and political in order to grapple with the complicated relationship between gender, feminism, race, migration and technology."

---

12 Klein, "Data Feminism: Community, Allyship, and Action in the Digital Humanities," keynote address, Digital Frontiers Annual Conference, October 4, 2018, Lawrence, Kansas, https://digital.library.txstate.edu/handle/10877/7839.

Chun acknowledged that experimenting with forms of dissemination is less hazardous for certain scholars; while for some scholars this work is an intellectual risk, for others, it could threaten their livelihood and ability to continue working within the academy.

3   Compensation

On June 30, 2019, sociologist Ruha Benjamin used Twitter to discuss how the material conditions surrounding a scholar's employment affect their possible scholarly outputs. Benjamin responded to a fellow Twitter user's compliment of her productivity and publication of two books within one year by centring the kinds of resources available to her.

> @ruha9 Jun 30: Truth be told—publishing is made infinitely easier w/ a sabbatical, low course loads, research funds to pay for several rounds of editing, many other intangible supports. "Productivity" is a byproduct of institutional inequality. In context, two books isn't that impressive.

Changing the way the tenure process considers public work is a laudable goal, yet this process will only affect those members of the academy that have tenure-track jobs. The majority of scholars work as adjunct faculty or in temporary contract positions: 50 percent in the Canadian context and

"Access" for the Scholar

70 percent in the United States.[13] For untenured, contingent, and adjunct faculty, most research and writing is unpaid. For those on the job market, however, peer-reviewed publications are valued more highly, as in the tenure process.[14] Changes to hiring practices that emphasize public scholarship would be beneficial. By recognizing the value of public scholarship, early career scholars and graduate students would be encouraged to engage in this work—or at the very least not be penalized for it.

Those more vulnerable within the institution, including those working without tenure and graduate students, do not benefit from the same level of academic freedom to publish without repercussion. In fact, their work, and primarily the form of their work, is greatly curtailed. Tenured scholars can use their position to model public scholarship. By showcasing this work, tenured scholars can grant both visibility and legitimacy to public scholarship. Doing so can benefit scholars who are still on the job market, who are applying for research grants, and/or are seeking fellowships.

Occasionally there is a divide in who has the skills to do this kind of work, especially when the scholarship involves technological skill sets. At the moment, rather than working collaboratively, public scholarship skills have been undermined and devalued, which allows more established faculty members

---

13   Kane X. Faucher, "Contractually Bound: Welcome to a New Space for Adjunct Faculty," *University Affairs,* February 5, 2014.

14   Mountz et al., "For Slow Scholarship."

Engage in Public Scholarship! 72

and other scholars who publish in traditional outlets to maintain their dominance. This does not have to be the case.

4 Skills

Researchers interested in doing public scholarship may be dissuaded if they do not have certain necessary skill sets. It is one of the great ironies that public-facing work is derided when the ability to communicate simultaneously with multiple audiences through different kinds of media and formats requires the laudable acquisition of numerous skillsets. Learning how to write about one's research in a manner that non-experts can engage with requires that scholars learn new forms of writing. The genre of blog posts differs from the genre of the op-ed. An article for a trade magazine differs from an academic article.

In addition to genre differences, some forms of public scholarship require learning how to use new technologies. The key is "learning" and not "knowing"; this deliberate word choice is to emphasize that these skills are possible for scholars to learn. However, scholars need support and resources in order to actually cultivate these skills. Universities can, and should, offer workshops on how to do this kind of work. The people leading these workshops should also be compensated for their time and labour. Attending these workshops could be included in tenure files and skill-set sections of curriculum vitae. The precariously

"Access" for the Scholar

employed scholars who piece together a living with multiple teaching contracts are not likely going to have the time to attend these events, so universities could even offer a stipend for attendance to adjunct employees.

Sometimes being a public intellectual includes the opportunity to speak with other producers of media. Radio, television, and newspaper interviews are other options for communicating one's research to the public. Here is one arena where many universities already have available resources. It is common for universities to have communications and public relations offices. These offices often build databases of employees at the university who are amenable to participating in interviews. They may also offer workshops on op-ed writing and media relations. Currently there is a disproportionate number of white male heterosexual scholars who are cited as experts in the media. Women only account for 29 percent of the experts cited in Canadian media and 38 percent in American media.[15] Organizations such as Femmes Expertes[16] and Informed Opinions in Canada and SheSource in the United States seek to empower women scholars to do this work. They offer training sessions and have a database of experts for the media to consult.[17] For more information on working with journalists, see chapter twelve.

---

15 These statistics come from Informed Opinions and The Women's Media Centre's SheSource and the Global Media Monitoring Program: https://womensmediacenter.com/about/learn-moreabout-wmcwmc-shesource.

16 Femmes Expertes, "About," 2019, https://femmesexpertes.ca.

17 Informed Opinions, "About," 2019, https://informedopinions.org/.

Engage in Public Scholarship!

Social media is another form of public scholarship. Whether scholars chose to utilize Twitter, Instagram, Facebook, or some other application, social media has the potential to allow scholars to communicate their work with larger audiences.[18] These networks can be particularly useful for collaboration and learning about new and related research. There can also be drawbacks to this work, as will be discussed later.

All of these various forms of media and publishing require specific forms of knowledge. Scholars need not engage with every type—certain kinds of scholarship lend themselves better to certain kinds of public engagement, and specific projects may be excluded. While learning the required skill sets may appear to be a daunting task, especially when this labour is undervalued by the university, public-facing work is still possible. Public scholarship lends itself to collaboration. Researchers do not have to be experts in all genres and formats. They can work with others, learn by attending physical and digital workshops, or even hire research assistants to build their websites and run social media accounts. The division between who can fund this labour speaks to another challenge of public work. There can be costs associated with this scholarship. Running a website requires more than computer skills and basic coding. Domain fees and hosting fees can be prohibitive for some individuals. Podcasting is a relatively accessible medium, yet it still necessitates purchasing or borrowing recording equipment. Filmmaking requires expensive equipment and will be out of reach for many researchers. However, there

18   Boyd and Ellison, "Social Network Sites."

"Access" for the Scholar   75

are often ways of doing this work on the cheap and oftentimes universities have underutilized AV equipment resources. These strategies will be discussed in greater detail in chapters eight and eleven.

5   Sexism, Heterosexism, and Racism Online

Apart from financial compensation, there is a cost to doing work in public spheres that is disproportionately paid by marginalized scholars. It is not rare for women academics and scholars of colour to face harassment online.[19] Especially for scholars who engage with the public through social media accounts, a writer's ideas are not the only thing attacked; threats of death and sexual violence can fill a scholar's inbox.[20] Racist trolls and gender-trolling can intimidate scholars and dissuade them from doing this work.[21] Doxxing—the act of broadcasting or identifying private information about an individual for the purpose of harassment—and racial and gender-based harassment have been well documented.[22] Women, gender non-binary

19   It is not just scholars who encounter cyberbullying and cyber-harassment. The media critic and creator of Feminist Frequency, Anita Sarkeesian, a survivor of the Gamergate cybermob, has spoken frequently about her own experiences with this violence.
20   Mulcahy, McGregor, and Kosman, "Whoops I Am a Lady on the Internet"; Megarry, "Online Incivility or Sexual Harassment?"
21   Mantilla, "Gendertrolling."
22   Harmer and Lumsden, "Experiences of Online Abuse."

Engage in Public Scholarship!

people, queer, and racialized peoples are more likely to not just have their ideas attacked, but their identities attacked. As journalist Amanda Hess explains, "'Ignore the barrage of violent threats and harassing messages that confront you online every day.' That's what women are told. But these relentless messages are an assault on women's careers, their psychological bandwidth, and their freedom to live online. We have been thinking about Internet harassment all wrong."[23] Online harassment diminishes the free speech of women and racialized scholars.[24] This kind of harassment, and the threat of potential harassment, curtails the desire to participate in public-facing work, especially online.

While scholars with marginalized identities are more likely to face harassment centred around their identities regardless of their specializations, certain research topics tend to draw particular ire. Communications scholar Adrienne Massanari asks,

> What does it mean to do ethical new media research, especially research that connects explicitly to issues of power, justice, and personhood, during the rise of this kind of right-wing extremism? What new risks do we face as scholars, and how must we reconceptualize research ethics to account for these risks? I contend

---

23 Amanda Hess, "Why Women Aren't Welcome on the Internet," *Pacific Standard*, June 14, 2017.

24 Jessica West, *Cyberviolence Against Women*, Battered Women's Support Services, 2014, http://www.bwss.org/wp-content/uploads/2014/05/CyberVAWReportJessicaWest.pdf

"Access" for the Scholar

> that we must attend not only to the new ways that
> White nationalist, Islamophobic, fascist, misogynistic,
> anti-immigrant, and anti-intellectual communities
> (often referred to in the United States at the "alt-right")
> are using social media, but also what impact this has
> on research into these technologies.

She continues that "scholars like Jessie Daniels have discussed the ways in which some of these groups have used online spaces as a communication and mobilization tool; however less has been said about the ways these same tools have been used to observe and potentially harass those researchers whose work is perceived as a threat."[25] Subject-matter differences make certain scholars more vulnerable to this kind of harassment.

Furthermore, even when harassment has not yet occurred, the fear of harassment can lead to a self-silencing. Gender studies professor Heather Savigny notes that many of the female academics she has interviewed have talked of how they made conscious decisions not to engage with media for fear of abuse. She argues that this silencing "becomes a form of symbolic violence; an expression of underlying relations of oppression and domination, which as Bourdieu suggests, becomes so normalized and routine that it occurs almost with the subordinate's own complicity," and thus, "women then are structurally positioned to be complicit in their own silencing" even when this can affect their career

---

25   Massanari, "Rethinking Research Ethics, Power, and the Risk of Visibility in the Era of the 'Alt-Right' Gaze," p. 2.

Engage in Public Scholarship! 78

trajectories.[26] Online harassment also comes with increased anxiety and long-term health effects.[27]

Universities are often not equipped to assist scholars who experience these kinds of attacks, and public scholars are often left to languish with these problems on their own. The Canadian Centre for Occupational Health and Safety (CCOHS) instructs employers that they should pay attention to online harassment.[28] Unfortunately, scholars often face cyberbullying and harassment alone. Researchers deserve to have support from their institutions' public-relations offices. During the workshop "Doing Feminism in a Man's World (Wide Web): Getting On, Switching Off, and Keeping Safe Online," at the OffScript Conference at McGill University in November 2018, film scholar Rebecca Harrison, who faced a barrage of cyber-harassment around her work on Star Wars, discussed the responsibility that universities have towards their employees.[29] Public relations offices can offer

26 Savigny, "Gender and the 'Impact' Agenda: The Costs of Public Engagement to Female Academics," https://blogs.lse.ac.uk/impactofsocialsciences/2019/06/14/gender-and-the-impact-agenda-the-costs-of-public-engagement-to-female-academics/.
27 Finn, "A Survey of Online Harassment at a University Campus." This phenomenon has received more attention regarding the harassment of young adults and youth. Films such as *Netizens* (2018) by Cynthia Lowen have documented the proliferation of cyber-harassment faced by women.
28 Unhelpfully, CCOHS also tells employees to use "gender neutral email addresses to curb harassment." Women and non-binary scholars cannot hide their gender identities—nor should they have to. (Canadian Centre for Occupational Safety and Health, "OSH Fact Sheets: Internet Harassment or Cyberbullying," December 23, 2020, https://www.ccohs.ca/oshanswers/ psychosocial/cyberbullying.html.)
29 Off Script Conference, "About," 2018, https://offscriptmtl.wordpress.com/portfolio/schedulehoraire/.

"Access" for the Scholar

79

to deal with large waves of attacking tweets and posts for their employees. These communications officers can also document the harassment by taking screenshots if legal action becomes necessary. Femtechnet provides resources for both survivors of this violence and employers who aim to support them.[30] Geek Feminism provides advice to survivors of trolling.[31] Crash Override provides additional support.[32] Although most advice is targeted at individuals, universities can assist scholars in undertaking necessary steps to mitigate these situations. While historically most scholars have faced this work alone,[33] or with the help of a few peers,[34] universities must assist their employees.

Although it might at first appear that universities, which are becoming increasingly unlikely to even hire their professors for tenure-track and secure contracts, will not allocate resources to a communications staff that will assist and help those precariously employed professors, these resources do exist at some universities.[35] However, as shown in chapter twelve and the "Report on the State of Resources Provided to Support Scholars Against Harassment, Trolling, and

---

30   Femtechnet, "About," 2019, http://femtechnet.org/csov/.
31   Geek Feminism, "Mitigating Internet Trollstorms," 2019, https:// geekfeminism.wikia.org/wiki/Mitigating_internet_trollstorms.
32   Crash Override Network, "About," 2019, http://www. crashoverridenetwork.com/contact. html.
33   Emily Contois, "I Was Trolled—Here's Why I'm Turning It into a Teaching Opportunity," *Nursing Clio*, July 17, 2018.
34   Hodson et al., "I Get by with a Little Help from My Friends."
35   For example, McGill University has a media-relations office that offers assistance to all levels of faculty in facilitating press interviews. However, when first questioned about the levels of protection offered, there was no plan in place.

Doxxing While Doing Public Media Work and How University Media Relations Offices/Newsrooms Can Provide Better Support," there is significant room for improvement.[36]

6 The Role of the University

If universities and grant agencies are going to encourage their researchers to engage with public scholarship, there must be support for scholars doing this work. As feminist theorist and engaged public scholar Sara Ahmed discusses, the university indicates its priorities by what jobs are made permanent positions.[37] Likewise, it is possible to know the university's priorities by looking at what type of labour is paid. If a university wishes to truly commit to more than nominal support of public scholarship, there are concrete steps that it can take. This kind of support includes valuing public scholarship as actual scholarship in the tenure, hiring, and promotion processes. Universities must provide resources for scholars facing cyber-attacks. Institutions can create workshops to train scholars in the skill sets

---

36 Alex Ketchum, "Report on the State of Resources Provided to Support Scholars Against Harassment, Trolling, and Doxxing While Doing Public Media Work and How University Media Relations Offices/Newsrooms Can Provide Better Support," 2020, https://medium.com/@alexandraketchum/report-on-the-state-ofresources-provided-to-support-scholars-against-harassment-trolling-and401bed8cfbf1.

37 Sara Ahmed, "Institutional as Usual," *Feminist Killjoys,* October 24, 2017, https://feministkilljoys.com/2017/10/24/institutional-as-usual/.

"Access" for the Scholar

81

necessary to work with new technologies, to do media outreach, and to write for new genres. Compensating this work is key. Institutions must establish grants and funds to support public-facing work. Until universities make these commitments, it is irresponsible to ask scholars to be public.

CHAPTER 5

Open Access

This chapter addresses the benefits and limitations of "openness" by looking at open-access movements. Beginning by addressing the issue of burying information behind paywalls, this chapter contextualizes the movements that advocate for open access. Next, the chapter examines the benefits and limitations of the idea of "openness." Librarian Alexia Hudson-Ward points to the manner in which "the professional discourse regarding open access appears to be dominated primarily by white males and large university presses; effectively 'pushing out' or marginalizing smaller presses, people of color, women, and the possibility of LGBTQ community," making the "open access movement closed, inaccessible, and privileged."[1] This chapter seeks to highlight these often-marginalized

---

1   Punctum Books, "Twitter Thread on Punctum," Twitter thread, September 22, 2020, 12:57 PM, https://twitter.com/punctum books/status/1308450285552119808.

Open Access

83

voices in the open-access discourse. Openness is not a synonym for publicly accessible scholarship, but it can be one strategy to work towards accessibility. Open is merely a starting point.

1   Closed and Paywalled

The majority of peer-reviewed academic articles sit behind paywalls. Over 53 percent of scientific research articles require subscriptions and institutional access.[2] In humanities the number is higher. In 2018 the European Commission's Open Science Monitor found that 76 percent of arts and humanities articles were not open access.[3] Scholars and students at larger or well-funded universities are the most likely to have institutional access through their library systems. People at smaller or less well-funded universities are not as likely to have institutional access, however. People who are not affiliated with a university are even less likely to have institutional access to academic journals. Individuals without subscriptions are required to pay upwards of 40 dollars per article. This means that only

---

2   Our Research, "When will everything be Open Access?" *Our Research Blog*, February 22, 2018, https://blog.impactstory.org/openaccess-by-when/.

3   European Commission, "Trends for Open Access to Publications," https://www.stm-assoc.org/20181004STMReport2018.pdf. The 2018 STM report notes that "The European Commission's Open Science Monitor uses a limited range of data sources, and thus presents a conservative picture of the proportion of OA content. However, it effectively demonstrates the wide variations in levels of OA at country level."

Engage in Public Scholarship!

a small percentage of the population is able to access these research materials.

The situation is further complicated by the fact that much of this research is publicly funded through taxes, which governments direct to universities or through grants to scholars affiliated with universities. Taxpayers essentially fund research that they are then unable to access. While research findings have applications outside of the confines of the nation state, the fact that the same public who funds the research cannot access it raises concerns. The paywalled, closed journal model restricts public access to scholarship. Paywalled research content is provided largely for free by researchers and peer reviewed by academics who are not paid for this work. Journal access is then made available to those same academics via their university libraries, which pay thousands of dollars per year for subscriptions.[4] Commercial publishers financially benefit from keeping knowledge paywalled.[5] This publishing model also results in other scholars being unable to access scholarship if their institutions do not subscribe to a particular journal—a phenomenon common at smaller institutions. Sometimes scholars do not even have access to their own articles.

Paywalled academic articles do not result in remuneration for authors, peer reviewers, or most editors. In fact,

---

4   Chris Wickham, "New Front in 'Open Access' Science Publishing Row," *Reuters,* June 12, 2012.
5   Roach and Gainer, "On Open Access to Research."

Open Access

scholarly journals have not paid authors for their articles since the first journals were launched in London and Paris in 1665.[6] With many scholarly journals now existing exclusively in online format, journal subscriptions paid by universities and individuals no longer need to cover the cost of printing and shipping. While there are costs to maintaining an academic journal, including website hosting fees, domain name fees, and paying copyeditors and website developers, these costs pale in comparison to the high cost of some academic journal subscriptions. At present, large universities pay yearly upwards of 6 million US dollars for journal subscription bundle fees.[7] Meanwhile, journal publishers, such as Elsevier, Springer, Wiley-Blackwell, Taylor Francis, and SAGE Publications —the largest publishers of research articles in the world—reap the profits.[8] Combined, these top five publishers account for more than 50 percent of all papers published with 70 percent of the papers from disciplines of the social sciences and 20 percent of the papers from the humanities, as of 2013.[9] The present, dominant model of academic journal publishing results in private entities controlling access to scholarship. As Canadian lead for Creative Commons Amy Buckland argues, "We built the scholarly publishing system

---

6   Guédon, "In Oldenburg's Long Shadow."

7   Bergstrom et al., "Evaluating Big Deal Journal Bundles."

8   Jessica Lange and Jenn Riley, "Open Access and Open Data," lecture for Disrupting Disruptions: The Feminist and Accessible Publishing, Communications, and Technologies Speaker and Workshop Series, Montreal, QC, October 21, 2019, https://drive.google.com/file/d/11Slbwu_XfnhCp5XduG8JfHi0lfSj_qVr/view?usp=sharing.

9   Larivière, Haustein, and Mongeon, "The Oligopoly of Academic Publishers in the Digital Era."

Engage in Public Scholarship!

because research deserves to be shared, but that intention has been lost in favor of financial and status motives."[10] Multiple strategies to ameliorate these issues have been proposed; the open-access movement has sought to address these challenges.

2   Resistance to Paywalls

Over the past decade, researchers have begun to resist paywall practices, particularly, but not limited to, scholars in mathematics and the sciences. In 2012, mathematicians started a petition to boycott Elsevier that has since been signed by more than 17,000 researchers.[11] Universities have initiated similar forms of resistance. In December 2016, universities in Germany stopped paying for Elsevier's journals. In 2018, the same thing happened in Sweden and then in Hungary. In 2019 the University of California, one of the largest research institutions in the world, left negotiations with Elsevier and decided that it would no longer pay Elsevier millions of dollars a year to subscribe to its journals.[12] However, on March 16, 2021, the University of California compromised and Elsevier granted universal open access to all UC research and agreed to contain the

---

10   Buckland et al., "On the Mark?"
11   Sarah Zhang, "The Real Cost of Knowledge," *Atlantic,* March 4, 2019.
12   Zhang, "The Real Cost of Knowledge."

Open Access

excessively high costs associated with licensing journals.[13] Some of the agencies that fund research have also begun to resist paywall publishing models.

Agencies that fund research have grown enthusiastic about open access as an alternative to paywalled research. In the United States, government agencies such as the National Institutes of Health and the National Science Foundation require grantees to deposit their papers in a public repository within twelve months of publication. In 2018, eleven European agencies that collectively fund 8.8 billion euros in research put forward a far more radical proposal: Plan S,[14] which requires all works be published openly.[15] As of 2020, these agencies have required their funded researchers to publish in journals that are free to read.[16] These initiatives are not restricted to the sciences. The Social Science and Humanities Research Council of Canada includes a mandate of public dissemination of findings as part of their grant requirements. All federal and provincial grants awarded after May 1, 2015, are required to have their peer-reviewed journal publications freely accessible online within 12 months of publication. For grants awarded in Quebec under the Fonds de Recherche du Québec (FRQ), a

---

13 University of California Office of Scholarly Communication, "UC and Elsevier March 16, 2021 Update," *Office of Scholarly Communication,* March 16, 2021, https://osc.universityofcalifornia.edu/ucpublisher-relationships/uc-and-elsevier/.

14 The S in Plan S stand for science, speed, solution, and shock.

15 Plan S, "Plan S," 2020, https://www.coalition-s.org/coalition-s-develops-rights-retention-strategy/.

16 Wickham, "New Front in 'Open Access' Science Publishing Row."

Engage in Public Scholarship! 88

similar policy applies to grants awarded after April 1, 2019.[17] In the United States, the Andrew W. Mellon Foundation has committed itself to numerous endeavours to make research available. These projects range from digitization efforts, open-access projects, and funding experimental publications. By mandating open access, grant agencies lend the open-access movement legitimacy—and even scholars without these grants are more likely to be encouraged to participate in open access. Open access serves as a counter to closed publishing practices, but there are different kinds of open access.

3   Open Access

The definition of open-access literature is that it is digital, online, free of charge, and free of most copyright and licensing restrictions. The Budapest Open Access Initiative coined the term, in 2001, as part of a conference of the Open Society Institute. The Budapest Open Access Initiative explains that

> an old tradition and a new technology have converged to make possible an unprecedented public good. The old tradition is the willingness of scientists and scholars

---

17   Communications Branch, "Tri-Agency Open Access Policy on Publications," Government of Canada website, December 21, 2016, https://www.ic.gc.ca/eic/site/063.nsf/eng/h_F6765465.html.

Open Access

89

> to publish the fruits of their research in scholarly journals without payment, for the sake of inquiry and knowledge. The new technology is the internet. The public good they make possible is the world-wide electronic distribution of the peer-reviewed journal literature and completely free and unrestricted access to it by all scientists, scholars, teachers, students, and other curious minds.[18]

The author of the book *Open Access*, Peter Suber, clarifies, "We know that open-access literature is not free (without cost) to produce. But that does not foreclose the possibility of making it free of charge (without price) for readers and users."[19] From the beginning, the open access movement has proffered complementary strategies including self-archiving and the creation of open-access journals.

There are numerous models of open access including "gold," "hybrid," "platinum," and "green" open access. In the gold open-access model, the publisher makes all articles and related content available for free immediately on the journal's website by requiring the author, rather than the reader, to bear the costs of publication. These publication fees, also known as "article processing charges," can range widely, with some journals charging upwards of two thousand US dollars to make an article "open."[20]

---

18 "Budapest Open Access Initiative," 2020, https://www.budapestopenaccessinitiative.org/read.

19 Peter Suber, "Open Access Overview (definition, introduction)," 2020, http://legacy.earlham.edu/~peters/fos/overview.htm.

20 Malakoff, "Opening the Books on Open Access."

Engage in Public Scholarship!

In 2020 the scientific journal *Nature* announced that it would charge $11,390 US to make individual articles "open," far surpassing other journals' fees.[21] Hybrid journals contain a mix of closed and open-access articles, often requiring authors pay high "open access" fees for their individual article to be made open. Open-access journals that do not ask authors for article processing charges are sometimes referred to as diamond or platinum open access. Publishers of these journals often rely on funding from external sources such as academic institutions, learned societies, philanthropists, or government grants.[22] For green open access, authors publish their work in a paywalled journal and also self-archive a form of their article to a website that is either controlled by the author, the research institution that funded or hosted the work, or to an independent, central open repository. These repositories are digital platforms that hold research output and provide free, immediate, and permanent access to research results for anyone to use, download, and distribute without paying. While most major funding institutions requiring their researchers to publish in open-access formats will accept green open access, a lack of public awareness about the existence of repositories continues to limit the number of people who ultimately access these pieces. Although there are numerous forms of open access, all speak to the idea of "open scholarship" which is "a commitment to create

---

21 Holly Else, "Nature Journals Reveal Terms of Landmark Open-access Option," 2020, https://www.nature.com/articles/d41586-020-03324-y. The highest fees elsewhere are 6,000 US dollars.

22 Fuchs and Sandoval, "The Diamond Model of Open Access Publishing."

Open Access

knowledge and share it as widely as possible for the benefit of all."[23]

A full history of the open-access movement is outside of the scope of this chapter. However, at its heart, the open-access movement argues that publicly funded research ought to be available to the public.[24] Open access ensures access to research without price barriers for readers and users. It increases the visibility of a scholar's research. To be clear, open access refers to free and unrestricted access to and re-use of articles, not to a business model.[25] This movement is linked to the open-data and open-source movements. John Willinsky argues that the debate over open access raises crucial questions about the place of scholarly work in a larger world and about the future of knowledge.[26] The open movement faces the challenges of finance, labour, and financing labour, while growing during a time when other sectors of academia face financial cuts. Information studies researcher Samuel Moore argues that "Open Access (in the UK but also elsewhere) has grown up in an era of austerity. Open publishing has the capacity to disseminate work much more effectively and, in many cases, much more cost efficiently."[27] The questions about who is getting paid,

---

23   Scanlon, "Scholarship in the Digital Age," p. 14.
24   Peter Suber, "Open-Access Timeline," 2007, http://www.earlham. edu/~peters/fos/timeline.htm.
25   "Budapest Open Access Initiative," 2020, https://www. budapestopenaccessinitiative.org/read.
26   Willinsky, *The Access Principle*.
27   Open Book Publishers, "Open Book Publishers Question," Twitter Thread, May 26, 2020, 2:35 PM, https://twitter.com/OpenBookPublish/ status/1265350768258961414.

3.1 Myths

One of the challenges for promulgating open-access practices is that there are deleterious myths about them. Since some forms of open access, such as gold, require that the author pays to make the article open, some critics view this as authors paying to publish, and believe that any journal that charges a publication fee is predatory. These critics also misunderstand or mischaracterize open access, believing that all open-access journals charge fees, all open-access journals are predatory, and that "reputable" publishers do not engage in predatory practices. Exploitative practices in publishing have nothing to do with whether a journal is paywalled or open access. There can be problems with a journal's peer-review process being less rigorous than it claims, or the existence of "peer review rings," in which authors positively cite each other's work to get published in closed and open journals alike. There are also pricing abuses in all types of journals. Not all of these issues are malicious, but they can be caused by carelessness or inexperience.[28] There is a myth that open-access journals do not utilize peer review, even though 98 percent of the over 12,000 journals in the Directory of

---

28 Smith, "Examining Publishing Practices: Moving beyond the Idea of Predatory Open Access."

Open Access

Open Access Journals perform some form of peer review.[29] Another myth is that open-access journals publish bad scholarship.[30] However, as librarians Jenn Riley and Jessica Lange argue, bad research can be everywhere. Open access is merely a dissemination method.[31] There are many legitimate open-access options.[32] These refutations do not mean open access is without recognized challenges, but that these myths are merely fallacies. Perpetuated by these myths, the negative perception of open-access journals as lower-quality publications is one of the greatest challenges, but not the only one.

3.2 Legitimate Challenges

Open access faces numerous legitimate challenges. Members of tenure and promotion committees may believe open-access myths or hold negative perceptions of open-access publishing. This can impact how these committees evaluate a scholar's work. Financial barriers present difficulties. While open access is free for the reader, there are still costs to cover. Financial challenges persist, with financial burdens placed on scholars, on the institution,

---

29 Niles et al., "Why We Publish Where We Do."

30 Peter Suber, "Open Access: Six Myths to Put to Rest," *Guardian,* October 21, 2013.

31 Jessica Lange and Jenn Riley, "Open Access and Open Data," lecture for Disrupting Disruptions: The Feminist and Accessible Publishing, Communications, and Technologies Speaker and Workshop Series, Montreal, QC, October 21, 2019, https://drive.google.com/file/d/11Slbwu_XfnhCp5XduG8JfHi0lfSj_qVr/view?usp=sharing.

32 McGill Library, "Finding Legitimate Quality OA Journals," 2020, https://www.mcgill.ca/library/services/open-access/legitimate-journals.

Engage in Public Scholarship! 94

potentially on taxpayers, and finally on the editor and journal staff. Open-access journals without stable funding sources raise concerns about stability, longevity, archiving, and how to coordinate access.

The myths surrounding open-access publishing create challenges. While open access is merely a dissemination method, articles published in open access journals are burdened by some scholars' perception that electronic publishing is of lower quality. This negative perception can have consequences in tenure and promotion decisions, although this is slowly changing.[33] As researcher of publishing practices Juan Pablo Alperin has shown, the response to open access in tenure and promotion decisions varies across universities, departments, and programs. He has found that when open-access articles are treated as having value, "it is strongly implied that it is a rigorous peer review process that confers value to an open access publication, not the increased access that it grants to the public."[34] So while university libraries and grant agencies may promote open access as part of a commitment to community engagement, tenure and promotion reviewers can veer from university policies.[35] As paywalled and open-access articles alike continue to be published in digital format, the form is less cause for concern, yet some naysayers persist. There is irony in grant agencies pushing

---

33 Chun and Thompson, "Issues in Publishing an Online, Open-Access CALL Journal."
34 Alperin et al., "Meta-Research."
35 François Shalom, "McGill Library Council Revises Open Access Statement," *McGill Reporter,* July 20, 2020.

Open Access 95

for open access, while committees evaluating grants, hiring, and promotion may penalize scholars for doing this work.

Journal publishing is also rife with financial challenges. Whether or not the journal is paywalled, authors, peer reviewers, and often even editors are not paid. While academic publishing always poses indirect financial burdens by requiring unremunerated labour, with open access there can be the additional direct financial burden on an individual scholar to pay for gold open access. Article processing charges have the potential to shift costs to the individual author, as opposed to being distributed in subscription models or requiring no direct cost, as is the case in platinum open access.[36] Sometimes a scholar can use grant money to pay the article processing charges. However, this practice results in a growing portion of research funds being spent on open access—publication fees, and can again encourage the cottage industry of low-impact, low-oversight journals.[37] As a result, publishing fees do not disappear but merely shift around. In addition, researchers in the humanities and social sciences tend to receive less grant money than researchers in the sciences, and thus do not always have the ability to publish in journals with article processing charges. Scholars in the developing world and at smaller institutions may not be able to publish in well-known journals because of article

---

36 Smith, "Examining Publishing Practices."
37 Shea and Prasad, "Open Issues with Open Access Publication."

Engage in Public Scholarship!

processing charges.[38] Neil Shea and Vinay Prasad add that when open-access article processing charges are funded primarily by an author's own grants, which are often publicly funded, the public then indirectly pays a second time to make the article open. They argue that in both gold open access and traditional paywalled publishing models, there are similar costs for taxpayers, having to pay for both the research and research access.[39] Open-access funds exist at some universities, such as the University of British Columbia Open Access Fund, which assist faculty members to publish in open-access books and journals when they are required to pay article processing charges. These funds set up by public universities are another way in which taxpayers must pay indirectly for both research and research access.[40] Tahla Imam contends that the issue with this argument against open access is that it downplays the costs authors incur under traditional journal publishing because some academic journals, especially in the sciences, also require fees for submission. To add to this, the publishers of traditional journals also retain the copyright to the authors' work. Open journal publishers such as Public Library of Science allow authors to retain copyright, and publication fees for print journals are often paid by the author.[41] Green open access does not have the same potential for abuse, although it often still requires a

---

38 Smith, "Examining Publishing Practices."
39 Shea and Prasad, "Open Issues with Open Access Publication."
40 Scholarly Communications @ UBC, "Open Access Fund for Humanities and Social Sciences Research," 2020, https://scholcomm.ubc.ca/ubc-open-access-fund/.
41 Imam, "Response to the 'Open Issues with Open Access Publication.'"

Open Access

copyright transfer agreement with the publisher, not with the repository, which commercial publishers request to discourage self-archiving more polished drafts.[42]

Open-access publishing, of all types, is not truly accessible for everyone, including the scholars who are doing this labour. Paywalled and open-access journals alike do not pay authors, peer reviewers, and most editors. This model is unsustainable. It is built on the idea that service work is part of a scholar's academic responsibilities and is considered in tenure and promotion decisions. However, while the majority of scholars in Canada and the United States no longer secure tenure-track jobs, journals still rely on a model in which it is assumed that editors, reviewers, and authors do not have to be paid for their labour because these are the expectations of tenure-track or tenured scholars. The offer of a course reduction in order to be the managing editor of a journal is meaningless if you are an adjunct without a stable salary and are paid per course. Herein lies the most convincing argument for open access. In 2018, the private publisher Elsevier had an operating-profit margin of 37 percent in 2019. At the publisher Taylor and Francis the operating profit margin was 29 percent, while Wiley's research publishing arm was 27 percent, and Springer Nature was 23 percent. For comparison, the 2019 operating margin at famously profitable Google was 26 percent.[43] These publishers made their profits by keeping

---

42 Smith, "Examining Publishing Practices."

43 Justin Fox, "How Scientific Journals Like Elsevier Need to Open Up," *Bloomberg*, June 6, 2020.

Engage in Public Scholarship! 98

articles behind paywalls, charging universities millions
of dollars in subscription fees, and requiring that authors
pay article processing charges to obtain gold open access.[44]
If authors, peer reviewers, and editors are going to do this
work without pay, at the very least the article should not be
published behind a paywall. If articles stay behind paywalls,
Elsevier and similar companies should pay for the expertise
of peer reviewers, as argued by James Heathers, founder of
the 450 Movement. He explains that based on his consulting
fees, profit-making paywalled journals should pay peer
reviewers $450 US. Heathers makes clear that he does not
think that this policy should apply to community journals
and open-access journals and that "it will not even occur to
me to charge them money. That is unthinkable and unfair."[45]
Heathers supports open-science movements but clarifies
that if paywalled journals continue to act as companies, with
their fiduciary responsibility resting with their shareholders
and not being accountable to the research community
and public, he will continue to ask to be paid. Following that
same logic, paywalled journals should pay editors. At
present, closed and open-access publishing is not financially
accessible for many authors, peer reviewers, and editors.
Each model shifts the meaning of access.

The different models of open access lead to various types of
access for different users and communities. Gold and hybrid
open access are not accessible for many authors who cannot
pay article processing charges and the journals might still

---

44   Lund and Zukerfeld, "Profiting from Open Access Publishing."
45   James Heathers, "The 450 Movement," *Medium,* September 3, 2020.

Open Access

99

profit from other people's free labour. Platinum open access does not result in pay for authors, reviewers, or editors, but at least authors do not have to pay article processing charges and readers and users can access the materials for free. These journals are less financially secure, however. Under green open access, authors are not paid but are unlikely to pay article processing charges, peer reviewers are not paid, journals profit, and readers must know how to find articles in various repositories. Further, the version of the article that users have access to in repositories will differ from the formatted version in the paywalled journal. As the Budapest Open Access Initiative argued, there are two complementary strategies: creating open-access journals and self-archiving in repositories. Both face challenges, from the perspectives of the scholars publishing and in terms of the ability to sustain a journal.

Platinum open access journals face financial uncertainty. They lack income from subscriptions and article processing charges, and thus depend on money from grants and donations. One potential solution is for university libraries to pool money to collectively fund open-access journals, creating much lower costs than paying the subscription fees from conglomerates such as Elsevier.[46] This strategy is one potential solution for the research journal—affordability problem. At present, journal prices are rising so libraries can only afford to grant access to a limited number of them. This results in the article-access/impact problem, in which the research impact is lost because potential readers do not

---

46   Goodman and Foster, "Special Focus on Open Access."

Engage in Public Scholarship!

have access to the material in traditional journals. As self-proclaimed "open access archivangelist" Stevan Harnad et al. write, "these problems are connected but different: even if publishers did not make a profit, libraries could not afford to pay for all journals."[47] University libraries working collectively could theoretically ameliorate these problems.

The other strategy proposed by the Budapest Open Access Initiative, self-archiving, has challenges as well. Harnad et al. argue that open access's best potential is self-archiving through institutional repositories, where all material is tagged in the same way—author, title, date—in order that these repositories can be combined into one searchable, open-access archive. However, coordinating access to different versions of material is still a problem.[48] Librarians David Goodman and Connie Foster argue that the preservation of open-access materials should be dealt with mainly through national libraries—like other electronic materials—and that most plans for article databases should have money supplied from government or institutional funding.[49] Essentially, the challenges for repositories are ensuring their stability, coordinating access, archiving, and maintaining longevity.

Open-access publishing faces struggles in actually being accessible and sustainable. There are also issues with delivering the material—making it accessible for those

---

47 Harnad et al., "The Access/Impact Problem and the Green and Gold Roads to Open Access," p. 37.
48 Goodman and Foster, "Special Focus on Open Access."
49 Goodman and Foster, "Special Focus on Open Access."

Open Access

101

with various disabilities, or in different languages, can be difficult. In some cases, such as articles that include multimedia, an archivable fixed version and an interactive version are needed. Open-access models often lack these facilities.[50] Thus, for open access to be a viable model, it must address these issues. There are benefits, however.

3.3 Benefits of Open Access

Despite its limitations, there are numerous benefits of open access: open-access scholarship is used more; open-access articles have a higher citation impact than paywalled articles;[51] and publishing in an open-access venue can lead to increased visibility. As Dorothy Chun and Irene Thompson argue: open-access articles can be read and cited more frequently; they can be accessed around the world; readers do not need to be affiliated with an institution or academic library (a concern of growing importance as non-tenure track and independent scholars lose institutional access); open access allows less-affluent institutions in developed countries the same access as institutions that can afford journal subscription fees; and scholars can retain some or all of their copyrights.[52] As stated in the introduction to the Tri-Agency Open Access Policy on Publications,

---

50 Goodman and Foster, "Special Focus on Open Access."
51 Harnad et al., "The Access/Impact Problem and the Green and Gold Roads to Open Access."
52 Chun and Thompson, "Issues in Publishing an Online, Open-Access CALL Journal."

Engage in Public Scholarship! 102

> Societal advancement is made possible through widespread and barrier-free access to cutting-edge research and knowledge, enabling researchers, scholars, clinicians, policymakers, private sector and not-for-profit organizations and the public to use and build on this knowledge ... Open access enables researchers to make their publications freely available to the domestic and international research community and to the public at large, thereby enhancing the use, application and impact of research results.[53]

Open access can further enable libraries and smaller institutions. Elizabeth H. Wood argues that open access has implications for libraries including the impact on subscription costs, institutional subsidizing of authors' fees, and libraries' negotiations with administrators.[54] Most optimistically, Chun and Thompson add that by publishing in open-access formats, researchers can contribute to societal good by providing scholarly content to a global audience.[55] At the very least, abstracts should be made open access, as argued by the Open Abstract Initiative.[56]

---

53 Communications Branch, "Tri-Agency Open Access Policy on Publications," Government of Canada website, December 21, 2016, https://www.ic.gc.ca/eic/site/063.nsf/eng/h_F6765465.html.
54 Wood, "Open Access Publishing."
55 Chun and Thompson, "Issues in Publishing an Online, Open-Access CALL Journal."
56 Initiative for Open Abstracts (@open_abstracts), "We're thrilled to announce the launch of the Initiative for Open Abstracts," Twitter thread, September 24, 2020, 10:20 AM, https://twitter.com/open abstracts/ status/1308984744080740352.

Open Access

103

Open access benefits from being online. The online format has numerous advantages, as argued by Chun and Thompson, including: more extensive dissemination and access; easy tracking of readership; impact (increased accessibility results in greater citation); virtually unlimited space through hypermedia (can link to other material/media without cost); quicker turnaround of manuscripts; lower cost of production; and the ability of editors and staff to live in different locations. For authors who then publicize this work, they can get ongoing feedback through social media, as online open-access journals can take advantage of online multimedia capabilities.[57] Open-access material is typically accessed electronically, which results in a lower cost per additional user than print formats. Although not everyone has access to the internet, this number is decreasing and often those without internet access have even worse access to printed scholarly publications.[58] Open access can also solve the problem of "versioning" (having multiple versions of a document, without knowing if your copy is the most recent) when used in concert with cross-indexing devices like OAISter that catalogue millions of records by harvesting open-access collections worldwide using the Open Archives Initiative Protocol for Metadata Harvesting (OAIPMH).[59] Open access would not be possible without the internet and this method of distribution confers additional benefits.

---

57 Chun and Thompson, "Issues in Publishing an Online, Open-Access CALL Journal."
58 Goodman and Foster, "Special Focus on Open Access."
59 OCLC, "The OAIster Initiative," 2020, https://www.oclc.org/en/oaister.html.

3.4 Pre-prints, Post-prints, Repositories, and Author Rights

Open access raises questions regarding author rights. With traditional academic journal publishing, authors transfer their rights to the publisher, sometimes resulting in not being able to use their own tables in later work. Copyright limits the possibility for published pieces to be used and authors may have to buy their work back from publishing companies.[60] The website SHERPA/ROMEO is a database of publisher policies.[61] Depending on the model of open access, a scholar does not necessarily need to pass rights to a publisher.[62] Questions of copyright are important when considering the role of self-archiving and repositories in open access.

Under the green open access model, authors deposit a version of their publication in an open-access repository without paying fees. Deposit can happen prior to or following formal publication. Open-access repositories have formed an important part of open-access implementation since the beginning of the open-access movement.[63] Using OpenDOAR data reports, librarian Stephen Pinfield's analysis of the global growth of open-access repositories from 2005 to 2012 shows a 1,660 percent rise of repository numbers, from 128 in December 2005 to 2,253 in December 2012.[64] Pinfield

---

60   Roach and Gainer, "On Open Access to Research."
61   Sherpa Romeo, "Index," 2020, http://www.sherpa.ac.uk/romeo/index.php.
62   Goodman and Foster, "Special Focus on Open Access."
63   Björk and Solomon, "How Research Funders Can Finance APCs in Full OA and Hybrid Journals."
64   Pinfield et al., "Open-Access Repositories Worldwide, 2005–2012."

Open Access

has also found 83 percent of repositories to be institutional, with a much smaller proportion of other sorts of repositories, particularly with 11 percent as subject repositories.[65] Repositories may have a disciplinary or an institutional focus. Hundreds of these repositories exist, and if you are a scholar seeking to follow a green open-access model, several could meet your needs. A few options include the Directory of Open Access Repositories, Canadian Academic Research Libraries (CARL), and SPARC Canadian Author Addendum (available in both English and French). A scholar's university may host their own repository. These are more likely to be stable or safe for longer than a personal website. If a researcher plans to submit their work to a repository, librarians Jenn Riley and Jessica Lange argue that you should automatically archive your versions and your author agreements.[66] The pre-print is the initial submission. The post-print is the version that has been accepted for publication and undergone full peer review, but has not been through the copyediting, typesetting, and proofreading process. This may lead to slight differences between the pre-print version and the version of record. The post-print version saved by the researcher can typically be posted to repositories, but often the author agreement requires that an author include a digital object identifier (DOI), a link, or a citation to the original article. Authors are rarely allowed to submit the publisher's version—the final copy with

---

65 Pinfield, "Making Open Access Work."

66 Jessica Lange and Jenn Riley, "Open Access and Open Data," Presentation for Disrupting Disruptions: The Feminist and Accessible Publishing, Communications, and Technologies Speaker and Workshop Series, Montréal, QC, October 21, 2019, https://drive.google.com/file/d/11SlbwuXfnhCp5XduG8JfHi0lfSj qVr/view.

Engage in Public Scholarship! 106

layout—to a repository. The Canadian Association of University Teachers advisory on retaining copyright in journal articles provides more details in its author rights guide.[67] Scholars need to select a repository where their work is most likely to be safe over the long term and can most effectively reach their desired audience.

Repositories ensure access to anyone with an internet connection, increase research visibility, satisfy open-access mandates of funding agencies, and provide long-term access to academic works, but they are not without challenges. Most publishers allow author-institution self-archiving, but Stevan Harnad argues that more researchers need to do it.[68] This could be accomplished with more institutional pressure to self-archive. An author survey by Alma Swan and Sheridan Brown showed that the majority of authors would self-archive if their employers mandated it.[69] Universities or research funders should support open access by implementing green open access self-archiving mandates. As Harnard explained in 2008, "about 10 percent of journals are gold, but over 90 percent are already green ... yet only about 10–20 percent of articles have been self-archived."[70] Despite this success, repositories face financial challenges. While some advocates

---

67 Canadian Association of University Teachers, "CAUT Intellectual Property Advisory," *CAUT Intellectual Property Advisory* 1, 2008, https://www.caut.ca/docs/default-source/copyright/intellectual-property-advisory---retaining-copyright-in-journal-articles-(july-2008).pdf.
68 Harnad et al., "The Access/Impact Problem and the Green and Gold Roads to Open Access."
69 Swan and Brown, *Open Access Self Archiving*.
70 Harnad et al., "The Access/Impact Problem and the Green and Gold Roads to Open Access."

Open Access

like Harnad argue that "it costs almost nothing: you just need a server, free software, and a few hours of a technician's time to set it up. Some of those who operate OA repositories would say it costs a small fortune to run an effective OA repository—for example, an ARL [Association of Research Libraries] study found that, for these very large university libraries, the mean cost of IR [information retrieval] implementation was more than 180,000 [US dollars] and the mean annual cost of operation was more than 110,000."[71] Again, repositories open up access to readers and users, and to a cohort of scholars who cannot afford gold open access. Meanwhile, the hosts of repositories must find funding. This is not the only challenge.

For repositories to be a trusted option for research dissemination it is necessary that documents are clearly marked to indicate their status. There must be a clear delineation between pre-prints that have not yet benefited from evaluation, and post-prints that have undergone peer review. The quality of the information contained within a document differs little between a post-print version, which might have a few typos and use simple formatting, and the version of record. However, the material in pre-prints may be disputed or rejected during the peer-review process. During the COVID-19 pandemic, the erosion of public trust in scholarship through the circulation of unreviewed pre-print articles became evident as pre-prints were impacting healthcare and public-health decisions.[72] This is not to

---

71   Crawford, *Open Access*, p. 36.
72   Vlasschaert, Topf, and Hiremath, "Proliferation of Papers and Preprints During the COVID-19 Pandemic."

Engage in Public Scholarship! 108

say that there is no value in circulating pre-prints; in the sciences it has been used as a technique for undergoing a form of crowdsourced open review.[73] Clear markings explaining the stage of the work offer researchers the opportunity to benefit from making research available earlier, while also mitigating confusion. Furthermore, clear markings can lend credence to repositories.

There is also the issue of the materials in repositories being spread out and hard to find. Open access means libraries have to rethink how to provide materials and teach the skills necessary for people to find them.[74] Several services already exist for searching repository materials. Pre-prints and post-prints in repositories appear in Google Scholar, but Google has recommendations to better facilitate discoverability in searches, including: that authors should upload a PDF where the filename ends with ".pdf"; that the title of the paper should appear in a large font on top of the first page; that the authors of the paper should be listed right below the title on a separate line; and that there should be a titled bibliography section, e.g., "References" or "Bibliography" at the paper's end.[75] For university repositories to facilitate their appearance in searches, Google recommends that they use the latest version of Eprints (eprints.org), Digital Commons (digitalcommons. bepress.com), or DSpace (dspace.org) software to host their papers. In addition to Google search results, Unpaywall is a browser extension that finds legal, free versions of (paywalled)

---

73   Sarabipour et al., "On the value of preprints."
74   Goodman and Foster, "Special Focus on Open Access."
75   Google Scholar, "Google Scholar Help," 2020, https://scholar.google.ca/intl/en/scholar/inclusion.html.

Open Access 109

scholarly articles. In July 2018 Unpaywall was reported to provide free access to 20 million articles, which accounts for about 47 percent of the articles that people search for with Unpaywall.[76] In June 2017 Unpaywall was integrated into Web of Science and in July 2018 Elsevier announced plans the same month to integrate the service into the Scopus search engine. In 2019, GetTheResearch was announced as a search engine for open-access content found by Unpaywall, with machine-learning features to facilitate discoverability. As evidenced by these existing services, green open access offers low-cost access without the risk of pirating.

3.5 Informal Access Shadow Libraries, Social Media Networks, and PDF Sharing

Repositories enable authors to legally adhere to publishing agreements while making their work open, however, some scholars have resorted to informal and at times illegal forms. The proprietary websites Academia.edu and ResearchGate can both serve as a kind of repository, where the understanding is that no documents uploaded will violate copyright. This does not mean that all users respect copyright laws.

Other platforms disregard copyright restrictions entirely. Sci-Hub is a platform for free access to scientific papers, founded by Alexandra Elbakyan, who is considered by some a Robin Hood figure. Sci-Hub is a shadow library, which is a pirate website that ignores intellectual property restrictions.

---

76   UnPaywall, "About," 2020, https://unpaywall.org.

Engage in Public Scholarship! 110

The illegality of shadow libraries makes them different from open-access platforms, but they are sometimes associated through the moniker "Black Open Access," referring to the black market. Sci-Hub is both a repository and a script to download open-access papers, which obtains access through users' voluntary contribution of credentials, or phishing. The site is decentralized though mirror sites and changes its domain name and host location periodically. Jeremy S. Faust finds that the main users of Sci-Hub are in countries with less institutional access, although many requests come from rich countries as it is faster to download from Sci-Hub than to request though a library. He argues that Sci-Hub is a wake-up call—it is not the solution to the problems with paywalled scholarship, but it is a reaction to inequality in publishing. Faust argues further that shadow libraries such as Sci-Hub have the potential to scare publishers into participating in open access or at least decreasing their subscription rates.[77] In a kind of nod to the success of the open-access discourse, and perhaps the threat of shadow libraries, some journals have adapted by giving out access codes to authors for fifty free reads. Providing this link is a limited acknowledgement to accessibility issues facing scholars without fully addressing them. It is also a strategy to discourage more informal or illegal resistance strategies.

While Sci-Hub is popular due to its simplicity and reliability, more informal networks of article sharing exist. Before Sci-Hub, people circumvented paywalls by requesting documents directly from the author or using the Twitter

---

77. Faust, "Sci-Hub."

Open Access 111

hashtag #ICanHazPDF. Facebook groups for sharing PDFs enable users with institutional access to share articles to people who cannot go beyond the paywall. Articles are not the only kinds of research that need to be shared, however.

4 Open Monographs and Open Textbooks

This chapter has been primarily concerned with the question of open-access journal articles. However open-access monographs face similar challenges. Open-access monographs are like other scholarly monographs in that they are single-volume books written for academic audiences. The difference is that open-access monographs are made freely available with Creative Commons licences. Though there are several types, all Creative Commons licences enable the free distribution of an otherwise copyrighted work and enable authors to grant other people the right to share, use, and build upon a work that they have created. Just as open-access journals have several publishing models, there are different business models for funding open-access books, including publication charges, institutional support, library publishing, and consortium models.[78] Open-access monographs seek to make knowledge more widely accessible, while at the same time addressing the monograph publishing crisis.

---

78   Newton et al., "Snapshots of three open access business models."

Engage in Public Scholarship!

Traditional models of monograph publishing are under threat; open-access monographs seek to address some of these issues. As with journals, university libraries struggle to assemble adequate collections of monographs and, since the 1990s, sales of monographs have shrunk by 90 percent, causing prices to rise dramatically as fewer copies are sold.[79] As founder of the (then) not-for-profit global library consortium Knowledge Unlatched Frances Pinter argues, open access monographs "can play an important role in ensuring both access to knowledge and encouraging the growth of new markets for scholarly books ... by facilitating a truly global approach to funding the up-front costs of publishing and open access, there is a sustainable future for the specialist academic 'long form publication.'"[80] As of mid-2014, a small number of presses have enabled green open access for books.[81] Presses such as the Amsterdam University Press allow green open access deposit for monographs, usually with an embargo of 18 to 24 months. For immediate access scholars must pay 6,950 euros.[82] Other presses publish a mix of ebook and print books, with presses such as Concordia University Press releasing electronic books "without any restrictions, via JSTOR, Manifold, and Project MUSE."[83] Green open access for monographs has yet to be implemented at the scale of journals, in part because "the economic structures for monograph production are

---

79 Pinter, "Open Access for Scholarly Books?"
80 Pinter, "Open Access for Scholarly Books?" p. 183.
81 Directory of Open Access Books, 2020, https://www.doabooks.org.
82 Amsterdam Open Access Books, 2020, https://www.aup.nl/en/publish/open-access.
83 Concordia University Press, 2020, https://www.concordia.ca/press/about.html.

Open Access

tightly bound into editorial and gatekeeping functions, yielding a high cost to reach first copy."[84] However, there is promise in the endeavour.

Open-access monographs encounter challenges that both open-access journals and traditional scholarly monographs face. Like open-access journal models, there is also a gold open-access model for monographs with book processing charges. At present, the current rates requested by established presses under such a system are high and pose real, possibly insurmountable challenges for unfunded research, costing upwards of $2,000 US per chapter.[85] These book processing charges pose the same funding challenges as gold open-access publishing for articles. It should be noted that it is often necessary to offset publication costs with subventions for print books without an open-access component as well, due to the declining sales of scholarly monographs since the 1990s. The publication subvention has become a routine part of the publication process, whether a book is open access or not, meaning that these challenges are not limited to open-access books. If a book processing charge is necessary regardless, at least creating an open-access monograph increases access for readers. There are other experimental models, however, that do not rely solely on publication charges to produce gold open-access books. These models can be similar to platinum open-access journals, which rely on grants for the press, and fundraising. Scholar of publishing Martin Paul Eve remarks that, "As with OA journals, it is also worth noting that some

---

84   Eve, *Open Access and the Humanities*, p. 136.
85   Eve, *Open Access and the Humanities*.

Engage in Public Scholarship! 114

open-access book efforts are scholar-led and subsist entirely on volunteerism, a model that certainly will not scale to cover the entire field but does seem to work within niche contexts."[86] Open-access books offer new possibilities for publishing, and have the potential to aid both digital and print publishing, with research showing that open-access book versions actually increase print sales.[87] Funding this work remains a challenge.

Monographs are not the only form of open-access books. The Rebus Foundation has invested in open-access textbooks. Zoe Wake Hyde and Apurva Ashok note in their guide for open-access textbooks that "knowledge shouldn't be contained, and knowledge should never come from only one source."[88] Open access textbooks are a form of open educational resources (OER), which are freely accessible, openly licensed text, media, and other digital works that are useful for teaching, learning, and assessing. Philosophy professor Jonathan Jenkins Ichikawa has made an open-access introductory logic textbook, produced under a Creative Commons licence. He explains that because the textbook is free for all students and instructors to use, the course is made more financially accessible.[89] Open-access textbooks face similar challenges to open monographs and open-access articles. These challenges rest in the publication of finished works.

---

86 Eve, *Open Access and the Humanities*, p.131.
87 Peter Suber, "Open Access Overview (definition, introduction)," 2020, http://legacy.earlham.edu/~peters/fos/overview.htm.
88 Ashok and Hyde, *The Rebus Guide to Publishing Open Textbooks (So Far)*.
89 Jonathan Jenkins Ichikawa, "forall x: UBC edition," 2018, http://jichikawa.net/ forall-x-ubc-edition.

Open Access

4.1 Paywalls Outside of Academic Journals

While other sections of this book will discuss writing forms other than journal and monograph writing, the question of paywalls and closed publishing is relevant here as it applies to non-academic journals, newspapers, and publications. Paywalls are not solely a concern with academic journals. As scholars carefully decide what academic journals are worthy of their articles and labour, scholars must also consider the paywalls of non-academic resources. Free online content is often subsidized by subscriptions or advertising space. The shift from digital content has meant that while content consumption has increased, users are no longer willing to pay for it. Hence the recent increase in the popularity of paywalls, as digital journalism requires direct financial support. In the 2000s, paywalls were seen as a way of protecting the print business. The *New York Times* was one of the first to introduce a paywall meant to generate a profit in 2011.[90] Online subscriptions can drive readers away from online content and can limit ad revenue. Paywalls decrease the engagement of online readership but increase print circulation.[91] So even when a scholar chooses to do the work of knowledge translation, there may be new barriers. These are merely strategies that are part of the larger project of accessibility.

---

90 Alexis Madrigal, "Prepare for the New Paywall Era," *Atlantic*, November 30, 2017.

91 Pattabhiramaiah, Sriram, and Manchanda, "Paywalls."

4.2　Knowledge Translation and Open Does Not Mean Accessibility

Uploading a PDF to a website is not the same as accessibility —whether that PDF is hosted by a hybrid journal, an open-access journal, or is held in a repository. Just because an article is no longer paywalled does not mean that it is accessible. One barrier has been removed, and that is an important step towards accessibility. The article may still only be read by a small group of scholars, however. One issue is that many members of the public are not trained in how to find these resources, whether in academic journals or in repositories. Another issue is that even when people can find the article, the language within the article may not be accessible. Putting a PDF online or pasting scrollable text on a web page is not the same as knowledge translation. A piece can be "open" but still be inaccessible. To be clear, I am not arguing against the need to, on occasion, write highly discipline-specific work for a small group of scholars. Articles like these have their utility. However, we should not mistake open access for being the same thing as accessibly published scholarship. Openness is just a start, or as podcaster Hannah McGregor discussed in relation to Moya Bailey's work, openness is not the goal but the result of an ethical framework.[92]

92　Hannah McGregor, "Secret Feminist Agenda: Podcasting Public Scholarship and Accountability," *Secret Feminist Agenda,* November 23, 2017, https://secretfeministagenda.com/2017/11/23/bonus-episodepodcasting-public-scholarship-and-accountability/.

Open Access 117

Unfortunately, academic journals constrain a scholar's ability to write in accessible language or forms. With the exception of experimental journals, the typical academic journal follows disciplinary format expectations, with little variation: an introduction; a literature review; an outline of methodology; a presentation of data or findings; an analysis; and a conclusion. Some disciplines discuss epistemology and some will refer to data analysis as textual analysis. However, the general format remains. When scholars deviate in form or language, they are often met with resistance. As graduate student Casarina Hocevar writes, "I have been deliberately trying to write more straightforward and prioritize accessible language in my academic writing—and I think I've achieved this [very] well with my most recent paper," but she feared not being taken seriously as a scholar. Historian Lynn Kozak responded that she "just got a paper rejected which apparently 'reads more like a magazine piece.' I was like 'oh no' and 'yes!!!' at the same time." Hocevar responded, "It's silly that making our work more accessible can be seen as a downside."[93] Scholars who aim to make their writing more accessible are often pressured in the peer-review process to restructure their articles to fit academic norms. While some resistance can occur within academic journals, and can be achieved by restructuring peer reviewers' expectations, journal procedures, and editorial decisions to make research findings more accessible, scholars may also look to writing in different genres and outlets. While there

---

93   Lynn Kozak (@lynnashleykozak) and Casarina Hocevar (@Casarina), "Just got a paper rejected which apparently 'reads more like a magazine piece'," Twitter thread, May 7, 2020, 1:39 PM, https://twitter.com/lynnashleykozak/status/1258451513791467520.

Engage in Public Scholarship!

118

was once a journalistic network that would help with the conveyance of scholarly thought to a public audience, those media roles have been drastically diminished and the labour of knowledge translation now must be done by scholars themselves.

5 Conclusion

Open access is not the same thing as justice, or as A Bee with a Blog writes, "The open movement failed when it centred freedom over justice. It failed when it placed abstract principles above actual human lives ... [and when] it failed to understand structures of oppression and chose instead to emphasize individual solutions to collective challenges."[94] Open access is not the same thing as accessible public scholarship and this form of distribution must address issues around labour equity and various levels of social injustice in order to be truly accessible. These issues are apparent in open-source and open-data discussions as well. The next chapter attends to these challenges.

---

94   A Bee with a Blog, "Open Is Cancelled," *Medium,* January 13, 2020, https://medium.com/@beewithablog/open-is-cancelled-da7dd6f2aaaf.

CHAPTER 6

Open Data and Open Source

The open movements are not restricted to the model of open-access literature; there are also the open-data and open-source movements. This chapter will look at the role of open data and open source in disseminating research and knowledge. Although this chapter does not focus on the open-source movement, particular lessons from the open-source movement are elucidating. The chapter particularly challenges the idea of "open" as meaning "accessible" by raising the issue of whether all data should actually be "open" and "open" for whom.

1   Open-Source Movement

The open-source movement supports the use of open-source licences for some or all software which enables, in theory, anyone to obtain and modify open-source code. The benefits of the open-source movement are that it promotes the creation of software that is not proprietary; that no one can discriminate against a group by failing to share the edited code, or hinder others from editing their already-edited work; and that it promotes working cooperatively with other people to improve open-source technology.[1] There are a few major drawbacks, however, relating to unequal skill sets, insufficient maintenance, and a lack of diversity. Participants need to have programming expertise in order to engage in open-code modification and exchange, and people interested in supporting the open-source movement may lack this skill set. Production can be very limited, and because no one is paid to maintain projects many of them are never completed, a topic raised frequently on the Maintainers listserv.[2] The open-source community is not representative of the general population; the majority of programmers in open source communities are men.[3] Researchers found that only 1.5 percent of all contributors are women.[4] Ashe Dryden argues that one factor for the gender disparity is that "marginalized people in tech—women, people of color, people with disabilities, LGBTQ people, and others—have less free time for a few major reasons: dependent care, domestic work and errands, and pay inequity," and thus are less able to spend time

---

1   Open Source Initiative, "Open Source," 2020, https://opensource.org/docs/osd.
2   Andrew Russell and Lee Vinsel, "Hail the Maintainers," *Aeon,* April 7, 2016.
3   Nafus, "'Patches Don't Have Gender.'"
4   Nafus, Leach, and Krieger, "Gender."

Open Data and Open Source

on unpaid open-source labour.[5] As Mozilla fellow Caroline Sinders argues, "Open source isn't perfect and isn't a panacea when it comes to technology inflicting harm in society, but a focus on better, more accessible, and more usable designed open source tools can help provide alternatives to for-profit tools maintained by companies with questionable values."[6] Here Sinders points to how the open-source movement distributes power and control. Similar benefits and problems are evident in the open-data movement. The question of power remains salient.

2 Open Data

The open-data movement promotes the idea that data should be freely available for everyone to use and republish as they wish, without restrictions from copyright, patents, or other mechanisms of control. At present, large swaths of data are controlled by private companies.[7] While data collection has the potential to benefit communities,[8] journalist Ben Tarnoff argues, "Big data is extractive ... Extractive industries

---

5   Ashe Dryden, "The Ethics of Unpaid Labor and the OSS Community," *Ashe Dryden Blog,* November 13, 2013, https://www.ashedryden.com/blog/the-ethics-of-unpaid-labor-and-the-osscommunity.

6   Caroline Sinders, "Examining the Human Labor Behind AI," Mozilla Foundation, May 14, 2020, https://foundation.mozilla.org/en/blog/examining-human-labor-behind-ai/.

7   Helbing et al., "Will Democracy Survive Big Data and Artificial Intelligence?"

8   Actionable Intelligence for Social Policy, 2020, https://www.aisp.upenn.edu.

Engage in Public Scholarship!

need to be closely regulated because they generate all sorts of externalities—costs that aren't borne by the company, but are instead passed on to society as a whole." He adds, "Regulating big data is a good start, but it's far from revolutionary. In fact, it's already begun." The General Data Protection Regulation (GDPR) that took effect in the European Union in 2018

> embodies aspects of this approach, imposing new obligations on companies that collect personal data. [US] Congress isn't anywhere close to passing something similar, but it's not impossible to imagine some basic protections around data privacy and algorithmic transparency emerging within the next decade. More public oversight is welcome, but insufficient. Regulating how data is extracted and refined is necessary. To democratize big data, however, we need to change who benefits from its use.[9]

He argues for democratizing or nationalizing data control. Tarnoff is not alone in arguing for public control and access to data. The Obama administration's Open Data Directive pushed federal agencies to make data available, and also served as a catalyst for many cities to open data sets.[10] The Canadian National Research Councils (SSHRC, NSERC, and CIHR) have also put forward calls for researchers to make their data sets

---

9   Ben Tarnoff, "The Data Is Ours!" *Logic,* April 1, 2018.
10 Costanza-Chock, "Design Justice, AI, and Escape from the Matrix of Domination."

Open Data and Open Source

accessible in order to encourage innovation.[11] While under the current model data is largely owned by big companies and used to generate profit, the push for a more democratic model is only one step to consider.

The key benefit of open data is that both the public and researchers can build on others' work—holes and gaps in the research can be more readily found—and as Rufus Pollack, pioneer in the Open Data movement, argues, "The best thing to do with your data will be thought of by someone else."[12] There are some fields, such as astronomy, in which data reuse has been significant.[13] Large-scale astronomical data collection is expensive, and the field benefits through data sharing.

However, when data relates to human experiences the matter is more complicated. As Lauren Klein and Catherine D'Ignazio's book, *Data Feminism*, argues, "in a world in which data is power, and that power is wielded unequally, data feminism can help us understand how it can be challenged and changed."[14] They continue, "This potential for good, on the one hand, and harm, on the other, makes it essential to ask: Data science by whom? Data science for whom? Data science with whose interests in mind?"[15] While the open-

---

11 Communications Branch, "Tri-Agency Statement of Principles on Digital Data Management," Government of Canada Website, January 21, 2021, https://www.ic.gc.ca/eic/site/063.nsf/eng/h 83F7624E.html.

12 Rufus Pollack (@rufuspollack), "The best thing to do with your data will be thought of by someone else," Twitter, April 20, 2017, 9:43 AM, https://twitter.com/rufuspollock/status/855054231153369090.

13 Canadian Astronomy Data Centre, 2020, https://www.cadc-ccda.hia-iha.nrc-cnrc.gc.ca/en/ about.html.

14 D'Ignazio and Klein, *Data Feminism*, p. 9.

15 D'Ignazio and Klein, *Data Feminism*, p. 14.

Engage in Public Scholarship! 124

data movement directs scholars to share their data sets, the *Feminist Data Manifest-No* "is a declaration of refusal and commitment. It refuses harmful data regimes and commits to new data futures." This Manifest-No includes a refusal "to operate under the assumption that risk and harm associated with data practices can be bounded to mean the same thing for everyone, everywhere, at every time. We commit to acknowledging how historical and systemic patterns of violence and exploitation produce differential vulnerabilities for communities."[16] Thus, while making data open can enable underfunded scholars and researchers to have access to sets that they wouldn't have the resources for, not all data should be reused.

Open data requires limitations. Ben Tarnoff acknowledges that even with the push for open data, "there are certain kinds of data we shouldn't be extracting. There are certain places where we shouldn't build data mines. And the incredibly complex and opaque process whereby raw data is refined into knowledge needs to be cracked wide open, so we can figure out what further rules are required."[17] There are also limitations in open-data repositories including: personally identifiable information; legal privacy constraints; contractual obligations; ownership of intellectual property; and Indigenous peoples' data. These categories show that not all data can be legally open, yet these categories continue to remain under consideration. Furthermore, there are restrictions on when certain data can be accessed. For

---

16 *Feminist Data Manifest-No*, 2020, https://www.manifestno.com.
17 Tarnoff, "The Data Is Ours!"

Open Data and Open Source

example, full census data in the United States is not available for seventy-two years and Canada's census data is not made public for ninety-two years.[18] However, we must move beyond questions of legality, as "open data standards are political, yet they are built in technical spaces devoid of political or social implications."[19] Not all data should be open.

Open data can hurt marginalized communities. Data collection has been used to criminalize and police.[20] It has limited access to credit, jobs, and housing.[21] It has been used to gerrymander political districts in order to politically under-represent Black communities,[22] limit access to healthcare,[23] and magnify gender bias in hiring practices.[24] As AI researcher Deborah Raji makes clear, "Data will always be a subjective interpretation of someone's reality, a specific presentation of the goals and perspectives we choose to prioritize in this moment. That's a power held by those of us responsible for sourcing, selecting, and designing this data and developing the models that interpret the information."[25] Data collection can cause harm.

---

18 In 2006, Canadians had to consent to have their information released ninety-two years later.
19 Ana Brandusescu, Michael Canares, and Silvana Fumega, "Open Data Standards Design Behind Closed Doors?" *IDLA*, August 21, 2020.
20 Richardson, Schultz, and Crawford, "Dirty Data, Bad Predictions."
21 Petty et al., "Reclaiming Our Data."
22 Waymer and Heath, "Black Voter Dilution, American Exceptionalism, and Racial Gerrymandering."
23 Shraddha Chakradhar, "Widely Used Algorithm for Follow-Up Care in Hospitals Is Racially Biased, Study Finds," *Stat News*, October 24, 2019.
24 Jeffrey Dastin, "Amazon Scraps Secret AI Recruiting Tool That Showed Bias against Women," *Reuters*, October 10, 2018.
25 Deborah Raji, "How Our Data Encodes Systematic Racism," *Technology Review*, December 10, 2020.

Engage in Public Scholarship! 126

Where there is harm, there is resistance. The efforts against certain kinds of data collection have been led by Yeshimabeit Milner, founder and executive director of Data for Black Lives. Milner discusses how

> Big Data is more than a collection of technologies and more than a revolution in measurement and prediction. It has become a philosophy, an ideological regime, one that determines how decisions are made and who makes them. It has given legitimacy to a new form of social and political control, one that has taken the digital traces of our existence and found ways to use them to sort and manage populations. Big Data is part of a long and pervasive historical legacy of scientific oppression, aggressive public policy and the most influential political and economic institution that has and continues to shape this country's economy: chattel slavery. Algorithms and other data technologies are the engines that have facilitated the ongoing evolution of chattel slavery into the Prison Industrial Complex, justified the militarization of schoolyards and borders alike, and continued the expansion of contemporary practices of peonage.[26]

Milner's work serves as a call to action to reject the concentration of Big Data in the hands of a select few.[27] Similarly, artist-researcher Mimi Onuoha's project,

26 Yeshimabeit Milner, "Abolish Big Data," UCIBrenICS, March 8, 2019, YouTube video, 58:09, https://www.youtube.com/watch?v=26IM2RGAdIM&t=596s.
27 Data for Black Lives, 2020, https://d4bl.org.

Open Data and Open Source

127

Missing Datasets (2018), shows holes in data collection, particularly concerning women, people of colour, and LGBTQ communities. She shows how metrified societies require the fluid, organic messiness of people to be secured, tagged, categorized, and abstracted. In Missing Datasets, Onuoha emphasizes that not all data should be collected and if or when it is collected it should not be made open to everyone, because making certain data sets endangers marginalized communities.[28] For example, data sets on immigration status could increase deportations if they fall into the wrong hands.

There are multiple popular metaphors for data. Laudatory metaphors include the idea of data as the new oil. Users of this metaphor focus on the economic value of oil and data.[29] However, oil as a commodity is imbued with a politically charged history. More critical metaphors build on this idea, using the concept of data as violence[30] and data as radioactive.[31] Journalist Stacy-Marie Ishmael takes this data as radioactive metaphor seriously and asks, "How will you treat it? How will you dispose of it safely? What will you do if there is a breach?"[32] There are limits to the degree that data

---

28 Refer to Mimi Onouha, *Library of Missing Datasets 2.0*, 2018, https://mimionuoha.com/the-library-of-missing-datasets-v-20.

29 Kiran Bhageshpur, "Data Is the New Oil," *Forbes,* November 15, 2019.

30 Hoffmann, "Terms of Inclusion."

31 Cory Doctorow, "Personal Data Is as Hot as Nuclear Waste," *Guardian,* January 15, 2008.

32 Rose Eveleth (host), "Should I Let My Company Put a Chip in My Hand?" *Advice for and from the Future* (podcast), August 25, 2020, https://www.listennotes.com/podcasts/advice-forand/should-i-let-my-company-put-3byr-GFmAOe/.

should be open. Certain degrees of openness actually limit access by actively harming other people or communities.

3   Should Everything Be Open?

There are limits to openness. As part of a discussion for Open Publishing Fest on May 26, 2020, organized by the Account for Labor Implications of Open Publishing, educator Monica Brown writes, "I think there are some concerns around the appropriation of knowledge in open publishing. Historically, when so many marginalized communities have had their ideas and contributions stolen, it makes venturing into #openlabor risky." This was expanded upon by open education technologist Lorna M. Campbell, writing, "Equitable access to and participation in the creation of open knowledge absolutely has to take this into account. This is critical." Sociolinguist Lauren B. Collister responded, "I'm a linguist and work with lots of linguists on data. The phrase 'as open as possible, as closed as necessary' means a lot to the researchers I work with in their communities. Participants need to be involved to understand how closed is 'necessary.'"[33] Marginalized communities risk further marginalization through certain frames of openness, especially, but not limited to, open data. The historical

---

33   Monica Brown (@EssentiallyEmBe), "I think there are some concerns around the appropriation of knowledge in open publishing," Twitter, May 2, 2020, 2:47 PM, https://twitter.com/EssentiallyEmBe/status/1265353837725904897.

Open Data and Open Source

and current extraction of knowledge from marginalized communities necessitates limits on openness, as do concerns about safety and labour.

Not all work should be made open because not all knowledge is for everyone. Indigenous knowledges have the right to be closed to community outsiders. As Abigail Echo Hawk, who works on decolonizing data, states, "When we think about data, and how it's been gathered, is that, from marginalized communities, it was never gathered to help or serve us. It was primarily done to show the deficits in our communities, to show where there are gaps."[34] Echo Hawk discusses how data collection is so often used against Indigenous communities, noting that "for many native communities, there's hesitancy to participate in government funded data gathering and state-funded and county-funded data gathering, because that information has always been used against us, never for us."[35] She argues that it is important to recover the

> traditional value systems of what data is and how it is meant to be used, and reclaim that we have always been data gatherers, we have always been the scientists who analyzed the data, and we have always been the community that participated in the analysis of that to ensure the well-being of our future generations ... Our way of being, acting,

---

34 Manola Secaira, "Abigail Echo-Hawk on the Art and Science of 'Decolonizing data,'" *The Crosscut,* May 31, 2019.
35 Rose Eveleth, "Dollars for Data," *Flash Forward* (podcast), July 21, 2020, https://www.flashforwardpod.com/ 2020/07/21/dollars-for-data/.

driving, living is sacred knowledge. And the only folks who should and do have any purview over that is our communities, and so we live in a society as Indigenous people where we think as a community. And how do we as individuals benefit that community as a whole.[36]

She is not alone in making this argument.

The Indigenous Protocol and Artificial Intelligence Working Group is invested in the question of data sovereignty. Their position paper considers who should be the knowledge keepers of this data.[37] Members of the working group, Indigenous researchers Peter-Lucas Jones and Keoni Mahelona, who worked to create the first automatic speech recognizer (ASR) for te reo Māori using DeepSpeech, speak to the importance of data stewardship. To be a steward is not the same as owning data; rather, stewardship is a different kind of relationship in which Indigenous people are able to be guardians of their community's data and care for it.[38] The question of who should steward Indigenous data continues to be discussed. The topic was raised repeatedly during the Indigenous in AI Affinity Workshop on December 10, 2020, at the NeuroIPS conference, organized by Michael Running Wolf, Caroline Running Wolf, Shawn Tsosie, and Caleb Moses, and during the Indigenous Protocols and Artificial Intelligence

---

36   Evelyth, "Dollars for Data."
37   Lewis et al., "Indigenous Protocol and Artificial Intelligence Position Paper."
38   Caroline Running Wolf, Michael Running Wolf, Shawn Tsosie, Caleb Moses, and Jason Lewis, "Indigenous in AI Affinity Workshop," 2020, https://indigenousinai.org.

Open Data and Open Source

Working Group Roundtable as part of the Resistance in AI Workshop that included Suzanne Kite, Ashley Cordes, Oiwi Parker Jones, and Jason Lewis in March and May 2019.[39] These panelists returned to the idea that decisions surrounding Indigenous data should be made in consultation with the communities, and that this is only possible by building relationships and trust. While acknowledging the harm data usage can cause, Hawaiian scholar Noelani Arista writes that it is possible to use "data in ways that allow us to synthesize ancestral knowledge and rebuild systems of knowledge keeping and transmission."[40] However, the use of data about Indigenous communities should be stewarded by these communities. Settlers have a long history of extracting knowledge from Indigenous communities; Indigenous communities have the right to keep some knowledge closed when making it open is not safe to do.[41]

Openness is a project in which it is not safe for every group to participate. LGBTQ2S+ communities risk certain kinds of exposure. Historian of gay and lesbian bars Greggor Mattson worries that, by publishing images of gay bars online as part of his public history work, he might inadvertently out someone who is closeted.[42] This is a challenge also encountered by public-facing, open digital collections managed by archives that house LGBTQ2S+ materials. Elspeth Brown of the Canadian queer archives, ArQuives, discusses this challenge

---

39 Neural Information Processing Systems Conference, "Public Schedule," 2020, https://nips.cc/virtual/2020/public/cal_main.html.
40 Lewis et al., "Indigenous Protocol and Artificial Intelligence Position Paper."
41 Tuck, "Suspending Damage."
42 Ketchum, "Lost Spaces, Lost Technologies, and Lost People."

in making LGBTQ2S+ oral histories more accessible online.[43] Geographer Julie Podmore shares in this challenge for queer and lesbian archives in the age of archival digitization.[44] LGBTQ2S+ communities are not alone in facing risks if data, resources, and materials about them are made open. As discussed previously, Mimi Onuoha, Yeshimabeit Milner, and others show how open data poses risks to immigrant and racialized communities. Camille Acey, through her work with the Collective for Liberation, Ecology, and Technology (COLET), points to the overlapping struggles of Black people, women, people from the Global South, poor people, Indigenous people, queer people, trans people, imprisoned and trafficked people, and those persecuted for their documentation or religious status. Acey shows that while open source can lead to empowerment, there are limitations.[45] It is not safe for all communities to have their writings, data, and resources made open. Openness can exacerbate disparities.

When considering openness, certain groups are asked to perform more labour than others. Education writer Audrey Watters raises this point when she reflects on why she decided to remove Creative Commons licensing at the footer of each article on her website, writing, "As a woman who writes online about technology, I have grown far too tired of 'permission-less-ness.' Because 'open' doesn't just mean using my work for free without asking. It actually often means demanding I do more work—justify my

---

43   Brown and Davidmann, "'Queering the Trans Family Album.'"
44   Podmore, "Gone 'Underground'?"
45   COLET, "Work with Us," 2020, https://colet.space/work-with-us/.

Open Data and Open Source

decisions, respond to accusations, and constantly rethink how and where I want to be and am able to be and work on the Internet." She continues, "So I've been thinking a lot, as I said, about 'permissions' and 'openness.' I have increasingly come to wonder if 'permission-less-ness' as many in 'open' movements have theorized this, is built on some unexamined exploitation and extraction of labor—on invisible work, on unvalued work. Whose digital utopia does 'openness' represent?"[46] Openness creates possibilities for readers, as advocate of open access Peter Suber writes, but, as this chapter makes clear, it also creates new barriers and new burdens. The labour of openness shifts from one group to another, depending on the model. It is important to be cognizant of whom is being asked to do this work, and to think of the gendered, classed, and racialized labour required in doing this work.

4   Conclusion

In *The People's Platform: Taking Back Power and Culture in the Digital Age*, author and filmmaker Astra Taylor shows the contradictions inherent in the word "open." "Openness" is an ideal espoused by techno-utopianists ranging from John Perry Barlow in his manifesto "A Declaration of the Independence of Cyberspace" (1996) to Facebook founder

---

46   Audrey Watters, "Invisible Labor and Digital Utopias," *Hack Education*, May 4, 2018.

Engage in Public Scholarship! 134

Mark Zuckerberg in his claim that he designed Facebook to make the world more "open and connected." The concept of "openness" overlooks issues around ownership and equity. While "openness" can indeed enable the spread of knowledge, it is important to recognize who actually benefits from "openness." Although the internet theoretically levels the playing field and offers the promise of democratic access to knowledge and the ability to spread it, the reality is quite different.[47]

The open-access, open-data, and open-source movements are important contributions to the conversation about who gets access to knowledge. As the public funds much academic research, this work should be made available to them. However, the open-access, open-data, and open-source movements do not address all of the barriers to accessibility. For work to be accessible, the work itself needs to take new forms. This requires different forms of scholarly outputs. The next chapter will look to these other kinds of scholarly outputs.

---

47   Morozov, *The Net Delusion*.

PART II
Toolkits

Part II offers practical strategies for doing public scholarship. Readers may elect to read these chapters in non-sequential order, deciding to prioritize some forms of public scholarship above others. These toolkits are unable to wholly escape the problematics discussed in earlier chapters, but instead offer examples of best practices given the limitations under which we work. Digital technologies will continue to evolve. As a result, the specificity of future tactics and forms of public scholarship may change. Nevertheless, the underlying lessons of the following chapters will remain relevant.

CHAPTER 7

Proprietary Platforms, Corporate Influence, and Social Media

This chapter begins by exploring how to choose the form or forms of public scholarship with which you wish to engage. This is followed by a discussion about the limitations of any medium, particularly the challenges surrounding proprietary platforms and corporate influence in various communication technologies. The chapter applies these lessons by analyzing popular forms of social media and their utility within research dissemination. In this way, the chapter treats social media as a serious form of public scholarship.

1 Choosing the Medium

Public scholarship can take a variety of forms, so choosing the medium for your public scholarship should take into

Engage in Public Scholarship! 138

account the needs of the individual scholar, the intended audiences, and the subject matter. A scholar must account for the financial, time, and infrastructural resources required by a particular medium. Consider the skills, training, and tools required to work in a particular form, and your energy and willingness to learn them. The form you choose will impact the audiences you reach and the ways you are able to display your materials. If the community that you wish to reach does not have computers, it does not make sense to publish digital materials. If your audience is primarily on the social media platform Facebook, you might choose to use Facebook even if you have reservations about the proprietary nature of that tool. Meet your audience where they already are—or expect to spend resources on training audiences to use new platforms.[1]

The ideal medium for your public scholarship will also fit the kinds of materials that you wish to share. If your work relies on visual imagery, audio formats of public scholarship such as podcasts may be impractical. This does not mean that an audio format cannot work, but it might need to be creatively supplemented. By considering the nature of your content and your desired target audiences, the form you choose will work to assist your public engagement goals. If possible, soliciting feedback from your intended audiences in the form of community consultation earlier in the process of creation can facilitate choices around

---

1   Artist Alamac, "Collaborators," 2020, https://sites.google.com/alum. calarts.edu/ almanac-workshop/home.

Proprietary Platforms, Corporate Influence, and Social Media   139

form.[2] With any medium there will be compromises, and no solution will be perfect. It may be necessary to undergo a process of trial and error in order to find the types of public scholarship that work best for you, your audiences, and your subject matter. The tools used for this work can also raise ethical questions.

2   Trigger Warnings and Content Warnings

If your public scholarship includes work with content that includes physical, verbal, emotional, sexual, or racial violence, consider using content or trigger warnings. Content warnings are verbal or written notices that precede potentially sensitive content. These notices flag the contents of the material that follows so readers, listeners, or viewers can prepare themselves to adequately engage or, if necessary, disengage with the content for their own well-being.[3] Trigger warnings are intended to give people with post-traumatic stress disorder and others who have experienced trauma an idea of what is included in the content. These warnings can appear

---

2   A full discussion of community consultation is outside of the scope of this chapter. For more information on community consultation, see Norton and Hughes, *Public Consultation and Community Involvement in Planning*.

3   LSA Inclusive Teaching Initiative, "An Introduction to Content Warnings and Trigger Warnings," 2020, https://sites.lsa.umich.edu/inclusive-teaching/inclusive-classrooms/an-introduction-to-content-warnings-and-trigger-warnings/.

Engage in Public Scholarship! 140

at the start of a publication or in front of a particular section.[4] Both content and trigger warnings enable individuals to choose when or if they want to interact with the work. While there are debates about the utility of trigger warnings,[5] the debate stems primarily from a misunderstanding regarding what these warnings are and what their intention is. Rather than being a form of censorship, they can make materials more inclusive.[6] As feminist disability studies scholar Angela Carter argues, "Trigger warnings provide a way to 'opt in' by lessening the power of the shock and the unexpectedness, and granting the traumatized individual agency to attend to the affect and effects of their trauma."[7] Providing a trigger warning above content, as Alice Wong did above certain chapters in *Disability Visibility*, did not prevent anyone from reading the text. Instead, she argues that within the book, there are "a lot of things that are really serious and disturbing and readers should have a head's up and to protect themselves and to read it or not ... It does not take anything away from the content. It just adds to it and I think this is absolutely the future in terms of just ways we can really be thoughtful in our

---

4   Critical race scholars have made clear that it is important to be intentional about the use of violent images and content, such as videos of police brutality, in your scholarship due to its ability to re-traumatize or traumatize oppressed communities. (Scott, "Introduction: Black Images Matter.")

5   Kelli Marshall, "Trigger Warnings, Quentin Tarantino, and the College Classroom," *The Chronicle of Higher Education,* March 7, 2014.

6   LSA Inclusive Teaching Initiative, "An Introduction to Content Warnings and Trigger Warnings."

7   Carter, "Teaching with Trauma."

work."[8] Content warnings provide people with information so they can make informed decisions.

3 Proprietary Platforms and Corporate Influence

The technologies behind self-publishing, website design, social media, and other digital communicative technologies that scholars use for public scholarship are not neutral. It is vital that scholars engage with research that critically analyzes technology if we seek to truly expand accessibility and create ways of communicating our scholarship in an accessible, feminist, and socially just manner. The technologies we use for public scholarship can reinforce pre-existing power dynamics.

The internet undergirds a significant portion of digital public engagement and thus it is important to be cognizant of the power dynamics behind it. The optimistic view of the internet is that it is a democratic and open space for knowledge sharing, a view shared by its original creators.[9] Scholars such as technology historian Joy Lisi Rankin

---

8   Alice Wong, "Alice Wong on Disability Visibility: A Fireside Chat," Disrupting Disruptions: The Feminist and Accessible Publishing, Communications, and Technologies Speaker and Workshop Series, November 3, 2020, YouTube video, 1:33:22, https://www.youtube. com/watch?v=UHLwMUrRVx4.
9   Hetland, "Internet between Utopia and Dystopia."

Engage in Public Scholarship! 142

have demonstrated that the internet and its predecessors, personal and social computing networks, never lived up to this ideal.[10] The internet has been a space where sexual and racial harassment has occurred, inequalities have flourished, and the digital world has replicated hierarchies of the physical world due to unequal access to resources, training, time, and funds.[11] Over the past decades internet usage has surged globally.[12] Corporate influence on the internet has intensified during this time. The networking equipment company Sandvine, which uses its vastly installed footprint of equipment across the internet to generate statistics on connections, upstream traffic, downstream traffic, and total internet traffic, reports that in 2019, 43 percent of the internet was consumed by just six companies: Netflix, Google, Amazon, Facebook, Microsoft, and Apple.[13] When digital public scholarship occurs on the internet, scholars are forced to engage with these systems.

Digital communication methods for public scholarship, such as designing websites and using social media, may pass through corporately controlled entities at multiple points: in the form of website builders; hosting services; proprietary software and plug-ins; browsers; platforms; and search engines. Depending on your technological skills and method of digital communication, you may have to rely more on

---

10   Rankin, *A People's History of Computing in the United States.*
11   Morozov, *The Net Delusion.*
12   Max Roser, Hannah Ritchie, and Esteban Ortiz-Ospina, "Internet," *Our World in Data,* 2015, https://ourworldindata.org/internet.
13   Cam Cullen, "Over 43 Percent of the Internet is Consumed by Netflix, Google, Amazon, Facebook, Microsoft, and Apple," *Sandvine,* August 30, 2019.

Proprietary Platforms, Corporate Influence, and Social Media 143

corporate platforms. This phenomenon is abundantly clear in the case of social media sites and applications owned by companies such as Facebook, Instagram (a subsidiary of Facebook), and Twitter, each of which has a for-profit model built upon data extraction. In the dramatic and stark words of Shoshanna Zuboff, with social media platforms, "you are not 'the product' but rather the abandoned carcass. The 'product' derives from the surplus data ripped from your life"[14]—an idea which she expands upon in *The Age of Surveillance Capitalism*. This data extraction is the root of further challenges.

The algorithms, or mathematical models, underlying data extraction and the repurposing of data have the ability to intensify social inequalities. In *Weapons of Math Destruction: How Big Data Increases Inequality and Threatens Democracy*, Cathy O'Neil demonstrates how the algorithms being used today are unregulated and uncontested, and, importantly, reinforce discrimination. Lauren Klein and Catherine D'Ignazio show how data can be used to discriminate, police, and surveil.[15] Data-extraction practices also influence the way that people access information while online. In her book *Algorithms of Oppression*, information studies scholar Safiya Umoja Noble writes about the problem of data discrimination in search algorithms. Noble argues that the combination of private interests in promoting certain sites, along with the monopoly status of a relatively small number of internet

---

14 Shoshanna Zuboff, "Facebook, Google and a Dark Age of Surveillance Capitalism," *Financial Times,* January 25, 2019.

15 D'Ignazio and Klein, *Data Feminism*.

Engage in Public Scholarship! 144

search engines, results in a biased set of search algorithm results that privilege whiteness and discriminate against people of colour, specifically women of colour. In this way, data extraction impacts the way that people find information, have access to your work as a scholar, and even impacts the information you use to inform your own research.

These models of data extraction are also key to understanding the role of machine learning (ML) and artificial intelligence (AI) in social media networks. ML is a subset of AI and is a series of algorithms that enable computers to identify patterns in data and classify them in clusters. ML is well adapted to social media's unstructured data, as social media posts are, depending on the platform, usually a mix of text, images, sounds, and videos. The machine learning-enabled analysis provides social media companies insights into the selected users, which can be used for marketing.[16] Web-scraping tools gather all the posts that may be associated with certain terms, products, or brands and put them in a data lake from which they are fed into the algorithms. (A data lake is a repository of data stored in its natural/raw format.) This process relies upon natural language processing (NLP), which purports to provide information about the age, gender, location, and preferences of the authors of posts on social media.

Marketers can then use the data coming from an NLP API (natural language processing application programming interface) as part of their customer segmentation based

---

16 Sophia Brooke, "How to Make Sense of Social Media Using Machine Learning," *Towards Data Science*, January 9, 2018.

Proprietary Platforms, Corporate Influence, and Social Media   145

on the social media data instead of statistics or educated guesses. As the Berkmen Klein Center for Internet and Society writes, "the concern is that the vast amounts of individually-identifiable data about users will allow ever-improving algorithms to refine the stream of content that individuals receive" from the targeted behavioural marketing powered by algorithms and machine learning.[17] Notably, this phenomenon occurs on social media platforms.

Advanced machine learning is used by social media companies for more than targeted advertising. Facebook uses machine learning to do everything from serve you content to recognizing your face in photos, and Instagram uses AI to identify visuals. As Data and Society's report argues,

> AI technologies hold great promise in advancing society and addressing existing problems. However, the potential benefits must not obscure the potential perils of these technologies. These perils have nothing to do with "killer robots" or the coming of "robot overlords." Instead, they will be found in the everyday structuring potentials of AI that will benefit some members of society but leave many others behind.[18]

Joy Boulamwini and Deborah Raji show the way that machine learning systems related to facial recognition do not work as well on people with darker skin, particularly

---

17   Benkler et al., "Understanding Media and Information Quality in an Age of Artificial Intelligence, Automation, Algorithms and Machine Learning."

18   Mateescu and Elish, "AI in Context."

Engage in Public Scholarship!

146

women of colour.[19] Numerous scholars such as Ruha Benjamin,[20] Virginia Eubanks,[21] and Morgan Klaus Scheuerman,[22] have shown how AI magnifies systematic bias against specific groups, respectively: people of colour; the poor; and transgender and non-binary people. Mimi Onuoha shows how holes in data collection, particularly concerning women, people of colour, and LGBTQ communities, lead to biased data sets which further bias the algorithms.[23] Efforts to combat these issues range from the creation of synthetic data,[24] the regulation of algorithms,[25] and the establishment of digital sovereignty—the idea that parties must have sovereignty over their own digital data. As Laurence Butet-Roch, creator of the Slow Net Toolkit, writes, "Concerned with how trivially knowledge is treated online, as snippets of information that can be accessed, consumed and acquired by all at any time in just a few mindless clicks, and its concomitant threats to digital sovereignty, I find myself imagining an alternative digital atmosphere, one that prioritizes and encourages both attentiveness and reflexivity."[26] The current climate of Big Data, machine learning, and AI through platforms was not inevitable.

---

19   Raji and Buolamwini, "Actionable Auditing."
20   Benjamin, *Captivating Technology.*
21   Eubanks, *Automating Inequality.*
22   Scheuerman, Paul, and Brubaker, "How Computers See Gender."
23   Onuoha, "On Missing Datasets."
24   Harrod, "How to Make Synthetic Data—Synthetic Data Generation for Machine Learning," October 5, 2020, YouTube video, 12:21, https://www.youtube.com/watch?v=vUoRZgWKUw.
25   Shalini Kantayya, Coded Bias (Salt Lake City, UT: Cinetic Media, 2020).
26   Laurence Butet-Roch, *Slow Net Toolkit*, 2020, https://www.laurence.virtualgrounds.zone/about.html.

Proprietary Platforms, Corporate Influence, and Social Media   147

This challenge of overcoming or altering these systems is not insurmountable, but it affects digital public scholarship as it shapes the digital environment and the choices scholars can make. Big Data and machine learning, are not, however, the only challenges for undertaking digital public scholarship.

Corporate-controlled tech platforms also raise labour concerns. Anthropologist of tech economies Sareeta Amrute writes that "as digital labour becomes more widespread across the uneven geographies of race, gender, class and ability, and as histories of colonialism and inequality get drawn into these forms of labour, our imagination of what these worlds contain similarly needs to expand."[27] Anthropologist Mary L. Gray and computer scientist Siddharth Suri likewise draw attention to the unregulated labour and the human workforce that powers the web.[28] This workforce is often underpaid,[29] and the actual labour is hidden behind marketing.[30] By utilizing these technologies for public engagement and research communication, scholars, however inadvertently, participate in an exploitative system.

As scholars interested in undertaking digital public scholarship, our work is embedded within this technological ecosystem based on exploitative labour practices; racial, class, and gender bias; not to mention the environmental issues

---

27   Amrute, "Of Techno-Ethics and Techno-Affects," p. 56.
28   Gray and Suri, *Ghost Work*.
29   David Lee, "Why Big Tech Pays Poor Kenyans to Teach Self-driving Cars," *BBC News*, November 3, 2018.
30   Astra Taylor, "The Automation Charade," *Logic*, August 1, 2018.

Engage in Public Scholarship!

that will be discussed in chapter ten. There are limitations to the degree that it is possible to do digital public scholarship outside of this system, especially if your audience is already using certain platforms and technologies. The ubiquity of certain social networks and platforms restrains scholars' ability to create public scholarship outside of these networks. Technological skills, training, and resources restrict the ability to work outside of these systems. To what degree is it realistic or desirable to maintain your own server? How much energy do you want to allocate to developing new platforms rather than utilizing imperfect pre-existing platforms and interfaces?

4 Social Media

Social media has become a powerful tool for knowledge dissemination, research promotion, and public scholarship. Social media can be useful for promoting academic research for scholars and interested members of the public. For example, research shows that scholars who post their academic articles to Twitter receive more citations than if they had not promoted their work in the first place.[31] If you choose to use websites, videos, podcasts, or apps to broadcast your scholarship, it is advisable to also share all of your updates on a corresponding social media account. Furthermore, social media can be a generative space itself,

---

31   Luc et al., "Does Tweeting Improve Citations?"

Proprietary Platforms, Corporate Influence, and Social Media 149

where research is not only shared, but produced. On these platforms, scholars can work through ideas, share initial findings, and solicit feedback from peers and the public. Scholars can communicate about their research on various social media platforms to different communities, based on the platforms that they use. Social media can be a useful tool, yet, as these platforms are controlled by large corporations, you are subject to their terms, conditions, policies, and their own corporate lifespans. Your account depends on the whims of an external, for-profit organization, whose business model typically rests on data extraction, as explained at the beginning of this chapter.

Social media's benefits and limitations relate to the profile of an individual scholar. In a study on scholars' social media use, Deborah Lupton found the benefits of social media included "connecting and establishing networks not only with other academics but also people or groups outside universities, promoting openness and sharing of information, publicizing and development of research and giving and receiving support."[32] However, while Lupton found that the majority of the respondents were positive about using social media, they also expressed concerns about becoming a target of attack, the possible plagiarism of their ideas, the commercialization of content, and copyright issues. This leads to self-censorship, a phenomenon discussed by geographer Arrianna Marie Planey.[33] Previous chapters have discussed the gendered and

---

32 Lupton, *'Feeling Better Connected,'* p. 3.
33 Arrianna Marie Planey (@Arrianna_Planey), "Self Censorship on Twitter," Twitter thread, December 4, 2020 10:26 AM, https://twitter.com/ArriannaPlaney/status/1334881752251305985.

racialized attacks that can happen on social media platforms. Scholars also worry about the increase of their workload if they are required to take on the work of social media communication—a common concern with public scholarship.

It is not uncommon for scholars to have accounts on more than one social media platform, but to use some for professional purposes only and maintain others for private or personal use. Researchers such as George Veletsianos, Nicole Johnson, and Olga Belikov have found that scholars' social media use over time is associated with individual, relational, cultural, and political factors.[34] There are also generational and cultural divides in who chooses to engage with social media and particular platforms.[35] As media scholar Sherri Williams shows, "Twitter is often a site of resistance where Black feminists challenge violence committed against women of color and they leverage the power of Black Twitter to bring attention and justice to women who rarely receive either."[36] André Brock's research shows similar findings. He notes that Black Twitter proves that Black discourses "can be employed effectively over a medium designed for a small, technologically proficient, mostly White user base"—a topic he discusses more in further work.[37] As the choice of medium for public

---

34 Veletsianos, Johnson, and Belikov, "Academics' social media use over time is associated with individual, relational, cultural and political factors."
35 Manca and Ranieri, "Networked Scholarship and Motivations for Social Media Use in Scholarly Communication."
36 Williams, "Digital Defense," p. 343.
37 Brock Jr., "From the Blackhand Side," p. 534. Refer also to Brock Jr., *Distributed Blackness.*

Proprietary Platforms, Corporate Influence, and Social Media 151

scholarship is determined by audiences, the platforms a scholar chooses to engage with can also depend on the research community that already exists on these platforms.

Consider differentiating between your public social media accounts and keeping your personal social media accounts more private. You can delineate these accounts both through the content you post and through privacy features available on the platforms. You can even create two accounts on the same platform: one that is for your public scholarship and one for your personal life.

4.1 Twitter

Twitter is one of the most common platforms for public scholarship. Users have a handle, which is a kind of username that serves to identify their account. Twitter functions as a feed of status updates in which users can follow others to see their 280-character posts, called "tweets." By creating a thread, a scholar can write out a chain of points, each within the confines of 280 characters (i.e., the total number of letters, numbers, spaces, and symbols in a post). Users can retweet other users' tweets, as a form of knowledge dissemination. Retweets also encourage users to share their own perspective on an idea, which can lead to a form of written correspondence between users. Other users can tweet comments or responses to tweets, creating another form of written correspondence. Twitter primarily relies on text, with the option to include images and videos. Anyone can read tweets on public Twitter accounts,

Engage in Public Scholarship!

even if they do not have their own Twitter account. As a result, Twitter lowers the barriers for people to access the information that is being shared there.

Twitter is a powerful tool for sharing ideas, distributing resources, and networking. Scholars such as corvid researcher Kaeli Swift, who tweets under the handle @corvidresearch, can use their Twitter accounts to communicate their research findings with the public. Swift tweets specifically about her research on crows, but she also creates interactive tweets about science to engage her over sixty-two thousand followers (as of December 2020). Once a week, Swift does #CrowOrNo in which she posts a picture of a bird and people have to guess whether it is a photo of a crow or not. Afterwards, Swift will explain to readers how they can know if it is a crow or another kind of bird by looking at the certain identifying features. She also uses her account to share links to her peer-reviewed research. In this way, her Twitter account allows her to speak to multiple audiences with different backgrounds and levels of expertise in her topic in one space. Swift also uses her Twitter account to amplify the voices of other scholars. She tweets about the work of other researchers and re-tweets their work, which can be particularly helpful in drawing attention to scholars with fewer followers.

Twitter can be a useful tool in expanding access to certain events, conferences, and spaces. One technique is live-tweeting conferences, in which scholars will tweet about the papers, lectures, and events at a conference they are attending. Readers of these tweets might not be able to

Proprietary Platforms, Corporate Influence, and Social Media   153

attend the conference in person, yet they can glean some understanding of the research that scholars share there. Media scholar Emily Contois has created a guide with information about how scholars can use Twitter in order to live-tweet conferences, events, and information about research.[38] Live tweeting creates a digital record of an ephemeral event on a proprietary platform. It increases access to these events, but again has limitations.

The privacy settings on Twitter can impact how users can engage with the platform. Tweets from a public account can be read by anyone, and thus the information shared on the platform is readily accessible. Users who make their accounts private create barriers for access, yet the decision to go private can protect scholars who are facing a barrage of trolling or cyberbullying comments. Even public accounts can restrict features such as direct messaging and photo tagging, which can protect a user's privacy, but also make it more difficult to contact them. A new feature in 2020 allows users to restrict who can comment on their tweets. Twitter has policies against harassment: harassing accounts can be deleted entirely, suspended (with content made unavailable pending appeal or specific changes), or sent a warning. Critics argue that these policies are not evenly applied.[39] Advocates against cyberbullying and cyber-harassment continue to pressure

---

38   Emily Contois, "Twitter and Instagram: A Quick How-To Guide," personal website, 2019, https://emilycontois.files.wordpress.com/2019/05/foodstudies19 guide.pdf.
39   Matias et al., "Reporting, Reviewing, and Responding to Harassment on Twitter."

Engage in Public Scholarship! 154

social media platforms, such as Twitter, to do more to combat online hate speech and online harassment.[40]

Privacy features on social media platforms typically mean that the platform can become more accessible for users who are facing harassment. However, it also means that the content that they produce is less accessible to audiences. The challenge for scholars is in navigating the level of privacy that works for them. Fortunately, scholars can experiment with these privacy and security features on their account by clicking a few buttons.

4.2 Facebook

Facebook is one of the most ubiquitous social media platforms, outfitted with individual user profiles, Facebook groups, Facebook pages, and Facebook events. While personal profiles on Facebook allow an individual to privately or publicly share photos, words, and links with a network of other users on the platform, Facebook pages are public profiles specifically created for businesses, brands, celebrities, causes, and other organizations to communicate with followers. Users with personal profiles or Facebook pages can share information about events by creating Facebook events. (In 2020, the platform also enabled users to host web-based virtual events through the Facebook platform itself.) Facebook groups are digital spaces where users with individual user profiles can

---

40   Gagliardone et al., *Countering Online Hate Speech.*

Proprietary Platforms, Corporate Influence, and Social Media 155

connect with one another. Facebook groups can be public or private.

For public scholarship, Facebook can be useful for sharing ideas, texts, images, and links. Public and private groups can be useful for community building around your research topic. Facebook groups like the Punk Scholars Network help scholars across the world connect to discuss their area of expertise. On the Punk Scholars Network Group, members share links to forthcoming articles, ask for leads on archival sources, and share information about upcoming conferences. The group is set to private but is visible. In this way, people who might want to join a group like this can find it by using the search bar within Facebook, yet the group can restrict access in order to mitigate harassment and spam. You might decide to create your own Facebook group in order to connect with other scholars or members of the public who share your research interests.

Facebook pages are less interactive, but can be useful for sharing information. It is possible to share information about your research on a Facebook page rather than creating a personal website. This could be an advantageous choice if your intended audience is already on Facebook. The issue is that Facebook is a proprietary platform and you are subject to the whims of the company. If Facebook decides to remove the Facebook page feature, you could lose the work and the community that you have created on the Facebook page.

One of the most useful features of the Facebook platform is Facebook events. Even if you have a website related to your

Engage in Public Scholarship! 156

public scholarship, Facebook events are a useful tool for publicizing any related events. Users can RSVP to the event, helping you have a sense of the number of people who will attend.[41]

4.3 Instagram

Instagram specializes in image sharing, accompanied by text. Instagram captions can extend to 2,200 characters, but the platform revolves around the visual. Users, who have unique handles to identify their accounts, can share images and videos as stories, which disappear (unless saved) after twenty-four hours, or they can share images on their "grid," which remain visible unless the images are later removed. This platform is particularly useful for scholars whose work has a strong visual component. It is less useful for sharing links.

4.4 TikTok

TikTok is an application for sharing short videos, accompanied by short text. At present, scholars are less likely to use TikTok to share public scholarship. There are some scholars, however, who have made use of the short video format. Casey Fiesler uses TikTok to create videos about academia and her

---

41 However, unless you charge for entrance to the event, from personal experience I can attest that Facebook RSVP numbers typically are double or triple the number of people who will actually attend.

Proprietary Platforms, Corporate Influence, and Social Media 157

scholarship, which she also shares through her Twitter feed.[42] Her December 2020 video, in which she held up books on technology and ethics while lip synching the song "Rät" by Penelope Scott, garnered over 105 thousand views in under twenty four hours.[43] TikTok videos are useful for sharing small amounts of content across platforms.

4.5 Across Platforms

Sharing similar information between platforms is commonplace. In the past, social media manager applications enabled you to create a single text and post, tweet, and/or share it on all of your platforms at once. Yet there are barriers to this working effectively due to the different ways that each platform works.[44] If you want to share your work across platforms, you might have to create slightly different versions of the same posts. For example, if you want to share the same information on Twitter as on your Facebook page, you will need to change the Twitter handles to Facebook handles. You will also have to make adjustments to your content based on the various accessibility features of each platform.

---

42 Casey Fiesler, "Professors on TikTok," Twitter thread, November 24, 2020, 7:41 PM, https://twitter.com/cfiesler/status/ 1331397531734077442.

43 Casey Fiesler (@cfiesler), "Someone on TikTok asked if I could recommend books about tech ethics and I have never been so hyped to create a piece of content in my life," Twitter, December 8, 2020, 9:30 AM, https://twitter.com/cfiesler/ status/1336317217034612737.

44 Barbara Krasnoff, "How to Post to Multiple Social Networks," *The Verge*, June 24, 2019.

Engage in Public Scholarship! 158

4.6 Accessibility

Using social media accounts can make your scholarship more visible to the public, and certain practices can make the public scholarship you do on these platforms more accessible. If you are using images on social platforms, write alt-text (also referred to as alt-tags or alt-descriptions), which is written copy that appears in place of an image on a web page if the image fails to load on a user's screen. Using alt-text helps screen-reading tools describe images to readers who are Blind or have limited vision, and allows search engines to better crawl and rank your website. For Twitter, you must write the alt-text before tweeting. On Facebook, alt-text is auto-generated on posts of photos, but you can override the alt-text with your description. Choosing to write your own alt-text can ensure more accurate descriptions. Caption your videos if you include them as part of your Facebook posts, Instagram grid or stories, or within your tweet. Upload transcriptions for audio that you share on these platforms, either as part of the post or shared as a link.

For potential audiences to find your work more readily, use hashtags, a form of keyword metadata marking made with the hashtag sign, followed by words, to label your posts. For the benefit of screen readers, when using a hashtag, capitalize the start of each letter. By writing #BlackLivesMatter instead of #blacklivesmatter, the screen reader can more easily differentiate between the words. Disability technology—rights advocates such as Chancey

Proprietary Platforms, Corporate Influence, and Social Media   159

Fleet want platforms to require these practices, but in the meantime, you can opt-in.[45]

4.7   Finding the Right Tool

Utilizing the most conducive features for creating content on a given social media platform makes for effective communication. Each social media platform has different strengths. The particularities of each platform enable scholars to do different kinds of public scholarship. For example, text-heavy posts do not work as well on Instagram as they do on Facebook or Twitter. These are not the only forms of social media that exist at present, yet they are some of the most ubiquitous.

Even in writing this chapter, the popularity of specific platforms has ebbed and flowed. It is less important to focus on the specifics of each platform. Rather, it is more useful to think about the ways that social media platforms enable scholars to share and produce particular forms of digital public scholarship, while being cognizant of the ethical issues raised at the start of the chapter.

---

45   Chancey Fleet (guest) and Sareeta Amrute (host), "Dark Patterns in Accessibility Tech," *Databites* (podcast), episode 121, June 5, 2019, *Data and Society*, https://datasociety.net/library/dark-patterns-in-accessibility-tech/.

5 Conclusion

This chapter discussed the pros and cons of working with certain technologies. It is this kind of thoughtful engagement with communications technologies and publishing that this project hopes to elicit. Corporate control of new media and web platforms will continue to be a challenge due to algorithms, data selling, and issues around data sourcing and bias. There is a limit to the technologies that we use; these are tools and should be treated accordingly. As should be clear by now, making public-facing scholarship accessible and feminist is complicated. These conversations continue in the next chapter, which pays particular attention to self-produced digital forms of public scholarship including websites, blogs, videos, and podcasts. Each section includes practical information about how to utilize these mediums. Their benefits and limitations are taken into account.

CHAPTER 8

Self-produced Digital Public Scholarship

This chapter considers the range of possibilities for self-produced public digital scholarship, with practical information about how to pursue various forms of media. Self-production here refers to work that is not produced by centralized media. This work may include collaborators, as Amy L. Chapman and Christine Greenhow explain that "public scholarship also includes collaboration, which can occur during the research or creative process through to the many ways in which the results of the collaboration are communicated to the public."[1] This book rejects a hierarchy between digital and physical forms of public scholarship, and instead advocates for using whichever medium makes sense for an individual scholar, their intended audiences, and the subject matter at hand. This chapter will focus on the creation of websites, videos, podcasts, and apps, whereas chapter nine will address physical public scholarship.

---

1   Chapman and Greenhow, "Citizen-Scholars," p. 4.

The analysis of the technological affordances and limitations of these forms intersects with a review of their accessibility.

1 Websites and Blogs

Websites are a useful way to share large quantities of information in a format that is relatively quick to update and revise. Since the popularization of the internet in the 1990s, the web has grown to be an important information repository and is one of the first places many people turn to when searching for information.[2] These web queries are intermediated by search engines such as Google; search engine use is the most popular approach to online information seeking.[3] Optimizing the position of one's website within search results, known as "search engine optimization," or SEO, can lead people to your public scholarship more readily. One simple effort to improve SEO includes keyword tagging. Developing websites is a useful form of public scholarship that can be cost effective. This section explores strategies to enable this endeavour.

Website design can require various skill sets. However, it is possible to build a website without knowing how to write or edit code by using proprietary website builders. Website

---

2   Morris, Teevan, and Panovich, "A Comparison of Information Seeking Using Search Engines and Social Networks."

3   Deborah Fallows, "Search Engine Use," *Pew Internet and American Life Project*, August 6, 2008.

Self-produced Digital Public Scholarship 163

builders are online platforms that enable you to build websites with from readymade editing interfaces. Website builders' features include professionally designed website templates, drag-and-drop editors, widgets, and elements for customizing and enhancing the functionality of your site, such as blog functionality, social media buttons, photo galleries, and a shopping cart. Proprietary website builders such as Squarespace, Wix, Weebly, and Wordpress often include hosting and easy-to-purchase domain names. You may still purchase your own domain name from an outside broker so that you can move the domain name to a future site if you decide to stop using a specific platform.[4] These services offer reliable server maintenance, meaning that your site is less likely to "go down." Premium accounts that are advertisement-free require fees of upwards of 10 to 50 US dollars a month, depending on the plan and website builder. Basic plans may require you to have advertisements on your site and include branded content. Website builders, such as Blogger, are free blog-site builders that do not require fees. Blogger is hosted by Google and does not require hosting fees or any other fees to use. There is no need to worry about software updates. As part of Blogger services, blogspot.com URLs (universal resource locators) are free to use, but you can also use a customized domain name bought through Blogger or another broker.[5]

---

4   Dana Fox, "How to Set Up a Custom Domain in Blogger," *Wonder Forest Blog,* February 2020, https://www.thewonder forest.com/2017/02/how-to-set-up-custom-domain-in-blogger.html.

5   A URL is a complete web address used to locate a particular web page. While the domain is the name of the website, a URL will lead to any one of the pages within the website.

Engage in Public Scholarship! 164

No coding skills are required, but you are able to edit the HTML,[6] so some basic coding skills can be useful. While the platform can be used for other kinds of websites, Blogger is specifically designed for blogs—a style of website comprised of discrete, often informal diary-style text entries in the form of posts, usually displayed in reverse chronological order so that the most recent post appears first, at the top of the web page. Blogs can also include "pages," which are stable, and used for static, unchanging content such as contact information or an author bio. It is possible to customize Blogger pages further by changing the favicon —the small graphic icon that many browsers, such as Firefox, Safari, and Chrome display as a visual reminder of the website identity in the address bar or in tabs. One issue with the Blogger platform is that it directs users towards Google products. Google can also decide to suspend your website at any time and even decide to cancel the Blogger service altogether, as the company has discontinued prior Google products. Depending on your budget and skill set, website builders may be a useful option. The downside of using proprietary website builders is that you lose independence and can be liable to a corporation's policy changes.

There are various ways to categorize websites. Static websites have web pages stored on a server in the format that is sent to a client web browser and they display the same,

---

6   Hypertext Markup Language (HTML) is the standard markup language for documents designed to be displayed in a web browser. HTML can be assisted by technologies such as Cascading Style Sheets (CSS) and scripting languages such as JavaScript.

Self-produced Digital Public Scholarship

consistent information to all visitors for an extended period of time. Static websites can, of course, be edited or updated periodically, but this is a manual process. These websites are primarily coded in HTML and CSS, which is used to control appearance beyond basic HTML. Static websites can include images as part of the main content. If audio or video plays automatically or if it is generally non-interactive, the website can be considered static. On the other hand, dynamic websites change or customize themselves frequently and automatically. They can display different content and provide user interaction by using advanced programming and databases in addition to HTML. The server-side dynamic pages are generated reflexively by computer code that produces the HTML. Here, the CSS is responsible for the appearance of the website and functions as static files on the dynamic site. Common Gateway Interface, Java Servlets and Java Server Pages (JSP), ASP.NET, and ColdFusion (CFML) are software systems that can be used to generate dynamic web systems and dynamic sites. Perl, PHP, Python, and Ruby are programming languages that can assist in creating dynamic websites. Static websites usually load more quickly than dynamic sites. The choice between static and dynamic websites impacts the kind of coding that you will need to undertake, however, both options can be useful for your public scholarship.

Before designing your website, it is important to understand how a website's design can affect questions of sustainability, preservation, and accessibility (chapter ten will address these matters in more detail). Using proprietary website builders means that the existence of your site depends on the survival

Engage in Public Scholarship! 166

of that company, their policies, and their decisions about continuing to provide their services. Proprietary websites have deleted users' accounts because of their content or for violation of their corporate terms of service.[7] This can result in not being able to access years' worth of content. If you decide to use a proprietary website builder, create a back-up version of your materials and/or code. If your website uses proprietary plug-ins that require subscriptions, such as mapping software for websites that share scholarship on geography, when your subscription or your institution's subscription ends the content may not be retrievable. Proprietary plug-ins and software also make digital archiving more difficult, because without access to the plug-in or software, archivists cannot access or display the information.[8] Websites built in simple HTML are the easiest to preserve and accessible for users with a wider range of devices and internet access speeds.

Creators have demonstrated how simple HTML websites can expand accessibility without compromising on content. Valeria Graziano, Marcell Mars, and Tomislav Medak who, along with the rest of their collaborators, created the Pirate Care Syllabus, thought intentionally about the kind of code they wanted to use for their website in order to prioritize maintenance, the sharing of information online and offline, and replicability. They did not want for their site—written in the form of a syllabus—and others following a similar model to "go defunct once the dependencies for that Wordpress

---

7   Aja Romano, "A Writer Kept a Blog for 10 Years. Google Deleted It. Why?" *Vox,* July 30, 2016.

8   My thanks to the Critical Archivist Group for inviting me to speak at their meeting on November 20, 2020, and for sharing this information with me.

Self-produced Digital Public Scholarship

installation get broken, that the links to resources lead to file-not-found pages or that adapting them requires a painstaking copy and paste process." Instead, they wrote that

> to address these concerns, we have made certain technological choices. A syllabus in our framework is built from plaintext documents that are written in a very simple and human-readable Markdown markup language, rendered into a static HTML website that doesn't require a resource-intensive and easily breakable database system, and which keeps its files on a Git version control repository that allows collaborative writing and easy forking to create new versions out of the existing syllabi. This makes it easy for a housing struggles initiative in Berlin to fork a syllabus which we have initially developed with a housing struggles initiative in London and adapt it to their own context and needs. Such a syllabus can be then equally hosted on an internet server and used/shared offline from a USB stick, while still preserving the internal links between the documents and the links to the texts in the accompanying searchable resource collection.[9]

Mindy Seu, in creating the CyberFeminism Index, has likewise thought intentionally about designing for simplicity, longevity, and collaboration. Seu and Angeline

---

9   Tomislav Medak and Valeria Graziano, Pirate Care Syllabus, 2020, https://syllabus.pirate.care.

Engage in Public Scholarship! 168

Meitzler used the "least amount of extra tech as possible, such as vanilla JavaScript for client-side and only Python for server-side." Seu writes that while there is one additional library used for markdown, "other than this, we do not rely on third parties or additional libraries and plug-ins. One day, it will be incorporated into Rhizome's linked open data project Artbase."[10] They actively solicit collaborative editing and compilation through a "submit" button at the bottom of all pages. Although an increasing amount of online traffic passes through either corporate-controlled websites and sites built with proprietary web builders,[11] it is possible to build websites outside of these models.

Website design can impact accessibility. As discussed in earlier chapters, the WCAG (Web Content Accessibility Guidelines) is the main international standard for web accessibility. Things to consider include: the font size; the font-colour contrast between text and background; not embedding essential information in graphic formats, as assistive technologies such as screen readers may not be able to process the text; written descriptions of images; and keyboard navigation.[12] Blind assistive technology coordinator Chancey Fleet argues that these accessibility options should be built into the platforms rather than having users and designers opt into them. While Fleet

---

10   Mindy Seu, *Cyberfeminism Index,* 2020, https://cyberfeminismindex.com/about/.

11   Dahlberg, "The Corporate Colonization of Online Attention and the Marginalization of Critical Communication?"

12   W3C Accessibility Initiative, "W3C Accessibility Standards Overview," 2019, https://www.w3.org/WAI/standards-guidelines/.

Self-produced Digital Public Scholarship

explains that this "encoded inhospitality" is not intended to cause harm, accessibility should be at the forefront of digital communications.[13] Mozilla has created a guide for enabling accessible web design.[14] The website design you use for your public scholarship can influence different audiences' access to it.

With these constraints in mind, websites continue to be a valuable form of digital public scholarship. A site's layout can range in complexity. Perhaps you want to create a website that explains your research without jargon and that links to academic and popular articles you have written on the subject, such as The Feminist Restaurant Project.[15] Maybe you want to create a website where you will embed videos, podcasts, or other materials that you create. You may decide to create a blog, like media scholar Emily Contois, where you explore ideas relating to your research in a more informal way.[16] If you are interested in creating a collaborative website, you might create a blog where other scholars can contribute posts about their research, such as the Historical

---

13 Chancey Fleet (guest) and Sareeta Amrute (host), "Dark Patterns in Accessibility Tech," *Databites* (podcast), episode 121, June 5, 2019, *Data and Society*, https://datasociety.net/library/dark-patterns-in-accessibility-tech/.

14 MDN, "Handling common accessibility problems," 2020, https://developer.mozilla. org/en-US/docs/Learn/Tools and testing/Cross browser testing/Accessibility.

15 Alex Ketchum, "About," 2015, http://www.thefeministrestaurantproject.com.

16 Emily Contois, "Why I'm Still Blogging after 6 Years & Being Trolled," personal website, July 31, 2018, https://emilycontois.com/2018/07/31/blogging-6-years/.

Cooking Project.[17] Think about the benefits of the chosen web-based form, such as the ease of sharing images. You can use interactive features where users can scroll, zoom, or click. There are many forms your website can take.

2 Videos

The creation of videos explaining your topics of expertise can be an engaging form of public scholarship. Your video-editing skills, the time you want to invest into your film and video projects, and your budget will impact the kinds of videos you create and the platforms you use to share them. However, the creation of videos has become a relatively accessible form of public scholarship, as video capture and film equipment have become more reasonably priced over time. This section begins with a discussion of how to create videos, followed by information for uploading, streaming, sharing, and embedding videos. For accessibility, this section will include a discussion of captioning. The discussion of live-streaming video is reserved for chapter eleven.

Public scholarship videos can range in form. For example, Jordan Harrod, a graduate student at Harvard and MIT researching brain-machine interfaces and machine learning

---

17 Alex Ketchum, Carolynn McNally, Emili Bellefleur, and Kathleen Gudmundsson, "About," Historical Cooking Project, 2013, http://www. historicalcookingproject.com.

Self-produced Digital Public Scholarship 171

for medicine has a YouTube channel, on which, by November 2020, she had created over 128 videos explaining artificial intelligence, algorithms, and other new technologies. The channel has more than twenty-two thousand subscribers. Her videos are typically a steady shot of her speaking to the camera for 8 to 15 minutes, with a few images or text examples used to demonstrate her points. Additionally, she occasionally creates longer videos, does interviews with other scholars, and holds question and answer sessions with subscribers. Her channel is a paragon of public-scholarship videos. Nonetheless, this kind of format is possible to achieve with a phone and some basic editing software. Scholars may create animated films, dramatizations, interview shows, and more. The VL2 Center of Gallaudet University publishes brief videos as a resource for educators and parents, in order to inform the education community of research findings, to summarize relevant scholarship, and, in the form of practice guides, to present recommendations that educators and parents can use when addressing the multifaceted challenges of educating Deaf and hard of hearing people.[18] The affiliated VL2 Motion Light Lab makes animations with sign language for children in order to "create a space where creative literature intersects with digital technology to create new knowledge."[19] The research team works with illustrators, interpreters, and story creators.[20] The use

---

18   VL2 Center, "Research Briefs," 2020, https://vl2.gallaudet.edu/research/research-briefs/.
19   VL2/PEN Labs, "Motion Light Lab (MLB)," 2020, https://vl2.gallaudet.edu/labs/motionlight-lab/.
20   Motion Light Lab, "The Blue Lobster - A Preview," January 19, 2016, YouTube Video, 0:58, https://www.youtube. com/watch?v=Jfo7ENKVobg.

Engage in Public Scholarship!

of images, text, sounds, music, or clips depends on the time, energy, and resources you can and want to invest.

There are various strategies for filming and creating videos, but some techniques require using only your computer and simple, free software. As people dedicate their entire careers to the endeavour of video production, this section aims to merely provide an introduction to various techniques that require basic skills, software, and equipment. A simple form of video creation entails using video-conferencing software and recording your screen. You can use a video-conferencing software, such as Zoom, host a call with only yourself, and record it using the software's embedded recording options. You can choose to save the video to your computer or to the cloud. Some of these platforms will auto-generate captions, allow you to work with an auto-caption software, and/or write your own captions into the video for accessibility. Depending on the software, these options may only be available with the paid subscription version of the software. If you are hosting a Zoom video and recording it, you can use the "share your screen" feature to display images, other film materials, or a slideshow made with software such as PowerPoint or Prezi. You can switch between filming your face (if your computer has a built-in camera or if you have an external camera), the faces of the other speakers in your group, and sharing your screens. Some conferencing platforms, such as Zoom, generate transcripts, audio files, and video files. Another avenue is to record your screen. You can record audio over slideshow presentations in software such as PowerPoint and generate a video. You may decide to record your screen and add audio

Self-produced Digital Public Scholarship 173

in post-production editing. These techniques require the use of various programs, many of which have limited or free options. However, the use of proprietary software, such as Zoom, a company that has faced backlash due to privacy and security concerns, should be an ethical consideration.[21]

With basic recording equipment you can take your video production to the next level. Today's cellular phones are often equipped with cameras and recording capabilities that surpass early home-market camcorders. You will have various hardware and software capabilities depending on the model of your mobile device. You may also be able to purchase video-editing applications through your phone in order to do initial editing on your phone, circumventing any downloads to your computer and allowing you to upload directly from your phone. Many universities have audio visual (AV) equipment facilities. As an affiliated scholar you may be able to rent or borrow cameras, microphones, tripods, booms, gimbals, reflectors, and other equipment for free or low cost. The quality of these devices will range. If your university has a film program, you may be able to access more professional equipment and/or be able to work with film students. Your choices surrounding the film equipment you use can also impact the degree to which you are able to produce the videos on your own.

Editing films can be a time-consuming process. Simple decisions, such as cutting the ends of a clip, may take

---

21 Tom Warren, "Zoom Faces a Privacy and Security Backlash as It Surges in Popularity," *The Verge,* April 1, 2020.

Engage in Public Scholarship!

seconds, whereas editing a complicated film with numerous takes and cuts may result in hours, days, weeks, months, or years of work. Robust editing software, such as Final Cut Pro, provide professional-level editing capabilities. However, film-editing software may already exist on your computer or phone, such as iMovie. There are also free, open-source programs such as Blender and Openshot.[22] Some third party—video-hosting services, such as YouTube, now include basic video-editing capabilities.

There are numerous options for hosting your videos, but the current landscape of the internet rewards the use of third-party hosting services. Popular choices include YouTube and Vimeo. Uploading videos on these platforms is simple and, in the case of YouTube, free. You can create a channel with playlists to gather your videos in one place. The skills required to upload the video files on this platform are similar to the skill set required to attach a file to an email. As a proprietary software, YouTube raises concerns similar to other giant tech brands.

Self-hosting videos is difficult. Video artist and queer studies scholar Dayna McLeod used to host her own videos. She created the 52 Pick-Up video production challenge, an online video series where participants agreed to make one video a week for an entire year, which featured over 3,000 videos made by more than fifty international artists

---

22 Tom Wells, "24 Best Free Video Editing Software Programs in 2020," *Oberlo,* March 21, 2021.

Self-produced Digital Public Scholarship

between 2009 and 2014.[23] The problem is that there is not a single file format that is standard for web video. The current HTML5 draft specification does not specify which video formats browsers should support. This means that the major web browsers have diverged, each one supporting a different format. For example, Safari will play H.264 (MP4) videos, but not WebM or Ogg; Firefox will play Ogg or WebM videos, but not H.264.

If you want to ensure your video will play on all the major web browsers, you have to convert your video into multiple formats: .mp4, .ogv, and .webm. This means that for every video you want to upload, you have to upload three different video files, each one potentially hundreds of megabytes in size. To ensure playability on various platforms, however, you will actually have to upload even more files. For audiences watching videos from their desktop or laptop with the benefit of a high-speed internet connection, high-definition-quality files of 1080p or 720p at a high-streaming bitrate of 5,000 to 8,000 kbps is standard. For audiences watching on devices like phones and tablets, as well as for delivery to viewers with slower internet connections, you need to create smaller, lower resolution versions. This means that you need to upload six or more individual video files to ensure your video can be viewed on all the major web browsers and devices.[24] You will need a separate application to convert your files into all those formats

---

23 Dayna McLeod, "52 Pick-Up," personal website, December 1, 2014, https://daynarama.com/52-pick-up/.

24 Shawn Hesketh, "10 Reasons Why You Should Never Host Your Own Videos," *WP 101,* November 16, 2020, https://www.wp101.com/10-reasons-why-you-should-never-host-yourown-videos/.

Engage in Public Scholarship! 176

and, unfortunately, every app handles the conversion process slightly differently. This phenomenon results in varying quality between your video files. Your video may look great as an MP4, but may look grainy or bitmapped in another format.

The work does not end there. Since your site needs to know which of those files to serve to each person, this requires cumbersome code or shortcode. Even after assembling your shortcode, uploading all the video files to your server, and installing a video player to handle all of the "behind the scenes" detection, your video quality will vary across browsers. Now imagine trying to do all of this work for one video, let alone the 3,000 Dayna McLeod has for her 52 Pick Up project. On top of this, due to the popularity of YouTube, search browsers are more likely to direct audiences to videos hosted there. Even if you are hosting your own videos, it is unlikely that you own your own server, unlike the creators of *Low-Tech Magazine* that run their website via a solar-powered server.[25] As a renter of server space, you are subject to the whims of the company with which you enter into agreement.

While this section will not include a robust discussion of copyright law, when using third-party materials in your videos, make sure to abide by the local copyright law. In Canada, fair dealing is an exception in the Canadian Copyright Act that outlines the permitted unauthorized use

---

25   Solar Low Tech Magazine, "About this website: This website is a solar powered, self-hosted version of Low-tech Magazine. It has been designed to radically reduce the energy use associated with accessing our content," 2020, https: //solar.lowtechmagazine.com/about.html.

Self-produced Digital Public Scholarship

of copyrighted materials for specific, mandated purposes. These purposes include: research, private study, education, parody, satire, criticism, review, or news reporting. For research and private study, education, parody, and satire, no special requirements are necessary. For criticism, review, and news reporting, the source and author must be named to constitute fair dealing. In the United States, fair use provides similar guidelines. Copyright law is specific to each country, so different rules apply in different places regarding length of copyright, method of registration, specific classes of works covered. In a digital environment, these boundaries can become complicated. Educate yourself on the copyright law of your geographic context.

Videos are a fantastic way to share visual and audio content. Captions expand accessibility for audiences by creating a text from the audio content. Captions are important for Deaf people, people who are hard of hearing, people watching content in a second language, and people who have auditory-processing disabilities, sensory-processing disabilities, ADHD, autism, learning disabilities, and/or intellectual disabilities. YouTube and other third-party hosting platforms use speech-to-text reliant on machine learning to generate auto-captions.[26] These captions are imperfect, though improving. They can still be useful for people who are hard of hearing, Deaf, or are participating in a second language. The platform also enables creators

---

26 Sourish Chaudhuri, "Adding Sound Effect Information to YouTube Captions," *Google AI Blog,* March 23, 2017, https://ai.googleblog.com/2017/03/adding-sound-effect-informationto.html.

Engage in Public Scholarship! 178

to upload their own, human-made captions.[27] With the automated features, you do not have to opt-in for captions; instead, they are auto-generated. Vimeo and self-hosted videos require that you create your own captions, although there are a few workarounds. For example, you can record a video on Zoom, turn on audio transcription, post video files to Google Drive, click "manage captions" and add Zoom's .vtt file. This creates the captions as subtitles. Then you will need to rename the .vtt file as .txt, upload it as well, and share links to both the video and .txt file. The .txt file is searchable text with timestamps that viewers can read, or use as an index to find specific spots within the video based on keyword searches.[28] You can choose to burn the captions into the video itself, so that they are visible to all users at all times. It is also possible to hire professional captioners to caption videos. For more information on this process, see chapter eleven. The accessibility of written transcripts is not only relevant to videos but is also a useful consideration in the making of podcasts.

---

27 YouTube used to have a collaborative caption feature where audiences could help transcribe the videos of their favourite creators into other languages, but the company discontinued this feature due to cyberbullying and cyber-harassment. (Ken Harrenstien, "Automatic captions in YouTube," *Google Blog*, November 12, 2009, https://googleblog.blogs pot.com/2009/11/automatic-captions-in-youtube.html.)

28 Costello, "Recording PowerPoint Slides with Captions in Zoom," September 2, 2020, Vimeo video, 2:53, https: //vimeo.com/454147681.

3 Podcasts and Audio Storytelling

Podcasts are an invaluable form of digital public scholarship that can circumvent some of the issues that plague other forms of digital public scholarship. Hannah McGregor, creator of the peer-reviewed podcast *Secret Feminist Agenda*, collaborator on the *Spoken Word* Podcast, and co-creator of the *Witch, Please* podcast, has worked to create the Amplify Podcast Network. This network was created in partnership with Simon Fraser University's Publishing Program and Digital Humanities Innovation Lab, Wilfrid Laurier University Press, Wilfrid Laurier University Library, and The Documentary Media Society in order to develop Canada's first scholarly podcast network and to build awareness of the potential of podcasting as a form of scholarly communication.[29] Podcasts are MP3 files circulated on RSS feeds (Really Simple Syndication), which amalgamate feeds of serial digital media and have a low barrier to entry for producers and audiences. Podcasts can be downloaded quickly to phones and computers and their audio files require lower bandwidth than video files.[30] Podcasts continue to grow in popularity. The Canadian Podcast Listener 2020 found that 27 percent of Canadian adults listen

---

29 Amplify Podcast Network, "About," 2020, https://amplifypodcastnetwork.ca.
30 Alex Ketchum, "Introduction," *Intro to Feminist Studies Blog,* 2020, https://introtofeministstudies.blogspot.com/2020/07/ audio-and-transcript-1-introduction.html.

Engage in Public Scholarship!

to podcasts monthly.[31] As Gribbins argues, the contributing factors to the growth of podcast interest include "pervasive Internet activity, growth in broadband Internet access, access to multimedia capable personal computers, a blur between streaming and downloading media content, and the rapid adoption of portable MP3 playback devices."[32] While methods for production are discussed in more detail below, producers can create a podcast with minimal equipment: a cell phone's microphone; a simple sound-editing software (although technically even this is optional); and an account with a hosting service such as PodBean. While podcasts are still a digital technology and there can be corporate interests involved if the podcast is paywalled or produced by a podcast network, the medium enables producers to circumvent some of the proprietary barriers that plague other forms of digital public scholarship. As podcasting functions through RSS, which is an open web technology, there are no costs affiliated with a podcast feed being picked up by podcast apps, such as Apple Podcasts, that come pre-loaded on many phones. At present, many listeners use corporate-controlled podcast applications, such as Spotify, in order to listen to podcasts, yet this phenomenon is not inherent to or necessary for podcasting as a technology. This means that with a few simple tools anyone can create a podcast.

There are different genres of podcast creation. There are interview podcasts, fictional podcasts, journalistic

---

31 The Canadian Podcast Listener, "Report," 2020, https://www.canadianpodcastlistener.ca/home#report.
32 Gribbins, "The Perceived Usefulness of Podcasting in Higher Education," p. 1.

Self-produced Digital Public Scholarship

podcasts, conversational podcasts, audio documentaries, and experimental podcasts, to name a few. These genres can be used to cover any topic. Across genres, podcasts can range in production value and required labour. The time required to produce a podcast can depend on the genre, but also on decisions regarding audio editing. An interview or conversational podcast can be as simple as recording one or more people speaking into a single microphone on a single audio track. Perhaps you decide to record the audio at a distance and use a recording program, such as Zencastr, that creates multiple audio tracks that you can edit separately or together.[33] Your podcast could simply be the raw audio converted, as is, to a MP3 file, and uploaded to the hosting service. You might decide to cut up the interviews and splice the audio with scripted host narration. An example of a podcast with a complex narrative structure is the *Ologies Podcast*, hosted by Alie Ward, which intersperses the main audio with tangents and several archival and field recordings.[34] If you also choose to add background music or original scores, your podcast editing time will greatly inflate in comparison to a simple raw audio file. Choosing a genre, sound scheme, and general structure can help you estimate the production time. This will help you decide the kind of project to which you can feasibly commit. It is possible to also create one-off podcast audio stories or single, serial episodes. Without a set release schedule, it can be harder to build an audience. Podcasts as a medium include a wide range of possibilities—get creative! You can even teach a

---

33 Zencaster, "About," 2020, https://zencastr.com.
34 Alie Ward, "About," 2020, https://www.alieward.com/ologies.

Engage in Public Scholarship!

university course through a podcast, such as the Intro to Feminist and Social Justice Studies Course Podcast.[35] Maybe you will create podcast episodes based on presentations at an academic conference, such as Anna Sigrithur's *OxTales Podcast*, based on the Oxford Food Symposium.[36] Podcast creation can be undertaken by individuals, large production teams, and anything in between.

There are different roles in the creation of podcasts—host, producer, writer, editor, sound engineer, and publicist—all of which can be done by one person.[37] The host delivers the information and sets the tone for the podcast. Some public-scholarship podcasts, such as *Métis in Space*,[38]

---

35 During the COVID-19 pandemic, all courses during the Fall 2020 semester at McGill University were delivered remotely. In order to make this class as accessible as possible, I delivered all twenty-two lectures in the form of audio files/podcast files. Audio files have many benefits including that they require lower bandwidth, can be played on phones, and can be accessed no matter what time zone the students were in. All audio lectures are accompanied by transcripts that include links to additional material. Students could download the audio files and transcripts from the class web page or through popular podcast apps like Apple Podcast, Google Podcast, Podbean, Spotify, and Pandora, if they preferred. I wanted to make the transition to a podcast course as smooth as possible and enable students to use the tools with which they were already familiar. All of the transcripts are on the course website: https://introtofeministstudies.blogspot.com. For the Fall 2021 semester, I updated all twenty-two episodes and made the Fall 2020 audio archive available through Bandcamp. (Alex Ketchum, "Introduction," *Intro to Feminist Studies Blog*, 2020, https://introtofeministstudies.blogspot.com/2020/07/audio-andtranscript-1-introduction.html)

36 Anna Sigrithur, "Guest Post: Aural Fixation," *OxTales* (podcast), 2019, https://www.oxfordsymposium.org.uk/podcast/.

37 Anna Sigrithur, "Podcasting and Storytelling Workshop," 2020, https://docs.google.com/document/d/13c2z69LnCa1u_KGcmCbOqs82uAMXBrqbwFRjJXFOFvk/edit.

38 *Métis in Space*, "About," 2020, http://www.metisinspace.com.

Self-produced Digital Public Scholarship   183

have more than one host. Other podcasts rotate hosts, such as the food-justice podcast *The Racist Sandwich*.[39] The role of the producer is to develop the stories, book guests, and coordinate with other individuals involved in the podcast production. The producer will also make sure that the finished MP3 file is uploaded to the podcast-hosting service so that the episode can be distributed via RSS feeds. She will make sure that the transcript is made available. If the podcast is scripted, the writer creates the script. Conversational style podcasts and interview podcasts will not have a set script, but the writer and host may work together to create a list of questions and topics. Editors will take the raw "tape"[40] and will use audio-editing software in order to cut and mix the tape into the final MP3 audio file that will be distributed via the RSS feed. Sound engineers can be involved in the recording and post-production processes in order to ensure the audio quality. Tasks can range from holding microphones, watching audio levels during a recording, creating sound design, scoring a show, to making foley (sound effects). The publicity or public-relations person will advertise the podcast, write show notes, manage the show's social media accounts, and oversee branding. It is common for all of these roles to be fulfilled by one person, but each requires different skill sets and tools.

After you have determined your podcast's theme, genre, and topics, the next step is recording the audio. There are

---

39   *The Racist Sandwich Podcast*, "About," 2020, http://www.racistsandwich.com.

40   The word "tape" is still used in the digital era to describe an audio recording.

Engage in Public Scholarship! 184

a wide range of tools that you can use for audio recording, which range in price and the audio quality they produce. It is genuinely possible to use your phone to record podcast audio. As of November 2020, instructor in the Graduate Comics Program at the California College of the Arts Nicole J. Georges has used her iPhone's internal microphone in order to record over 220 episodes of her podcast *Sagittarian Matters*. In episode 201, Georges and her producer, Chris Sutton, discussed how after five years of using the podcast in order to elevate the voices of queer women and non-binary writers and artists, they have stayed committed to a DIY (do it yourself) or a DIT (do it together) ideology. For them, this has meant using phones to record and minimal edits.[41] This commitment to simple edits and tools may have contributed to the longevity of their collaboration; choices over equipment, labour, and structure can impact sustainability. Expensive tools are not necessary. For under 100 dollars, it is possible to buy microphones that can improve audio quality. There are microphones that plug into smart phones, which are useful for hosts who want to minimize equipment and/or use their phones for roving recordings. These microphones, such as the Rode Smart Lav, can produce better audio quality and control than the smartphone's own internal microphone.[42] USB computer microphones,

---

41 Nicole J. Georges (host) and Chris Sutton (guest), "Episode 201 - Produce Chris Sutton!!! Plus Vanport, Black Lives Matter, JK Rowling More!" *Sagittarian Matters* (podcast), June 12, 2020, https://sagittarianmatters.podbean.com/e/episode-201-producer-chris-sutton-plus-vanport-blacklives-matter-jk-rowling-more/.

42 Anna Sigrithur, "Podcasting and Storytelling Workshop," 2020, https://docs.google.com/document/d/13c2z69LnCa1u_KGcmCbOqs82uAMXBrqbwFRjJXFOFvk/edit.

Self-produced Digital Public Scholarship 185

such as the Blue Yeti Mic, enable you to plug the microphone into your computer, and are a fairly standard podcast tool. There are microphones that are useful to record ambient or background sound. Audio recorders, such as the Tascam DR100 mkii, are technical, professional gear that record high-quality audio, on which you can set different compression rates and file types. Other recording tools that can be useful are pop screens, also known as pop filters or pop shields, that reduce or eliminate the popping sounds caused by the mechanical impact of fast-moving air on the microphone during recordings. While tools can impact audio quality, the location in which you record also has an effect. Whenever possible, avoid recording next to a busy road. Putting a blanket behind you can block ambient sounds.[43] Some podcasters choose to record in their closets to mimic recording studios. The tools you use to record the audio can affect the podcast's quality but editing also plays a large role.

As with tools, you have a large range of options for audio editing. There are open-source and proprietary options. Audacity, for example, is an open-source audio editor,[44] yet the learning curve is a bit steeper than other software. The professional Hindenburg tools, which are directed towards journalists, radio producers, and podcasters, have a more intuitive interface. You can experiment with the software during a free trial, after which you pay a one-

---

43   Jonathan Sterne, "Recording Your Lectures 4: Techniques," *Super Bon!,* August 21, 2020, https://superbon.net/2020/08/21/recording-your-lectures-4-techniques/.
44   Audacity, "About," 2020, https://www.audacityteam.org.

Engage in Public Scholarship! 186

time download fee.[45] Many smart phones' and computers' operating systems already have some kind of audio-editing software included, such as Garageband.[46] Some tools, such as Logic Pro X, are made primarily for music editing, but can be used for podcasts. The right audio-editing software depends on your skill level and needs. Fortunately, there are many video tutorials available on how to use these programs, produced by individuals and by the companies building this software.

You may want to incorporate audio that you have not recorded yourself into the podcast. Firstly, it is important to be aware of the copyright law where you live. (For more information on respecting copyright, see the above section on video production.) There are also millions of royalty-free pieces of music and online sound repositories available at websites such as Freesound.org, Archive.org, and FreeMusicArchive. org. Many of these audio files are licenced under Creative Commons and may require attribution. It is also possible to commission or write your own theme-song music. It is fairly standard practice to include consistent theme-song music with each episode so that listeners will associate the episode with your podcast.

Once you have created your MP3 file, it is time to launch your podcast. You might decide to release one episode at a time or an entire season at once. The benefit of releasing a whole season at once is that you can take your time editing

---

45 Hindenburg, "About," 2020, https://hindenburg.com.
46 Garageband, "About," 2020, https://www.apple.com/ca/mac/garageband.

Self-produced Digital Public Scholarship 187

the audio and work to create a cohesive format and sound. The benefit of releasing episodes one at a time is that you can work to build an audience. You can also adapt to what works and what does not work. The most common way to share your podcast is through podcast-hosting platforms such as Podbean, Libsyn, and Transistor, which create a unique RSS feed for your podcast. For your podcast to then appear in aggregators such as iTunes/Apple Podcasts, Stitcher, and Spotify, you will need to connect your RSS feed to these aggregate platforms. This is a simple process that you only have to undergo one time per platform. After that, every time you upload an episode to your hosting platform, the RSS feed will automatically be captured by the aggregator apps. These hosting platforms range in monthly fees, beginning with free options for a limited number of hours. When making decisions about which hosting platform to choose, check the terms and conditions to see who retains the rights of the podcast, and if advertisements can be added without your consent. These issues are more common with hosting platforms that do not charge fees. It is possible to create audio and upload it to platforms such as Soundcloud, Mixcloud, and Bandcamp, which are more traditionally used for music. This audio is not technically a podcast, as it is not distributed via RSS feeds. However, these platforms have their own platform-specific audiences, and can be useful if you are interested in audio storytelling. These platforms also auto-generate embeddable audio players that can be useful for distributing your work on a website.

Podcasts and audio storytelling are useful in making scholarship more accessible to larger audiences, but they

Engage in Public Scholarship! 188

can also be used in traditional academic settings. Podcasts enable people from around the world to interact with your scholarship, free of paywalls. The audio format lends itself to a different tone than an academic journal article. You might take on a more conversational style to discuss your research on a podcast or have the time to expand upon ideas and definitions of concepts. It is possible to also use podcasts to make peer-reviewed academic articles open to audiences in an audio format. Historian of colonialism and Canadian food studies Ian Mosby has recorded audio versions of some of his academic articles in order to improve accessibility.[47] *BC Studies: The British Columbia Quarterly* academic journal has created audio versions of their articles to expand accessibility.[48] Similarly, *Hakai Magazine*, which explores science, society, and the environment from a coastal perspective, has created the Hakai Podcast to reproduce some of their articles in an audio format.[49]

The ability to record audio versions of one's academic articles by reading them aloud depends on the author's contract with the journal and the kind of copyright to which she has agreed. However, it is possible to talk about the work that you have written about without reading your article verbatim. This decision may lend itself to a livelier retelling, better suited for the podcast medium.

---

47 Ian Mosby (@Ian_Mosby), "Thinking about recording audio versions of some of my articles to improve their accessibility," Twitter thread, February 27, 2020, https://twitter.com/Ian_Mosby/status/1233092934213476352.

48 *BC Studies*, "Audio Articles," 2020, https://bcstudies.com/issues/audio-articles/.

49 *Hakai Magazine*, "Podcasts," 2020, https://www.hakaimagazine.com/category/podcasts/.

Self-produced Digital Public Scholarship

While podcasts are useful for making academic work more accessible, podcasts can also be productive pedagogical tools within university classrooms. Ernie C. Avila and Mary Kris S. Lavadia have demonstrated the efficacy of academic podcasts in a learning environment.[50] Similarly, Brock Peoples and Carol Tilley emphasize that "70.21 percent of students who participated in the study found that 'integration of podcasting can be useful in college curriculum'"[51] when incorporated into their learning alongside traditional methods, like lectures and textbook readings. Peoples and Tilley argue that "podcasts should be included in academic library collections, as research has shown that podcasts are becoming a trusted information resource."[52] Podcasts are valuable tools for pedagogy, research promotion, knowledge dissemination, and scholarship, in and of themselves.

Although podcasting as a tool can increase accessibility for some audiences, providing transcripts for podcasts is an important consideration for Deaf people, people who are hard of hearing, audiences connecting with your work in a second language, and people with auditory-processing issues. Transcripts also can provide audiences with useful references and a keyword-searchable tool for when they want to cite your work. Transcripts can also improve your search engine optimization, helping potential audiences find your

---

50 Avila and Lavadia, "Investigation of the Acceptability and Effectiveness of Academic Podcasts to College Students' Scholastic Performance in Science."

51 Peoples and Tilley, "Podcasts as an Emerging Information Resource," p. 47.

52 Peoples and Tilley, "Podcasts as an Emerging Information Resource," p. 46.

Engage in Public Scholarship! 190

work.[53] Transcripts also facilitate citation practices because researchers can more readily search through and quote from the transcript of audio materials. Providing a transcript is quite simple if your podcast is scripted, as the transcript is essentially the script. There are certain conventions, such as writing the name of the speaker before the audio and describing the background sounds and music. Nonetheless, generating a transcript for a scripted podcast is a streamlined process.

You have numerous options if your podcast is unscripted. It is possible to write your own transcripts or hire a professional transcriptionist. Similar to captioning, auto-transcriptors are useful, but imperfect tools. The *Disrupting Disruptions* podcast's transcripts were made by first running the audio at half speed while sometimes using the auto-transcriptor otter.ai, and at other times using SpeechTexter (https://www.speechtexter.com/). A human then proofread the transcript and cleaned up the grammar and text. It is also possible to run the podcast audio while using a program such as Zoom. Zoom can generate a transcript of the call and then you can manually clean it up. If these options are unavailable to you, you can upload your podcast in the form of a video file to YouTube, which will generate imperfect captions. From here, you can download a free auto-transcribed version. Numerous podcasts have solicited fan-created transcripts. The Bello Collective has created a useful guide with additional tool suggestions for creating podcast transcripts.[54] They

---

53 Listen Notes, "About," 2020, https://www.listennotes.com.
54 Bello Collective, "The Podcaster's Guide to Transcribing Audio," *Join the Party* (podcast), March 19, 2018, https://bellocollective.com/the-podcasters-guide-to-transcribing-audio-2121f9e7992f.

Self-produced Digital Public Scholarship

191

emphasize that "transcripts must be free. Accessibility should never depend on a listener's income," an idea reinforced by SimpleCast's post on accessibility.[55] Furthermore, the authors explain how audio-mixing choices can increase accessibility. They recommend that podcasters: expand their episode with mono audio; remove or remix sound effects and music to improve the intelligibility of your dialogue; compress the music and sound effects heavily to push the dialogue forward in your mix when someone starts speaking; and mix the episode with a limited dynamic range, which is another huge help for Deaf or hard of hearing listeners.[56] Once you have generated your transcripts and have undertaken other measures for accessibility, you can link to your transcripts in the show notes for each episode. You can make the transcripts publicly available through applications such as Google Docs; you can host them on a website made for the podcast; or you can post them on another kind of platform, such as Tumblr.

Podcast audio prioritizes the power of the voice over the visual. There are gender politics around the register and pitch of who is speaking. Voices that are considered "masculine," that are lower pitched, are often read as the voice of authority. As PhD candidate Stacey Copeland discusses in an episode of the podcast *Secret Feminist Agenda*, there is a particularly gendered policing of women's voices. Women's voices will receive criticism for being allegedly shrill or for having vocal

---

55 Caitlin Van Horne, "Three Ways to Make Your Podcast More Accessible," *Simplecast Blog,* May 31, 2019, https://blog.simplecast.com/three-ways-podcast-accessibility/?fbclid=IwAR0fVV1HWPPKNQunwgRdXQEkOuhX Bjm2bFiHRuZt7G4WSqLAySoLLe6k.

56 Join the Party Podcast, "The Podcaster's Guide to Transcribing Audio."

Engage in Public Scholarship! 192

fry.[57] Renowned feminist writer bell hooks questions the idea of the liberated voice. hooks wants us to think about the voice of power, particularly of liberatory power. She questions whose voices are listened to, who has the voice of power, and how technology has changed or reinforced the way we think about voices.[58] Podcasts can increase access to public scholarship. They have the potential to challenge cultural ideas of what the voices of power and academic knowledge sound like. At the same time, scholars who engage in podcasting can face difficulty in being seen as authoritative in their realm due to their voices. As transcription software is most often trained on white, male voices, those voices are better understood by this software.[59] These applications continue to have racial and gender biases.[60] For more on these discussions, see the bibliography by Zed Adams and Shannon Mattern[61] and an illuminating Twitter thread on the inequality caused by the "normal voice" training of voice-to-text protocols.[62]

---

57 Hannah McGregor (host), "Secret Feminist Agenda and Stacey Copeland: Producing Queer Media," *Secret Feminist Agenda* (podcast), May 15, 2020, https://secretfeministagenda.com/2020/05/15/episode-4-20producing-queer-media-with-stacey-copeland/.
58 bell hooks and John Badalament, "bell hooks on Voice," March 6, 2011, YouTube video, 1:29, https://www.youtube.com/watch?v=j5ThEoA0ESA.
59 Perez, *Invisible Women.*
60 Li and Mills, "Vocal Features."
61 Adams and Mattern, "April 2: Contemporary Vocal Interfaces," 2019, https://www.wordsinspace.net/interfaces/2019/portfolio/april-2contemporary-vocal-interfaces.
62 Vanessa Heggie (@HPSVanessa), "Voice Inequality," Twitter, September 13, 2020, 3:19 AM, https://twitter.com/HPSVanessa/status/13050433 97925838848.

Self-produced Digital Public Scholarship 193

Podcasting is a fairly accessible medium for scholars interested in public scholarship in a digital form. Perhaps the time, training, skills, and energy required for creating your own podcast do not appeal to you. Even if you are not interested in producing your own podcast, it is still possible to participate in podcast-based public scholarship. You can reach out to podcasters that you admire who work in your field and let them know that you are available to talk about your research. This way you benefit from their already established audience. For example, podcasts such as *Anthrodish*[63] and *Femidish*[64] actively seek out researchers interested in food scholarship. There are also established podcast networks that exist to promote scholarly work, such as the New Books Network.[65] For tips on preparing to be interviewed by the media, including on a podcast or radio, see chapter twelve.

4   Apps and More

Scholars have even created apps in order to engage the public. For example, George Vrtis of Carleton University and Chris Wells of Macalester College developed the Minnesota Environments app in March 2016. The app is available on the Apple and Google Play app stores, and was made in collaboration with colleagues and students

---

63   Sarah Duignan, "About —Be A Guest," *Anthrodish* (podcast), 2020, https://www.anthrodish.com/beaguest.

64   *Femidish* (podcast), "About," 2020, https://www.femidish.com.

65   New Books Network, "About," 2020, http://newbooksnetwork.com/.

Engage in Public Scholarship! 194

at Carleton, Macalester, the Minnesota Historical Society, and the Minnesota Historical and Cultural Grants Program. The app and accompanying website use geo-located maps and multimedia presentations to explore the people, places, ecosystems, and developments that have shaped Minnesota's environmental history. The designers built the app on the Curatescape framework.[66] Curatescape is a web and mobile app framework that is user-friendly and enables small to mid-sized cultural organizations, preservation groups, or educational institutions to build apps in order to reconnect to their communities and audiences. It is particularly useful for public history.[67] Other examples of apps using this framework include the Emmett Till Memory Project[68] and Cleveland Historical.[69] Curatescape is not the only option. Omeka is a free, open source—content management system for the display of library, museum archives, and scholarly collections and exhibitions. Omeka Everywhere Mobile enables scholars and organizations to transform content from their Omeka Classic site into app form for Android and iOS operating systems.[70] Proprietary options, such as the tour and walking guide app-builder STQRY, exist, however, using them can cost thousands of dollars per year.[71] Museums and other cultural institutions have deployed apps, using Smartify and the Google Arts

---

66 Center for Community and Civic Engagement, "Minnesota Environments App," 2020.

67 Curatescape, "About," 2020, https://curatescape.org/about/.

68 Emmett Till App, "About," 2020, https://tillapp.emmett-till.org.

69 Cleveland Historical, "About," 2020, https://clevelandhistorical.org.

70 Omeka, "Omeka Everywhere," April 12, 2018, https://omeka.org/news/2018/04/12/omeka-everywhere/.

71 Stqry, "Products and Pricing," 2021, https://stqry.com/products/stqry-apps/.

Self-produced Digital Public Scholarship 195

Culture with mixed results. While some users enjoyed the augmented experience of using apps, others have claimed that the apps did not add to their experience and were a technological distraction.[72] Open-source and proprietary mobile-app frameworks can enable scholars to engage audiences on their mobile devices.

Building an app without a pre-existing framework requires coding skills but allows for even greater customization. Apps, podcasts, videos, and websites are not the only forms of digital public scholarship. With creativity, platforms and applications can be repurposed for public scholarship.

5   Conclusion

The forms of public scholarship available to you as a scholar will shift over time, depending on your interests, audiences, skills, and the resources that are available to you. As new technologies emerge, so too will new forms of public scholarship. The root of any choice surrounding self-produced public scholarship depends on the content and your goals for your public scholarship. Do not let the tools become deterministic. The next chapter will look at physical, self-produced public scholarship as well as the connection between the digital and physical.

---

72   Rachel Kraus, "Bring on Museum Companion Apps—But Only If They're Absolutely Awesome," *Mashable,* April 21, 2018.

CHAPTER 9

Self-produced Physical Forms of Public Scholarship

This chapter examines physical forms of self-produced public scholarship. Books, pamphlets, zines, reports, and exhibits are valuable forms of research communication, and are especially useful in reaching audiences that are not online.[1] Even if your audience has access to the internet, physical media opens up different ways to interact with content. This chapter builds on the framework of chapter eight and rejects any hierarchy between physical and digital public scholarship; rather, this chapter examines how the two can work together.

---

1   Yates et al., "Who Are the Limited Users of Digital Systems and Media?"

1 Books

Books are a fantastic way to communicate research and disseminate knowledge. The choice of publisher for your book will impact the accessibility of your text and the kinds of audiences that are likely to interact with it. Publishing with an established university press has benefits for scholars applying for tenure, promotion, or grants, and can contribute to ongoing dialogues within one's field. There are numerous guides for turning your research into an academic monograph, such as Melody Herr's *Writing and Publishing Your Book: A Guide for Experts in Every Field*, William Germano's *Getting It Published: A Guide for Scholars and Anyone Else Serious about Serious Books*, and Laura Portwood-Stacer's *The Book Proposal Book: A Guide for Scholarly Authors*. While some academic presses have a commitment to publishing texts written in a more accessible format, academic presses are focused on reaching academic audiences. Publishing with an academic press impacts the tone, content, design, marketing, and distribution of the book and will skew the book towards those academic audiences. There are some presses, such as the Feminist Press, which exist at the boundary between academic and non-academic publishing.[2] Their books do not undergo peer review but may deal with content similar to a scholarly monograph.

Crossover and trade books have the potential to reach wider audiences. Susan Rabiner and Alfred Fortunato's

---

2   Feminist Press, "Mission," 2020, https://www.feministpress.org/mission.

Engage in Public Scholarship!

Thinking Like Your Editor: How to Write Great Serious Nonfiction and Get It Published is useful for authors who are thinking of publishing crossover books that are aimed at both academic and non-academic audiences, and trade books that are targeted towards the general public. Courtney Maum, Anne Trubek, and Jane Friedman's guides are particularly useful for scholars who are interested in writing trade books.[3] Publishing with trade presses can expand the distribution of your content. Whereas scholarly monographs can be expensive for readers due to limited print runs, trade books are often priced more affordably. Writing for trade audiences does not mean simplifying your ideas or concepts.[4] However, you will likely use fewer citations, give broader context and examples, and have a shorter introduction. Books are not the only available physical written form and as W.W. Norton executive editor Alane Salierno Mason advises, a "book should not be one's first and only attempt to address the public."[5] It is useful to experiment with other forms of public scholarship in advance of book publication in order to cultivate your voice and audience.

---

3   Maum, *Before and After the Book Deal*; Trubek, *So You Want to Publish a Book?*; Friedman, *The Business of Being a Writer*.

4   Scott Montgomery, "Writing for General, Non-Academic Audiences: Benefits, Opportunities, Issues," The Henry M. Jackson School of International Studies, September 12, 2017, https://jsis.washington.edu/news/writing-general-non-academic-audiences-benefits-opportunities-issues/

5   Alane Salierno Mason, "10 Tips for Academics Writing for a General Audience," W.W. Norton & Company, May 13, 2016, https://wwnorton.medium.com/10-tips-for-academics-writing-for-ageneral-audience-d9f946fbd5de.

Self-produced Physical Forms of Public Scholarship 199

2 Zines, Bookettes, and Pamphlets

Writing a book is a huge time investment. Zines, bookettes (mini-books), and pamphlets enable you to create a publication for the public that is shorter, can be distributed for less money, and can be published quickly. Scholars can utilize these media in order to communicate with the public. Pamphlets, leaflets, bookettes, and zines are short, usually unbound publications that are used to cheaply distribute information.

Zines are DIY (do it yourself) publications, usually made on paper and reproduced with a photocopier or printer. Common production techniques include cut and paste, collage, or typing and formatting pages on a computer.[6] The Barnard College Zine Library explains that "zine creators are often motivated by a desire to share knowledge or experience with people in marginalized or otherwise less empowered communities."[7] While zines have historically been used to distribute knowledge across subcultures such as the Riot Grrrl and punk scenes, zines have since been taken up by other communities interested in knowledge sharing.[8] It is possible to create an eight-page zine from a single piece of paper, and many templates for printing and

---

6   Alex Wrekk, "Stolen Sharpie Revolution: A DIY Guide for Zines and Zine Culture," 2001, https://stolensharpierevolution.org/about/.
7   Barnard College, "Zine Basics," 2020, https://zines.barnard.edu/zine-basics.
8   Groeneveld, *Making Feminist Media*.

Engage in Public Scholarship!   200

folding exist online.[9] As a result, this kind of knowledge communication can be financially accessible and relatively sustainable from a labour and environmental perspective.

Zines can be self-published and distributed or published by zine presses. Some publishers, such as Microcosm Publishing, will use zines as a means to test the market and support a wider range of authors. Microcosm first publishes an author's work in a zine format and if the zine garners significant interest and has the potential to be expanded into a 100-page book or longer, the press will work with the author over the course of a few years to publish one.[10] Zines can circulate information in the present. They also present a valuable resource within libraries and archives, as they often speak to the social history of marginalized communities.[11] The tangible quality of zines, pamphlets, bookettes, and leaflets serve a different function than blogs and can reach audiences who would not otherwise find your work.[12] Writing a zine, pamphlet, leaflet, or bookette can enable you to communicate your scholarship with the public without having to commit to a longer-term project.

9   Anne Elizabeth Moore, "How to Make This Very Zine," 2020, https://zines. barnard.edu/zinebasics/how-make-zine.
10   Microcosm Publishing, "Why the Focus on Zines," 2020, https:// microcosmpublishing.com/ faq#why-focus-zines.
11   Barnard College, "Zine Libraries," 2020, https://zines.barnard.edu/zine-libraries.
12   Jenna Freedman, "Zines Are Not Blogs: A Not Unbiased Analysis," Barnard College, 2005, https://zines.barnard.edu/are-zines-blogs.

3 Comics, Cartoons, and Graphic Novels

Some scholars have utilized comics, cartoons, and graphic novels as a way to communicate their research through the use of text and images. For example, Ebony Flowers created a comic version of her doctoral dissertation. She was studying visualization practices in educational settings and comics enabled her to communicate her research in an accessible form that supported her research findings.[13] Due to her subject matter's emphasis on the visual, a comic format actually supported her argument. The usefulness of comics as a form extends beyond the subject matter, however. B. Erin Cole is a historian and the creator behind Little Brain Comics. She has a PhD in history and works at a museum, but since experiencing a traumatic brain injury she has shifted her scholarly communication away from long-form academic articles and books towards comics. In her comic "Am I Still a Historian?" Cole argues that the emphasis on publishing a scholarly monograph is harmful, ableist, and undermines other useful forms of research communication, such as comics.[14] The monograph can be an effective form of research communication, but the emphasis on long-form text is inaccessible to a wide range of scholars and audiences. Writing and reading books require time and space, which

---

13 Ebony Flowers, "Comics Based Dissertation," *Centre for Imaginative Ethnography,* June 24, 2017, https://imaginative-ethnography. com/2017/06/24/comics-based-dissertation-by-ebony-flowers/.

14 B. Erin Cole, "Am I Still a Historian?" *Little Brain Substack,* August 23, 2020, https://littlebrain.substack.com/p/am-i-still-a-historian.

Engage in Public Scholarship! 202

may not be available to people with children, busy work schedules, other commitments, and/or people with cognitive and learning disabilities.

Comics open up new ways of communicating information and new ways of thinking about and approaching a subject. This choice of medium impacts both the scholar's and the reader's relationships with the material. In her books *Syllabus: Notes from an Accidental Professor* and *Making Comics* renowned cartoonist and scholar Lynda Barry argues that the act of drawing and writing are one in the same. She rejects the hierarchy between script and illustration.

Cartoons, comics, and graphic novels encourage creative uses of images, drawing, paintings, and text done by hand or on a computer. By using these techniques, the creator and reader can interact with the subject matter on multiple levels. Rachel Crane-Williams's comic "Can You Picture This? Activism, Art, and Public Scholarship" describes her work as an artist and scholar in women's prisons. She writes that "comics are more than stories; this way of presenting experiences also allows me to succinctly share the sounds, sights, and even smells of prison, as well as the conversations and body language."[15] Cartoonist and graphic-novelist scholars range in the styles of art they utilize, which can draw different audiences to the work. Not all comics are created by a single scholar. Comics can be collaborative endeavours. For example, comics scholar Damian Duffy will work alongside artists, such as John Jennings, on the script

---

15 Crane-Williams, "Can You Picture This?"

Self-produced Physical Forms of Public Scholarship 203

and images in their books.[16] These image-based forms of research communication can be published both digitally and physically. They can be shared as webcomics on personal websites or on cartoon-publishing platforms. They can be physically published as part of an anthology, self-published, or published by a comics press. Comics, cartoons, and graphic novels can be a useful means of communicating research findings with the public by employing the power of words and images together.

4   Policy Briefs and Reports

If your research findings may be useful for informing policy and legislation, consider writing policy briefs and reports. Policy briefs and reports are documents intended for governmental and non-governmental organizations that deliver content in a manner that is concise, specific, objective, persuasive, and focused on practical decision making. These kinds of reports can be written alongside community organizations and governmental agencies or be released independently. In his guide, "Writing Policy Briefs and Reports," Mitchell McIvor of the University of Toronto explains that "compared to academic writing, a policy brief or report contains little to no theory and is instead focused on providing only necessary details—background, evidence, facts, and key logic. [The report's goal is to give] feasible

---

16   Duffy, Butler, and Jennings, *Kindred.*

Engage in Public Scholarship! 204

solutions or recommendations for the problem at hand."[17] Communications advisor Susan Doyle demonstrates the importance of writing policy recommendations in her guide, and argues that they are "in many ways the chief product of the ongoing work of government managers to create and administer public policy."[18] Guides for writing policy briefs consistently recommend that reports avoid jargon and focus on clear and concise writing.[19] It is useful if these reports are written in plain language.

5   Plain-Language Versions and Audiobooks

Plain-language writing is a form of writing that makes important information and ideas more accessible to people with intellectual and developmental disabilities, and others with disabilities affecting reading, comprehension, and other cognitive functions. As disabled journalist Andrew Pulrang explains, plain-language writing includes techniques such as: using more common words and words with fewer syllables; using shorter sentences and shorter

---

17   Mitchell McIvor, "Writing Policy Briefs Reports," 2018, https://www.utm. utoronto.ca/asc/sites/files/asc/public/shared/pdf/wdi/sample_course_ materials/soc/SOC_PolicyWritingGuide.pdf.

18   Susan Doyle, "Writing a Policy Recommendation," ENGL 302 —Writing for Government, 2013, https://web.uvic.ca/~sdoyle/E302/Notes/Policy%20 Recommendation.html.

19   The Writing Center, "Policy Briefs," 2020, https://writingcenter.unc.edu/ tips-and-tools/ policy-briefs/.

Self-produced Physical Forms of Public Scholarship 205

paragraphs; using active instead of passive voice; and cutting back on extra details or personal impressions. The complete information of the document should be included, yet it should be written in a more accessible way. As Zoe Gross of the Autistic Self Advocacy Network says, "A plain-language translation of a complex document should be a true translation: it should contain the same complex ideas and content expressed in a more accessible way, rather than removing ideas until things seem more simple."[20] On June 22, 2020, disability activist Alice Wong announced that disabled writer and journalist Sara Luterman would be releasing a free, plain-language version of Wong's book *Disability Visibility.*[21] Reflecting on this choice in an interview with Kendra Winchester of the *Reading Women* podcast, Wong stated,

> I commissioned Sara to write a plain-language version of the book because there a lot of people with different kinds of disabilities who process information differently. You know, self-writing can be very dense. And having clear language is a form of access that I don't think is talked about enough. And I've learned from other people. I've learned from people with learning disabilities, people with intellectual or

---

20 Pulrang, "Plain Language Writing: An Essential Part of Accessibility," *Forbes,* October 22, 2020.

21 Alice Wong, "Plain Language as Access," *Disability Visibility Substack,* June 22, 2020, https://disabilityvisibility.substack. com/p/plain-language-as-access.

Engage in Public Scholarship!

cognitive disabilities that plain language is absolutely the key to reaching all kinds of people.[22]

In order to create the plain-language version of the text, Luterman simplified sentence structure, stripped down the number of hard words, and employed a major principle of plain language: chronological writing.[23] She used tools such as the UpperGoer6 in order to check how common words were, with the idea "that the more common a word is, the more likely people are to understand what it means."[24] At times, Luterman would include a definition of a term if there was not a common equivalent. Writing in plain language is a form of knowledge translation that requires understanding the audiences and communities that you are writing for—as Sara VanLooy and Hannah Rudstam's webinar presentation, "Writing Pure and Simple," on plain-language writing in the disability field makes clear.[25] A term may be common for one audience and not another. When creating written publications for public scholarship, offline or online, consider the language you use. Consider creating a plain-language version of your texts.

---

22 Kendra Winchester (host), "Interview | Alice Wong," *Reading Women* (podcast), July 22, 2020, https://www.readingwom enpodcast.com/blog/interview-with-alice-wong.
23 Sara Luterman, *Plain Language Translation of Disability Visibility,* 2020, https://docs.google.com/document/d/180BSG2lEZHNOPhp9uH7dGN6Y Le9eNvkeSry6tEZJ0/edit.
24 Theo Sanderson, "The Up-Goer Six Text Editor," https://splasho.com/upgoer6/.
25 Sara VanLooy and Hannah Rudstam, "Writing Pure and Simple: Plain Language Communication in the Field of Disability," webinar at Northeast American Disabilities Act Center, December 3, 2014, https://www.northeas tada.org/media/play/0 6xre62dj.

Self-produced Physical Forms of Public Scholarship   207

As plain language can expand the accessibility of your content, audiobooks can similarly expand access. Audiobooks enable another mode of reading that is useful for, but not limited to, Blind and people with limited vision.[26] Listeners can interact with the materials while completing other tasks, such as commuting or doing errands. Audiences with lower-grade reading levels can have access to the work in a way that they otherwise would not. Furthermore, education researchers Beth A. Rogowsky, Barbara M. Calhoun, and Paula Tallal found no significant differences in comprehension between reading, listening, or reading and listening simultaneously.[27] In 2020, the W3C Publishing Working Group was in the process of developing a set standard for accessible audiobooks, and there is a public draft of their working document.[28] Creating a set of accessibility standards can significantly improve user experience, as only 10 percent of the over six-hundred people with print disabilities who participated in the 2020 "How do YOU Read?" study in Canada found that it was "very easy" to find sufficiently accessible books.[29] The distribution platforms available for audiobooks impact access. The Association of Canadian Publishers has committed to improving these platforms. In 2020, the association released

---

26   Sarah Pittaway and Michelle Malomo, "Audiobooks, Accessibility Tools and Universal Design for Learning: Breaking Down Barriers," paper presented at UKSG 42nd Annual Conference and Exhibition, Telford, UK, 8 to 10 April 2019, https://eprints.worc.ac.uk/id/eprint/7904.

27   Rogowsky, Calhoun, and Tallal, "Does Modality Matter?"

28   Wendy Reid and Matt Garish, "Audiobooks: WC3 Recommendations," WC3, November 10, 2020, https://www.w3.org/TR/audiobooks/.

29   Association of Canadian Publishers and eBOUND Canada, *Accessible Publishing Research Project,* April 2020, https://publishers.ca/wp-content/uploads/2020/06/ACP eBound Accessibility Report final.pdf.

Engage in Public Scholarship! 208

two reports regarding the accessibility, capacity, financing, and sustainability of audiobooks: *Audiobooks: Building Capacity for Canadian Creation and Publishing* and *Accessible Publishing Research Project*. In these reports there are numerous suggestions on how to improve distribution and raise awareness. Choices over whether to use proprietary or open platforms for hosting and sharing audiobooks will further affect access.

Audiobooks can also be an art form in themselves. Authors who choose to read their own books can enliven the text by adding emphasis to particular sections. Voice actors who may be hired to read aloud engage in a performance of the text. Some audiobooks incorporate other levels of audio production, such as sound effects or music. As with any form of public scholarship, it is important to consider the labour issues involved in creating audiobooks. Recording audiobooks requires specialized skill sets and dedicated time and labour. The Association of Canadian Publishers provides recommendations for more audiobook-specific training for actors, directors, editors, and studios.[30] Efforts to fairly compensate this labour are necessary to make audiobooks accessible for audiences and creators alike.

---

30 Susan Renouf, "Audiobooks: Building Capacity for Canadian Creation and Publishing," 2020, https://publishers.ca/wp-content/uploads/2020/04/2020-Symposium-Backgrounder.pdf.

Self-produced Physical Forms of Public Scholarship   209

6 Exhibitions, Art, Music, and Performance

Exhibitions, art, music, and performance can also be used as forms of public scholarship. Jon Bath argues that the "creation and exhibition of artistic works closely aligned with scholarly research, [can function] as a way to increase public engagement with academic research."[31] He relies on Sheila A. Brennan's "public first" framework, where the public's needs must be considered first if scholarship is to actually be public.[32] This is particularly applicable to artistic research—communication measures, where the art is created with the public's experience as the priority. A robust discussion of the potential of exhibits within public scholarship would involve debates occurring within museum studies,[33] archival studies,[34] library and information studies,[35] and public history.[36] This discussion would need to be conducted alongside a thorough literature review of curatorial practices within art and media studies[37] and research creation.[38] Music,[39] dance,[40] and performance studies likewise have robust literatures on the potential to engage audiences. Such a discussion is beyond the parameters

31 Bath, "Artistic Research Creation for Publicly Engaged Scholarship," p. 1.
32 Gold and Klein, *Debates in the Digital Humanities 2016*.
33 Buchanan, "Curation as Public Scholarship."
34 McCausland, "Archival Public Programming."
35 Novara and Novara, "Exhibits as Scholarship."
36 Sayer, *Public History*.
37 Joachim, "'Embodiment and Subjectivity.'"
38 Leavy, *Method Meets Art*.
39 Leonard, "Exhibiting Popular Music."
40 Overby, *Public Scholarship in Dance*.

Engage in Public Scholarship! 210

of this text. Rather this section exists to emphasize the manner in which scholars have utilized art, music, dance, performance, and exhibitions as part of their scholarship in order to make their work interesting and accessible to non-academic audiences. For example, A.D. Carson produced a thirty-four-song hip-hop album entitled *Owning My Masters: The Rhetorics of Rhymes Revolutions* for his doctoral dissertation.[41]

Working in other media, transmedia artist and Stony Brook University professor Stephanie Dinkins creates platforms, art, and robots in order to engage people in dialogue about artificial intelligence (AI) as it intersects with race, gender, aging, and our future histories.[42] Dinkins's *Project Al-Khwarizmi* uses art and aesthetics to help citizens understand how algorithms and AI systems intersect with their lives. Her AI sculpture, *Not The Only One (N'TOO)*, is "about broad engagement and attracting people to the AI space who might not be there otherwise."[43] Audiences can speak to the sculpture, listen to *N'TOO*'s answers, and reflect on their own role in what *N'TOO* calls "the technological future."[44] Dinkins uses art to invite audiences who may be uninterested in attending a lecture

---

41 Ashley Young and Michel Martin, "After Rapping His Dissertation, A.D. Carson Is UVa's New Hip-Hop Professor," *All Things Considered,* NPR, July 15, 2017.

42 Stephanie Dinkins, "Biography," *Stephanie Dinkins,* 2020, https://www.stephaniedinkins.com/about.html.

43 Stephanie Dinkins, "Project AI Khwarizmi," *Stephanie Dinkins,* 2020, https://www.stephaniedinkins.com/ project-al-khwarizmi.html.

44 Stephanie Dinkins, "Talking to Not the Only One," July 17, 2020, Vimeo Video, 1:58, https://vimeo.com/439410255.

Self-produced Physical Forms of Public Scholarship 211

or reading a book or article into conversations about race and technology. Art, music, performance, and exhibits can be practices of public scholarship if the public is a central part of the intended audience.

7 From Online to Offline

While this book has addressed many ways in which offline content can be uploaded or reconfigured for online formats, there has been less focus on how digital materials can be moved offline. Communications scholar Cait McKinney has documented the history of how AIDS activist Kiyoshi Kuromiya ran a website, bulletin-board system, and a twenty-four-hour telephone hotline, as well as offered nonprofit internet service provision and web hosting for AIDS service and activist organizations.[45] He also printed out online information in newsletters, in what McKinney calls a "digital-to-print practice."[46] This strategy improved what Elisabeth Jay Friedman calls "chains of access,"[47] for people who did not have access to the internet.

At present, there are several strategies for making online content accessible for offline audiences. Like Kuromiya's

---

45 Cait McKinney, "Crisis Infrastructures: AIDS Activism Meets Online Content Regulation," 2019, http://caitmckinney.com/wp-content/uploads/2020/06/McKinney-Crisis-Infrastructures-postcopyedit.pdf.
46 McKinney, "Printing the Network."
47 Friedman, *Interpreting the Internet.*

Engage in Public Scholarship!

activism, printing the internet remains a strategy. Sharing files in PDF format preserves the formatting when printed. While most of social media's ephemeral nature is incongruous with printing, there are a few options. Print My Tweet is an online service by Eric Kigathi that makes it easier to print tweets. The process is straightforward: users copy the Tweet URL, paste it on the Print My Tweet website, and click the "print it" button.[48] This is a pretty simple model of moving work from online to offline, however, more complicated models exist. Are.na is a social media tool with the mission to build a member-supported community for shared knowledge and lifelong learning, without advertising.[49] Mindy Seu, Charles Broskoski, and Ekene Ijeoma created Print.Are.na in order to print out Are.na channels.[50] When printing, you can choose whether or not to include a table of contents, display authors, display the source, display the description, and whether or not you want to use reverse chronological order. This website uses Bindery.js, an open-source library for creating books using HTML and CSS, created by Evan Brooks. Brooks's Bindery.js helps us think about books as an extension of the responsive web.[51] Bindery.js is intended to provide an approachable jumping-off point for HTML-to-print exploration, which can be considered a first step in improving chains of access.

48 Eric Kigathi, "About," *Print My Tweet,* 2020, https://printmytweet.com.
49 Are.na. "About," 2020, https://www.are.na/about.
50 The first version Print.Are.na was created by Callil Capuozzo for the 2017 Cybernetics Conference. (Charles Broskoski, Mindy Seu, and Ekene Ijeoma, *Print Are.na,* 2020, https://print.are. na/.
51 Evan Brooks, "About," *Bindery,* 2020, https://github.com/evnbr/bindery.

Self-produced Physical Forms of Public Scholarship 213

Scholars do not have to choose between online and offline forms of research communication.

8 Online and Offline at the Same Time

It is possible to make online and offline work simultaneously. If the goal of your scholarship is to reach a particular community, you might produce multiple forms of the same work in order to make it accessible for more people in the community. For example, the Detroit Community Tech project has worked with communities in Detroit that have limited internet access and low bandwidth.[52] As part of their work on data justice, the organization created six zines: three volumes of the *Opening Data* zine, two volumes of the *(Re)building Technology* zine, and the *How to DiscoTech* zine.[53] The organization has also released the *Equitable Open Data Report* with policy recommendations,[54] and the *Digital Defense Playbook* (a downloadable workbook of popular-education activities focused on data, surveillance, and community safety), all to co-create and share knowledge, analyses, and tools

---

52 Detroit Community Tech, "Equitable Internet Initiative," 2020, https://detroitcommunitytech.org/eii.

53 Detroit Community Tech "Data Justice," 2020, https://detroitcommunitytech.org/?q=datajustice.

54 Detroit Digital Justice Coalition and Detroit Community Technology Project, *Equitable Open Data Report*, 2017, https://datajustice.github.io/report/index.html.

Engage in Public Scholarship! 214

for data justice and data access for equity.[55] Additionally, Detroit Community Tech has worked with teenaged community members to create graphic novels. This organization has successfully created physical and digital materials that are available both online and offline.

By working in multiple media, Detroit Community Tech has translated their subject matter for subcommunities, age groups, and different demographics within Detroit. Having multiple methods of communication has made the ideas accessible for more people in Detroit. Furthermore, the organization has hosted workshops with community members to discuss the materials and to explore how to use and improve them. Their chosen mediums for communication were decided only after working with the intended audience to understand their needs. Similarly, in 2018, data artist Mimi Onuoha worked alongside Detroit-based artist, DJ, and educator Mother Cyborg (Diana Nucera) to create A People's Guide to AI. The guide contains information about AI, written in plain language and accompanied by illustrations of cats.[56] This project, and Detroit Community Tech, are sponsored by Allied Media Projects, which is a network of people and projects making media for liberation.[57] These projects serve to make information about technology available to communities

---

55   Lewis et al., *Digital Defense Playbook*.
56   Onuoha and Nucera, "A People's Guide to AI," *Allied Media,* August 2018, https://alliedmedia.org/speaker-projects/a-peoples-press.
57   Allied Media Projects, "Sponsored Projects Program," 2020, https://alliedmedia.org/projects.

Self-produced Physical Forms of Public Scholarship

in a physical form. Versions of the guides also exist online as PDFs.

Digital and physical forms can co-exist and benefit different community members—and can have different utilities even for the same person. Digital documents can be easily word searchable, whereas the tactile experience of flipping through a pamphlet can create another form of engagement. People who experience eye fatigue or migraines from prolonged screen use benefit from being able to interact with physical materials. By putting materials online, the information can circulate beyond the initially intended community. By making it possible to discover their links, this information written for the Detroit community can inform people around the world. The case studies of these two Detroit-based projects further demonstrate that the ability to make information accessible is not limited to the distribution of a PDF or pamphlet. The organizations wrote the materials in a manner that was accessible to the communities they aimed to reach. They defined terms within the text. They created interactive activities. Furthermore, they did not just produce one version of the information. The organization worked with youths, adults, and elders in order to get their perspectives and create materials that catered to them. Knowing the community you want to reach might actually require reaching multiple communities. Employing physical and digital forms of public scholarship can expand access.

9   Conclusion

Reflecting on an image of the massive metallic tubes that cool Google's servers, anthropologist Gabriella Coleman writes, "We don't think of the digital 'revolution' as industrial but it's as extractive and requires the same massive resource inputs: mining, energy and water."[58] The binary between physical and digital public scholarship is a somewhat false division. Public scholarship work can exist online, offline, and in both forms simultaneously. Furthermore, the tools and infrastructure needed to do this work blur the boundaries between the digital and the physical. Utilize the tools that best enable you to communicate with your audiences. This may include mixing and matching podcasts with zines, social media with books, or other combinations. It may be necessary to create workshops to train users and audiences on how to use products. Through experimentation you will be able to see what techniques are most appealing to your audiences. The next chapter explores the ways that the digital is always tied to the physical. It will address the questions of sustainability and maintenance of this work.

---

58   Biella Coleman, "Infrastructure," Twitter post, August 16, 2020, 8:38 PM, https://twitter.com/BiellaColeman/status/129515796 9454280706.

CHAPTER 10

Sustainability and Maintenance

For public scholarship to be feminist and accessible, it also must be sustainable. Here, the word "sustainable" functions in three ways. The first form of sustainability refers to the ability of scholars to sustain the effort of doing their publicly engaged scholarship. Earlier chapters addressed the challenges surrounding the valuation of public scholarship both as labour and as a valid form of research communication. Instead of viewing publicly engaged work as another task a scholar must pile upon an ever-expanding workload, valuing public scholarship as central to scholars' work can make public scholarship more sustainable as a whole—and for the scholar's work/life balance. To view public scholarship as "something extra on the side," makes it harder for scholars to sustain these efforts long-term, and more difficult to prioritize these endeavours. For non-tenure-track scholars and graduate students—an ever-growing class of people within academia—the question of sustainable labour loads is even more fraught.

As previous chapters have looked at these labour issues in more detail, this chapter will focus primarily on the two other forms of sustainability used here: maintenance and environmental impact. Maintenance, and the ability to upkeep one's public scholarship projects, goes beyond continually updating projects, because it applies to sunsetting (the process of decommissioning, shutting down, or phasing out projects), archiving, and preserving projects. This chapter will explore both the tools that can assist scholars in this process, such as working with academic institutions or web archives, and the limitations of these tools. The third application of sustainability considers the environmental impact of the tools that scholars use for their public scholarship. In order to do this, the material consequences of the digital realm are examined.

1   Maintenance

Some modes of public scholarship are meant to be ephemeral, such as a public reading or a presentation at a bookstore or library. However, other public-scholarship endeavours, especially those existing in digital forms, can be protracted and require maintenance, which, in turn, threatens their sustainability. Susan Brown, the director of a digital feminist literary history project, and her co-authors ask, "When can a digital scholarly project be considered finally 'done?' Perhaps

Sustainability and Maintenance 219

never."[1] Founders of The Maintainers network Lee Vinsel and Andrew L. Russell argue that most work is not in fact innovation but maintenance.[2] For example, having the idea to create a website in order to communicate research findings with the public is merely the first step. Upkeep requires labour and financial inputs. Vinsel and Russell's framework, when applied to public scholarship, explains how the cultural fixation with innovation results in the front loading of funding and resources for public scholarship, while neglecting the need for continual maintenance and preservation.

This section will address the challenge of maintenance, which plagues the sustainability of public scholarship, especially in digital forms. Rapidly changing file formats, lapsing ownership of domain names, and new technologies threaten preservation. The struggle to keep resources up to date and accessible has led historians and archivists to fear that the modern era will become the "digital dark ages" for future generations. Keeping websites working and up to date is a specific struggle that requires constant maintenance, necessitating labour and financial resources. When projects have come to term, it is necessary to properly sunset them. Archiving and preserving projects is another component of maintenance. This section of the chapter will discuss a case study in order to elucidate these challenges, followed by a longer discussion of the digital dark ages. The other challenge is to make these efforts "sustainable and scalable."[3] As this book seeks to

---

1 Brown et al., "Published Yet Never Done."
2 Vinsel and Russell, *The Innovation Delusion.*
3 Vinopal and McCormick, "Supporting Digital Scholarship in Research Libraries," p. 4.

Engage in Public Scholarship! 220

offer solutions, the explanation of these challenges will be followed by a discussion of strategies for sunsetting, tempered by a discussion of the difficulties of the right to repair.

1.1 Case Study: The Food Timeline

The case of the food history timeline, foodtimeline.org, demonstrates some of the challenges of maintaining public scholarship, particularly regarding digital resources. In 1999, Lynne Olver (1958—2015) founded the Food Timeline, which she maintained until her death. Olver was a librarian with a passion for food history. Through the timeline she collected resources with the goal to "make food history fun" and accessible to the public for free. Her sister stated in an interview, "I think she started on the internet as a way to reach a lot of people [because there are] a lot of people who wouldn't go into the library."[4] The Food Timeline is divided into two columns: "beginnings" and "recipes." The beginnings column explains when foods were first introduced, and the recipes column provides historical recipes for some of these foods. Each entry in the timeline links to either an external site or to another part of the Food Timeline for additional information or recipes. Some of the external links are scholarly, and others lead to popular media or news articles. As of 2020, the website continues to share valuable information.

The Food Timeline's scope grew from a single page in March 1999, with a sprinkling of links, to seventy web pages offering

---

4   Dayna Evans, "Who Will Save the Food Timeline?" *Eater,* July 8, 2020.

Sustainability and Maintenance   221

a wealth of historic information, primary documents, and original research. By March of 2014, the site served 35 million readers. The original Food Timeline site, circa 1999, is available through the Internet Archive's Wayback Machine. The site shared resources about the art of culinary research and research methodologies, with a page featuring popular requests and teacher resources. In 2004, the Food Timeline was named one of *Saveur* magazine's top 100 best food finds that year. It was recognized by the American Library Association as a Great Website for Kids and was reviewed in ALA's academic publication, *Choice*, in July 2009. Notably, Olver offered a question and answer service where people could post culinary reference questions. She promised a turnaround time of forty-eight hours. As of March 2014, Olver had answered twenty-five thousand questions.

According to her friend and fellow reference librarian Sara Weissman, Olver's comprehensive project began when she wrote a history of Thanksgiving dinner for children on the Morris County Library's Children's Department website.[5] The project continued to grow until it became too large for the county library's hosting resources. Weissman bought Olver an account and the domain name through their local internet service provider. Just before her death, Olver renewed foodtimeline.org for a decade.

Lynne Olver did her own coding in HTML 2.0. Olver noted on her site that "information is checked against standard reference tools for accuracy. All sources are cited for

---

5   Sara Weissman, email interview by Alex Ketchum, 2018.

Engage in Public Scholarship! 222

research purposes. As with most historical topics, there are some conflicting stories in the field of food history. We do our best to select and present the information with the most documented support."[6] Olver used two computers and most of her day to make sure that the links on her website worked. Since her passing, Weissman has noted that Olver's friends have, understandably, not continued to update the links and now the website is riddled with broken links.[7] Olver hoped that eventually her physical library of more than 2,000 books and the website would move to the Culinary Institute of America as a teaching tool, but it did not. From 2015 to 2020, no institution had undertaken the project or collection.[8]

After her death, Weissman and Olver's family settled upon which social media accounts to delete and which to maintain. By 2020, only the Food Timeline's Twitter account (@foodtimeline) and the website, with an attached mailbox, remained. There had not been any new tweets since 2018. Weissman stripped out all links to Olver's question and answer service from the site. As of August 2018, however, Weissman had continued to check the mailbox periodically for messages. The Food Timeline was still getting around 2 million hits per year, yet the domain name was set to expire in 2025. Fortunately, after continual efforts made by Olver's family and friends, the Food Timeline found a new home. In June 2021, Virginia Tech Special Collections and University

---

6   Lynne Olver, "Food Timeline," 1999, http://www.foodtimeline.org.
7   Sara Weissman, email interview by Alex Ketchum, 2018.
8   Evans, "Who Will Save the Food Timeline?"

Sustainability and Maintenance 223

Archives announced that, under the care of food historian Anna Zeide, they will preserve the timeline.[9]

The Food Timeline's history speaks to the difficulty of maintaining digital resources, especially those independent from large institutional resources.[10] While the internet has been touted as an arena for the democratization of knowledges and a tool for making knowledge more accessible, the ephemeral quality of digital resources challenges this narrative of accessibility and sustainability. How do scholars preserve digital public scholarship projects? Is this work fated to disappear? The Food Timeline's reliance on contemporary technology also speaks to the fear of the digital dark ages.

1.2 Digital Obsolescence and the Digital Dark Ages

Digital obsolescence is a phenomenon in which a digital resource is no longer readable because it was made in a format that has since become outdated. The software needed to access digital files can become obsolete and contemporary devices may no longer be configured to read data in older formats. In addition, the hardware needed to access a digital file can become obsolete and thus no longer available.[11] For

---

9   Tonia Moxley, "Food Timeline Serves Up Delicious Opportunities at Virginia Tech," *The Roanoke Times*, June 6, 2021.

10 Alex Ketchum, "Digital Dark Ages, Documenting Food Histories, and Honoring Lynne Olver," *Historical Cooking Project,* 2018, http://www. historicalcookingproject.com/2018/08/digital-dark-ages-documenting-food.html.

11 Ernie Smith, "The Internet of Trash," *Tedium,* February 18, 2018.

example, floppy disks are no longer commercially available and modern computers are no longer built with floppy disk drives. Information stored on floppy disks has thus become more difficult to access, as described on the page for Cornell University's Digital Preservation Management Project's tutorial, "Chamber of Horrors: Obsolete and Endangered Media": "Although the media may be able to physically survive for hundreds of years, the technology to read and interpret it may exist for only a brief time." Even this helpful tutorial from Cornell describes itself as "implementing short-term strategies for long-term problems."[12] The challenge of digital obsolescence is magnified by the fact that repairing hardware oneself can actually be illegal.[13] This has led to a movement of scholars, organizers, and activists to argue for the "right to repair." Digital obsolescence may lead to what some historians and archivists call the digital dark ages.

The digital dark ages refers to the idea that future generations will be unable to access historical information produced during the digital age as a direct result of outdated file formats, software, or hardware that becomes corrupt, scarce, or inaccessible as technologies evolve and data decays. In 2013, the Internet Archive stated that it was founded in part to combat the digital dark ages, noting, "without cultural artefacts, civilization has no memory and no mechanism to learn from its successes and failures. And paradoxically, with the explosion of the Internet, we live in what Danny Hillis has

---

12   Nancy Y. McGovern et al., "Chamber of Horrors: Digital," Digital Preservation Management, 2003, https://dpworkshop.org/dpm-eng/oldmedia/chamber.html.

13   Sinnreich, Forelle, and Aufderheide, "Copyright Givers and Takers."

Sustainability and Maintenance 225

referred to as our 'digital dark age.'" The Internet Archive is, in its own words, "working to prevent the Internet—a new medium with major historical significance—and other 'born-digital' materials from disappearing into the past."[14] Despite the Internet Archive's Wayback Machine preserving 341 billion web pages over the past twenty-five years, it is only useful if users know what they are searching for, such as the name of a website and an approximate date. Also, it seems precarious to depend exclusively on this single resource. It is not the only existing effort to preserve digital records, yet it is one of the most comprehensive. Smaller scale efforts are made to preserve specific endeavours, such as the British Library's web-archiving program, which preserves online records of 7.2 million UK domain websites. The head of the British Library's web archiving program, Stephen Bury, explained how the program preserved important records that only existed online, giving the example of British politician Robin Cook's site and noting that "if we hadn't done that, nobody would have access to the information, the photographs, the interviews on that site."[15] While the British Library has financial resources for this kind of work, many public-scholarship projects are maintained by individuals without any dedicated institutional funding. Maintaining digital resources, especially projects independent of large institutional resources, is difficult.[16] A discussion on the preservation of the entire internet is outside of the scope

---

14   The Internet Archive, "About," *The Internet Archive,* 2013, https://archive.org/about/.

15   Naomi Fowler and Jennifer Abramsohn, "For Historians and Archivists, Modern Era is a Digital 'Dark Age,'" *DW,* June 6, 2009.

16   Ketchum, "Lost Spaces, Lost Technologies, and Lost People."

of this chapter. Instead, this chapter will focus on what you can do in order to make your public scholarship sustainable.

2 Strategies for Maintenance

The sustainability of public scholarship is bolstered by planning. While your public-scholarship projects may grow and develop in ways that you did not previously imagine, it is useful to begin the endeavour by thinking about the intended size of the project or effort. What is its duration? What is the intended termination timeline? And what is the manner in which you want to or need to preserve it? The following section explores a variety of strategies for maintaining, sunsetting, and preserving public scholarship. In some cases, it can be useful to partner early on with an institution. One of the best ways to ensure the longevity of a project is to consult with university libraries or potential institutional partners during the planning or grant-writing processes, as they can offer infrastructure and feedback from the start.[17] However, many public-scholarship activities happen outside of institutional structures. Therefore, this section also provides ideas for individuals on how to preserve or maintain their work. The section will also touch on a philosophical question about the degree to which it is important or necessary to preserve or maintain all public scholarship, as everything is ultimately ephemeral. Finally, this section draws on the work of digital

---

17   Goddard and Seeman, "Building Digital Humanities Projects That Last."

Sustainability and Maintenance 227

humanities scholars, archivists, and librarians. Digital-humanities projects often lack end-to-end project support, and thus the field has already been reckoning with these questions.[18] Additionally, the challenge for preservation and maintenance is familiar to archivists and librarians.

Strategies for preservation, such as archiving in an institution, are more established for public scholarship in the form of print media such as zines, pamphlets, or posters. You may also choose to preserve a version as a digital file. Digital public scholarship endeavours, such as websites and podcasts, pose different challenges that require different strategies. The sections below explore physical and digital public scholarship preservation strategies.

2.1 Institutional Strategies

Preservation and maintenance may require funding and resources beyond an individual's capacity. One strategy, then, is institutional partnership. Institutions such as libraries and archives may be able to provide infrastructure, such as additional staff, work and storage spaces, and funding. There are several challenges to this approach, however. The first is finding an institution that is interested in this work of preservation. The second is determining whether the scholars feel comfortable institutionalizing their work, especially depending on the communities they serve. As Kirk Anne et al. show, different institutions offer varying degrees

---

18 Poole, "The conceptual ecology of digital humanities."

Engage in Public Scholarship! 228

of support for preserving digital work, because it is expensive, time consuming, and resource intensive (like support for other high-tech science and social-science research).[19] Grant applications may encourage scholars to think about sunsetting, preservation, and sustainability, especially encouraging scholars to partner with institutions, but there are limitations. For example, Susan Brown points out that funding bodies have policies requiring the public archiving of data, scholarship, and outreach, however "many researchers are unaware of this requirement and ... [Canada] lacks the standards and indeed the facilities to permanently archive digital material."[20] Moreover, even when scholars choose to work with institutions, there are issues.

Lisa Goddard and Dean Seeman write that in preserving work, especially in digital form, there is a basic tension between maintaining the materials in a standard way or allowing for a freedom of choice in the format.[21] This leads to what Goddard and Seeman call the "sustainability spectrum." The two options they present are preserving the content but losing the look and feel of the original formatting, or trying to preserve the content as well as the look and feel exactly as they were first implemented. Digital obsolescence plagues both options. For example, the Rhizome organization preserves art that was made for audiences using Netscape Navigator

---

19 Anne et al., "Building Capacity for Digital Humanities."
20 Brown et al., "Published Yet Never Done."
21 Goddard and Seeman, "Building Digital Humanities Projects that Last."

Sustainability and Maintenance 229

on Windows 98.[22] The collective uses emulators that recreate the appearance of digitally obsolete programs on modern applications. Rhizome has also curated a physical and web exhibit, and has published a printed book of the exhibition, *The Art Happens Here: Net Art Anthology.* All of these strategies are compromises, however. The task of preservation must take into account the quality of digital objects, and there can be issues with standards for resolution, colour management, and file formats. These questions are tied to the challenge of platform choice, issues of not having standard data models, and issues around the use of metadata.[23] Institutions partnering with individuals must verify any potential copyright and material usage, as well as manage the rights.

Another technical problem is software fees. Building a project that relies on an expensive software subscription may threaten the longevity and sustainability of a digital public-scholarship project, which is why some librarians and archivists argue for prioritizing open software.[24] This challenge is made significantly more difficult as much digital work has shifted away from an individual managing her own files to a reliance on bespoke, proprietary interfaces.[25] Partnering institutions may suggest infrastructure required for longer-term preservation and access, such as Archive-It, a subscription service of the Internet Archive that lets you

---

22 Eric Johnson, "How do you preserve art when it was made for people using Netscape Navigator on Windows 98?" *Tech News Tube,* February 25, 2019.
23 Goddard and Seeman, "Building digital humanities projects that last."
24 Smithies et al., "Managing 100 Digital Humanities Projects."
25 Simon Pitt, "Computer Files Are Going Extinct," *One Zero,* October 2, 2019.

Engage in Public Scholarship!

point to specific web pages and crawl them regularly.[26] (A web crawler is an internet bot that systematically browses the internet, typically for the purpose of web indexing. This process is called "crawling.")

If you are a scholar affiliated with a particular university, your public scholarship might be able to be classified as research data, particularly if you have structured data of some kind (i.e., things in spreadsheets). Your institution may have signed up with the Scholars Portal Dataverse service, which can house this kind of work. These are technical problems with which archivists and librarians continue to wrestle. Consulting archivists and librarians for resources, strategies, and tips specific to your digital public scholarship is advisable. The second challenge of working with institutions is more social, however, and involves the intended audience and communities that your public scholarship focuses on.

Scholars endeavouring to create public-scholarship projects about, by, or for marginalized communities may be wary of partnering with institutions, whether the projects are digital or not. For example, as scholars Marika Cifor and Stacy Wood demonstrate, archives and public-history projects centred on marginalized, particularly LGBTQ+, communities have often decided to remain independent and not join with an institution.[27] Historian Elise Chenier likewise explains that "one of the major concerns expressed about the current shift of LGBTQ materials from community-based archives

---

26   Internet Archive, "About Archive-It," 2020, https://archive-it.org.
27   Cifor et al., "'What We Do Crosses Over to Activism.'"

Sustainability and Maintenance 231

to institutional libraries, archives, and special collections is that collections will no longer be shaped by LGBTQ praxis."[28] Cifor and Wood report that organizations such as the Lesbian Herstory Archives (LHA) are "decidedly suspect of the long-term investment in and commitment to these initiatives [and as a result] many organizations chose to keep collecting efforts autonomous and community driven, ensuring that collections, policies, and materials were not subject to changing priorities within universities."[29] This sentiment is echoed in works by scholars Cait McKinney and Danielle Cooper.[30] However, as evidenced above, institutions provide more funding stability and are not subject to the same risks of changing circumstances as an individual.

Perhaps some compromise can be made. Ann Cvetkovich has proposed "Queer Archive Activism," which calls for something beyond the financial and infrastructural support of the institution by also requiring space for active engagement with materials, and space for housing materials that push against traditional archival notions of evidentiary value.[31] This debate between institution and community-driven projects continues.[32] For example, online public-history projects serve as a kind of counter-narrative to the erasure or marginalization of LGBTQ+ histories. However, with their creation comes new challenges. These digital history projects are different than community archives because they

28 Chenier, "Reclaiming the Lesbian Archives," p. 170.
29 Cifor and Wood, "Critical Feminism in the Archives," p. 7.
30 McKinney, "Body, Sex, Interface"; Cooper, "Welcome Home."
31 Cvetkovich, "The Queer Art of the Counterarchive."
32 Eichhorn, *The Archival Turn in Feminism*; Juhasz, "Video Remains."

depend on an individual, who will not have the same financial and technological resources to sustain or retain the project as a group institutionalized within an archive. To be incorporated within an institution would help maintain these projects, which serve as valuable resources for understanding LGBTQ+ histories. Moving away from a burden on the individual and towards institutionalization will give these projects a greater chance of survival. Ideally, community members will be included and benefit from the kinds of engagement that Cvetkovich proposes. Institutionalization and preservation of these projects can enable future scholarship that builds on prior work. However, if institutionalization is not possible or preferable, there are individual strategies.

2.2 Individualized Solutions

There are various scales of individual solutions to ensure maintenance and sustainability. Individuals can utilize some digitization solutions similar to the ones employed by larger institutions, depending on levels of funding. Ying Zhang, Shy Lie, and Emilee Mathews argue that in order to prevent sunsetting, digital projects can try different sources of support, like changing from a non-profit to a for-profit model (e.g., subscription fees).[33] This may only offer a temporary solution because, as Alex H. Poole argues, crowdsourcing also raises issues of sustainability—digitization will always raise issues of sustainability and accessibility, whether linked with

---

33   Zhang, Liu, and Mathews, "Convergence of Digital Humanities and Digital Libraries."

Sustainability and Maintenance 233

institutions or not.[34] However, most individuals engaged in public scholarship will likely employ smaller scale efforts of maintenance and preservation.

Smaller scale and more manageable solutions are readily available. Public scholarship in physical formats, such as books, pamphlets, zines, posters, flyers, t-shirts, and art projects, can be archived in large institutional archives or community archives in addition to being housed in your personal collection. It may be useful to create different versions of the work, which can also help the project exist beyond its culmination. Scanning zines, photographing or filming exhibits, recording audio, and embedding audio and video files on personal or institutional websites each provides another form of the work, and increase the likelihood of preservation and access.

The *Preserve This Podcast* zine provides useful resources for preserving podcasts. It explains the process for archiving podcast audio within the Internet Archive, on your personal computer, and in your personal file storage. The writers note, "Reality check: preservation is not easy. It takes resources (namely: your time, money, brain power). However, it can be manageable, and not only that, has many long-term benefits. Below are some suggested actions you might take in the next month, year, or over the long-term."[35] The options they

34   Poole, "The Conceptual Ecology of Digital Humanities."
35   Molly Schwartz, Sarah Nguyen, Margie Dana Gerber, and Mary Kidd, *Preserve This Podcast*, online zine, 2018, https://preservethispodcast. org/assets/ PreserveThisPodcastZineOnline.pdf.

Engage in Public Scholarship! 234

suggest will all take varying amounts of time and resources.[36] Speaking about this dilemma in personal correspondence, Grant Hurley, digital preservation librarian for Scholars Portal, the information technology service for the Ontario Council of University Libraries, writes,

> I wish there was an easy solution outside of partnering with established institutions who have access to the infrastructure required for longer-term preservation and access. But preservation is work and at the very least these institutions have (relatively more) resources to do this work, if not always the right priorities when it comes to working with marginalized communities. I'd say that the first thing to do is take advantage of the Internet Archive Wayback Machine's "Save Page Now" feature.[37]

Here you can submit the URLs of the sites you profiled and indicate they should be crawled.[38] Individualized web archiving of digital resources can be less time—and resource intensive, though there is the risk of relying on a single source.

---

36 Scott David Witmer, "Personal Digital Archiving Guide, 2019 Edition," *Bits and Pieces, Digital Preservation and Research Data,* December 19, 2019, https://apps.lib.umich.edu/blogs/bits-and-pieces/personal-digital-archiving-guide-2019-edition.

37 Grant Hurley, email correspondence with Alex Ketchum, 2019.

38 Internet Archive Wayback Machine, "Save Pages in the Wayback Machine," *Internet Archive,* 2020, https://help.archive.org/hc/en-us/categories/360000553851-The-Wayback-Machine.

Sustainability and Maintenance

2.3 Everything Is Ultimately Ephemeral

During an exploration of a book published on the early internet, journalist Ernie Smith checked the links and none of them worked.[39] A perusal of checking the links within the Internet Wayback Machine would have yielded more results. Unfortunately, these websites would likely have led to other broken links, incomplete media, and digitally obsolete programs. Preservation, maintenance, and archiving are definitely important practices for future generations. However, it is important to remember that ultimately everything is ephemeral. As an individual, part of the work of doing public scholarship is deciding what actually needs to be preserved and then directing your resources in a more targeted manner.

3 Environmental Impact

Public scholarship relies on a wide variety of forms of research communication: books, zines, podcasts, websites, social media accounts, and more. Each of these forms, whether physical or digital, has a tangible impact on the environment. Furthermore, the tools used to create this work have further environmental repercussions. Although in 1984 author William Gibson famously said of his new buzzword, "cyberspace," "There is no 'there,'

---

39   Ernie Smith, "I Bought a Book about the Internet from 1994 and None of the Links Worked," *Vice*, August 14, 2017.

Engage in Public Scholarship!

there,"[40] there *is*, in fact, a "there," there.[41] Both a scholar's research and the techniques for research communication rely on physical technological infrastructure: the desktop computer, laptop, tablet, or phone used to type; internet modems, wifi routers, underwater cables, and the cellular towers used to transmit tweets and upload web pages. These are all as tangible as the paper, ink, printer, and pen used to publish physical manifestations.[42] As Adi Kuntsman and Imogen Rattle add, the materiality of digital communication inflicts substantial environmental damage through the extraction of resources needed to produce digital devices, from the toxicity of e-waste to the rapidly increasing energy demands required to sustain data generated by digital communication.[43] Rather than thinking of a binary between the digital world and the IRL (in real life) world, digital geographer Jess McLean employs the phrase "more than real," in order to conceptualize the materiality of cyber, or virtual, life. McLean suggests that if we think of the digital as intangible or immaterial, we "sideline the environmental impacts that our digital lives have ... or the power of digital social interactions can be underestimated and the generative and destructive potential of these can be dismissed."[44] The physical and digital infrastructure in which we operate creates what geographer Dustin Edwards calls "digital damage."

40   Gibson, *Neuromancer.*
41   See Pilar Praba, Carrie Hott, and Maya Weeks, "Rare Earth: The Ground Is Not Digital," *Living Room Light Exchange* 5 (2020).
42   Crawford, *Atlas of AI.*
43   Kuntsman and Rattle, "Towards a Paradigmatic Shift in Sustainability Studies."
44   McLean, "Delivering Green Digital Geographies?"

Sustainability and Maintenance

Edwards uses the phrase digital damage "to designate how the material infrastructures of the internet and connected platforms and devices are tangled up with lands, waters, energies, and histories that are often unseen, un-felt, or unacknowledged in our everyday lives."[45] In order for public scholarship to ever be sustainable, feminist, and accessible, scholars must account for digital damage.

The digital damage caused, in part, by public scholarship and research communication contributes to a slow violence that is not equally felt by all. Rob Nixon defines slow violence as the "incremental and accretive" forms of violence that harm peoples and ecosystems around the world. The violence wrought by climate change, toxic drift, deforestation, oil spills, and the environmental aftermath of creating the tools for our digital technologies takes place gradually and often invisibly. Nixon focuses on the inattention we have paid to the gradual lethality of many environmental crises, in contrast with the sensational, spectacle-driven messaging that impels public activism today. He argues that "slow violence, because it is so readily ignored by a hard-charging capitalism, exacerbates the vulnerability of ecosystems and of people who are poor, disempowered, and often involuntarily displaced, while fueling social conflicts that arise from desperation as life-sustaining conditions erode."[46]

Nixon's understanding of slow violence, and employment of Ramachandra Guha's framework of the environmentalism

---

45　Edwards, "Digital Rhetoric on a Damaged Planet."
46　Nixon, *Slow Violence and the Environmentalism of the Poor*, p. 10.

Engage in Public Scholarship! 238

of the poor,[47] shows, as Edwards does, the ways in which digital damage is felt unequally by all human and non-human (or more-than-human) lives. Edwards and media theorist Jussi Parikka consider how digital devices require the mining of precious metals, whose modes of extraction, transportation, and refinement threaten the livability of specific ecosystems.[48] Likewise, the zettabytes of global data flows rely on millions of data centres worldwide, which require vast amounts of energy and water to power and cool their server spaces.[49] As Vincent Mosco argues, the ethereal metaphor of "the cloud" for offsite data management and processing hides the physical realities of mineral extraction from the Earth's crust, and the dispossession of human populations that sustain the Earth's existence.[50] The environmental impact is tied to a social impact, as some of the most purportedly environmentally sustainable and economically viable technology companies have gentrified neighbourhoods, exploited labour conditions, and perpetuated environmental racism in the places in which they are headquartered.[51]

This digital damage goes beyond e-waste, or the materials discarded from hardware devices such as televisions, cell phones, printers, and so on. In 2012, data centres worldwide used around 30 billion watts of electricity, roughly equivalent to the output of thirty nuclear power plants.[52]

---

47 Guha, "Environmentalist of the Poor."
48 Parikka and Richterich, "A Geology of Media and a New Materialism."
49 Hogan, "Data Flows and Water Woes."
50 Sullivan, "Vincent Mosco, To the Cloud: Big Data in a Turbulent World."
51 Pellow and Park, *The Silicon Valley of Dreams.*
52 James Glanz, "Power, Pollution, and the Internet," *New York Times*, September 23, 2012.

Sustainability and Maintenance   239

For context, at the start of the 2010s, if all of the data centres combined to form a country of their own, it would have been the fifth most power-hungry country in the world.[53] This energy consumption continues to intensify. In order to combat digital damage, scholars must be critical of the tools upon which we rely.

To counter the damage, the impact of the technologies we employ must be considered before beginning our work. Kate Crawford and Vladan Joler study the material resources, human labour, and data behind the creation of a technology to illustrate how difficult it is to trace all of the components in a technological device.[54] They describe how the semiconductor-chip manufacturer that supplies Apple with processors for their devices took four years just to understand its own multi-tiered supply chain. This chain consisted of more than 19,000 suppliers in over one hundred countries providing the direct materials for their production processes, the tools and machines for their factories, and their logistics and packaging services.[55] Rather than attempting to track the labour and environmental conditions of all the materials used for production, as well as understand the e-waste and other forms of digital damage created after a technology is made, Suzanne Kite argues that the onus begins before the technologies are even built.[56]

---

53 Cook and Van Horn, "How Dirty is Your Data"; Jones, "How to Stop Data Centres from Gobbling Up the World's Electricity."
54 Crawford and Joler, "Anatomy of an AI System."
55 Intel Corporation, "Intel's Efforts to Achieve a 'Conflict Free' Supply Chain," 2018, https:// www.intel.com/content/www/us/en/corporate-responsibility/conflict-minerals-white-paper.html.
56 Lewis et al., "Making Kin with the Machines."

Engage in Public Scholarship!

Drawing on Lakota epistemology, she argues that before building any technology, you need to think about what will happen at the end of its lifespan. How will it be disposed of? What will happen to it?[57]

Slow violence reminds us to be wary of techno-utopianism or techno-solutionism when thinking about creating feminist and accessible scholarship. Technological utopianism is any ideology based on the premise that advances in science and technology could, and should, bring about a utopia, or at least help to fulfill one utopian ideal or another. Data journalist Meredith Broussard makes the case against technochauvinism—the belief that technology is always the solution.[58] Broussard argues that "using technology is not inherently liberating—in fact, often the opposite is true."[59] Technology can be useful, but we must remember that there is no divide between the cyber and material world because the servers, the routers, the computers, satellites, and phones that enable our virtual communication and public scholarship are material objects made of metals, which are mined.[60] Chemicals from mining leak into the watershed. These toxins affect the bodies of current and future generations. They also impact other organisms in the environment. As Astra Taylor

---

57 Kite, "How to Build Anything Ethically."
58 Broussard, *Artificial Unintelligence.*
59 Broussard, "Meredith Broussard Discusses Artificial Unintelligence," lecture at Disrupting Disruptions: The Feminist and Accessible Publishing and Technology Speaker and Workshop Series, Montreal, QC, November 4, 2020.
60 Paul Mobbs, "The Invisible, and Growing Ecological Footprint of Digital Technology," *Resilience,* January 7, 2020.

Sustainability and Maintenance

reminds us, sustainability encourages us to think long term—for the environment, for workers, or for non-humans.[61]

Whether doing public scholarship or not, it is likely that you will still use your computer, the internet, and rely on data centres, underwater cables, and mining practices for your various technological needs. While these deleterious environmental and social impacts are not restricted to your public-scholarship work, it is important to keep them in mind. There will always be limits to the degree that our work is feminist and accessible. As long as we live in a world that relies on capitalist exploitation of the earth and its people, our work will always be connected with harm and violence. Feminist and accessible publishing is not an adjective, but rather a goal to strive towards. We must always be aware of the limitations of this work and focus on reducing harm.

4   Conclusion

This chapter approached the question of sustainability through the perspective of labour conditions, maintenance, and environmental impact. Making scholarship sustainable requires time, resources, and several ethical considerations. Understanding the quotidian and overarching problems one can face, and trying to adapt to them, is key. Moving

---

61   Taylor, *The People's Platform.*

forward, it is important to consider the ways in which public-scholarship efforts can be systematically sustained within academia for tenure-track and non-tenure-track scholars alike. Broader support for public scholarship is necessary. Training and resources provided for graduate students and faculty is an important step. Compensation for these efforts and a greater valuation in dossiers for tenure-track faculty will help. The next chapters will focus on media work and event organization. While these forms of public scholarship are ephemeral in nature, and thus are not plagued by the exact same issues around maintenance, the questions of labour and environmental damage remain.

CHAPTER 11
Events

Public scholarship also exists off the page and screen. As evidenced throughout this book, engaging a wide variety of publics requires a wide variety of methods. Readings, lectures, panels, and exhibits enable scholars to communicate their research with new audiences. The format of these events can vary, as can their level of formality. The following chapter will provide a framework for scholars to follow in order to make public events inclusive for academic and non-academic audiences alike. This chapter will also address ways to increase potential reach—before, during, and after the event—through various methods of dissemination. For the purposes of this chapter, accessible scholarship and public events will focus on inclusivity. Whether you are organizing an event to showcase other scholars' work or participating as a presenter, this chapter contains pertinent information for making events more accessible.

1 Event Formats

No event will ever be entirely accessible, since there is never going to be a single setup that works for literally everybody. However, as disability-justice advocate Lydia X.Z. Brown states, it is "less a matter of how can we make sure that literally everyone can participate in this one event and more how can we make sure that we bring this conversation or this opportunity for socialization or whatever it is, the kind of space that we're trying to create, to as many people in as many spaces and communities as possible, even if that means it's at different times and in different places and in different platforms."[1] There will always be people who have to work, need to parent, live far away, or are ill. However, as a person organizing or co-organizing an event, your choices around space, timing, format, technology, language, cost, publicity, and dissemination will increase accessibility for various communities, many of whom are often overlooked. Audience members, presenters, and performers alike may have various disabilities, care responsibilities, and needs, which is why this chapter refers to all these groups collectively as "participants."

This chapter addresses accessible, inclusive "events" in a broad sense and differentiates between events that are open to the public and events that are public-focused. Events that are open to the public are scholarly events

---

1 Patty Berne, Lydia X.Z. Brown, Leah Lakshmi Piepzna-Samarasinha, and Allegra Heath-Stout, "Podcast Episode 61: Organizing in a Pandemic: Disability Justice Wisdom," *Irresistible* (podcast), April 14, 2020, https://irresistible.org/podcast/61.

Events

that are advertised more broadly and which anyone can attend. However, the tone of the event remains targeted at academic audiences. The language used by presenters may include more jargon and follow traditional scholarly conventions and formats. Typically, these events also occur in more traditional academic spaces, such as lecture halls on university campuses. While these events are allegedly open and public, people may not feel comfortable entering these spaces, particularly if they do not have a connection with the university. Events that are public-focused have a different tone. The information shared is often less niche and is directed to multiple audiences at once. It is more likely that public-focused events happen in community centres, bookstores (particularly independent bookstores), and libraries. Occasionally cafes, clubs, or other event venues will host these events.

This chapter also discusses in-person and online (also referred to as virtual and/or cyber) events, presenting the benefits and drawbacks of each type. Based on your decisions around dissemination, your event may also be a hybrid format of virtual and in-person, or continue in perpetuity in a hybrid form. The choice of in-person or virtual events influence which communities and audiences you are able to reach. While a virtual event means that someone across the planet can participate, virtual participation often requires a greater access to technologies and not everyone has computers, phones, access to the internet, or a strong and stable wifi connection. If you hope to congregate folks from a local community, it is likely that you will choose to hold an in-person event. Hybrid formats allow you to

Engage in Public Scholarship! 246

disseminate aspects of the event so that individuals who would not otherwise be able to attend can still be involved. This chapter provides guidance on all three kinds.

The format of events centred on public scholarship can range widely. Options include, but are not limited to: lectures, panels of speakers, book readings, fireside chats, roundtable discussions, workshops, performances, and exhibitions. While this chapter focuses on these examples, the framework offered by the chapter can apply to other formats.

Universities have begun producing guidelines for organizers to consider when hosting campus events. Although it is unknown how often this information is consulted, these guides can serve as useful resources. While created specifically for academic conferences, the "Checklist for Planning Accessible Conferences," written by the Council of Ontario Universities, includes guidelines that speak to much of the discussion in this chapter, and is useful for inclusive events outside of the university context as well.[2] The University of Windsor has created its own downloadable checklist.[3] The University of British Columbia, Okanagan Campus, has produced a guide for event planning[4] and Cornell

---

2   Council of Ontario Universities, "A Checklist for Planning Accessible Conferences," 2016, https://www.accessiblecampus.ca/wp-content/uploads/2016/12/A-Checklist-for-Planning-Accessible-Events-1.pdf.
3   Equity University of Windsor Office of Human Rights and Accessibility, "Accessible and Inclusive Event Planning," 2017, http://www.uwindsor.ca/ohrea/ 155/accessible-and-inclusive-event-planning.
4   University of British Columbia Okanagan Equity and Inclusion Office, "Checklist for Accessible Event Planning," 2020, https://equity.ok.ubc.ca/resource s/checklist-for-accessible-event-planning/.

Events 247

University has its own checklist for accessible meetings and events.[5] In response to a lack of campus resources, disabled University of California students created the "UC Access Now Demandifesto," in order to implement universal design, accessibility, and inclusion for all disabled people in the UC campus community (and visitors to their campuses).[6] These guides inform this chapter and provoke important reflection, even though they are not targeted towards public scholarship and focus primarily on campus events.

1.1   Scheduling

Choices around scheduling impact the accessibility of an event. Knowing the target audience for an event helps organizers pick a time. If the event occurs midday, people might not be able to leave their 9 to 5 office job to attend. If the lecture happens after 5 p.m., parents or people who care for other family members might not be able to attend, especially if childcare is not provided. Facilities might not be free or available on weekends. Religious affiliations may prevent attendance. For example, scheduling an event on a Friday evening may prevent people who are Jewish from attending, or a Sunday morning event may limit attendance by Christians. There will never be a perfect time for the event, but some times will be more optimal depending on the

---

5   Cornell University, "Accessible Meeting and Event Checklist, " 2021, https://accessibility. cornell.edu/event-planning/accessible-meeting-and-event-checklist/.

6   UC Access Now, "UC Access Now Demandifesto," 2020, https://archive.org/details/disabilit y-equity-and-justice-demands/mode/2up.

Engage in Public Scholarship!   248

group you are hoping to target. Be thoughtful about whom you might inadvertently exclude when you consider the target audience and do not default to able-bodied individuals. The point of creating inclusive events is to actually be inclusive and accessible. If you are hosting a series of recurring events, one option is to schedule events of the series at a variety of times. This way, if one event's time is not an option for someone, hopefully another time will work for them. These choices can be constrained by the availability of venues.

1.2   Childcare

Depending on the time of the event, it may be necessary to provide childcare as an option in order to make the event accessible to parents. Grant agencies, such as the Social Science and Humanities Research Council, now allow participants to claim the cost of childcare or babysitting expenses while a nursing mother or single parent is travelling. However, the allowable cost for a single parent is limited to overnight childcare costs incurred while travelling.[7] Grant agencies and departments have widely different policies regarding childcare funding. If the event takes place at a university, there is a chance that the university already has a program that makes childcare available to allow parents to participate in programming on campus. If not, see if your town or city has an organization that subsidizes childcare.

---

7   Social Sciences and Humanities Research Council, "Using Your Funds," September 6, 2013, https://www.sshrc-crsh.gc.ca/funding-financement/usingutiliser/grant regulations-reglement subventions/conferences-colloques-eng.aspx.

Providing childcare often requires asking participants to RSVP in advance. The importance of parents having access to childcare for participation in events and any aspect of public scholarship cannot be overstated.

1.3 Tickets and Cost for Attendees

Ticket cost can prohibit attendance and access. Ideally it will be possible to offer attendance free of charge or on a sliding scale. Organizing events may incur costs, and without funding sources it may be necessary to charge for entrance. Pay-what-you-can, tiered-cost tickets (i.e., different prices for children, students, elders, and the general public), or "no one turned away for lack of funds" models can expand access if a free event is not possible. Economic considerations will impact and be impacted by choices around the venue of the event.

2 In-person Events

Events that happen in-person require a venue. The choice of venue will impact the accessibility of an event. Depending on the region in which you are hosting the event, some of the considerations below may already be legally required or already incorporated into the building code. For example, the Americans with Disabilities Act and the Accessibility for Ontarians with Disabilities Act, require some of the following components.

2.1 Accessibility of Space

Venue choice impacts the audience. If you host an event at a university with which you are affiliated, you likely have free or subsidized access to rooms or spaces. Not everyone is going to feel comfortable attending an event at a university, however. Consider also hosting events in other public or semi-public spaces. Among these spaces, options may include libraries, bookstores, and community centres. Libraries offer more than books; your local library may have a room for gatherings, have maker-spaces, and/or provide other resources. Your local independent bookstore can be a great place to hold readings, panels, and lectures. Many offer their spaces for free or low cost. "Community centre" is a broad term that can refer to a wide range of resources and spaces available. They are typically public or semi-public locations where members of a community tend to gather for group activities, social support, public information, and other purposes. They are sometimes open for use by the whole community or may only be for a specialized group within the greater community. In addition, your city or town might have a cafe, restaurant, pub, bar, or gallery that offers free or low-cost space, or has a sliding scale for events. Depending on the local music or arts venue, there can be a wide range of fees. Businesses that are explicit about their feminist, social justice, educational, or anarchist politics tend to have more affordable options. The cost of renting or using a space can impact whether or not you charge for the event, and this in turn can impact who can attend. Depending on the community you are trying to reach, various venues may encourage or dissuade participation.

Events

The actual room, building, or outdoor venue chosen impacts an event's accessibility. The space you choose will also impact and be impacted by the date and timing of the event, costs and decisions over entrance or ticket fees, and the kinds of programming that you offer. By making accessibility requests of venues, you are not only raising awareness to venue staff about your own event's needs, but also influencing what may be offered to you and other event organizers in the future. Your choices around accessibility can set precedents for future events and encourage venues to make their own spaces more accessible.

2.2   Access to the Venue and Transport

It is important to consider how participants can access the venue when choosing a space for your event. Not everyone has a car, so choosing an event that is accessible by public transit will enable participation from non-drivers and offer a transportation option with lower environmental impacts. Granted, not every town or city has robust public transit. If your event will be in a major metropolitan area, however, it is easier to ensure that there are accessible routes following Google Maps' addition, in 2018, of wheelchair accessible routes to both the desktop and the mobile versions of their app.[8] Curbs on parking lots and a lack of designated parking spots near the entrance for disabled people will limit access for

---

8   Rio Akasaka, "Introducing 'Wheelchair Accessible' Routes in Transit Navigation," *Google Blog*, March 15, 2018, https://www.blog.google/products/maps/introducing-wheelchairaccessible-routes-transit-navigation/.

Engage in Public Scholarship! 252

people with mobility disabilities. Ensure a barrier-free path for people to travel from the parking lot or drop-off area to the venue entrance. If you are hosting the event in a place with snow or ice, check that the paths will be cleared.

The venue's layout can pose further limitations to accessibility. If the room can only be reached by stairs, people with reduced mobility and wheelchair users will not be able to attend. If there are elevators, they must be wide enough for wheelchairs and scooters, at least 32 inches or 82 cm (preferably wider). Door frames of the venue must be equally wide enough for a wheelchair or scooter to pass through. Even a 1-inch or 2.5-cm bump over a threshold can pose an issue for wheelchair users. Threshold ramps can mitigate this problem. If the front entrance or event room's doors are closed, do the doors have lever handles and/or are they equipped with an automatic opener? If not, you need someone at the entrance to welcome people into the room. If the main entrance is not accessible, have clear signage at the front of the building that indicates the location of an accessible entrance. Make sure to circulate this information in advance of the event as well. If the event is being held at an outdoor site, ensure that the surface is accessible for persons using wheelchairs and scooters.

2.3 Design of the Room

Within the venue, the layout of the room can affect accessibility. Provide chairs for people who may need to sit. This can be particularly important for, but not limited to,

Events   253

people with various disabilities, the elderly, and pregnant
individuals. The spacing of the chairs will affect whether or
not wheelchair or scooter users can have a seat at the table
and be able to move about the room. If audience members
are facing a presenter or panel, make sure that there is space
near the front of the stage for people to be able to view a
sign-language interpreter, and that the interpreter is well lit.
Consider where the presenter or presenters will be located
and how their materials will be displayed. Will audience
members have to stare into the sunlight to try and see slides?
Service animals require space, and service dogs need access
to the outdoors. Good lighting, re-arrangeable furniture,
and good acoustics will enable more audience members to be
able to participate in the event.

2.4   Bathrooms/Washrooms and Lactation Rooms

Bathrooms affect access. The ability to access a washroom
is a basic human right. Does the venue have an all-gender
washroom/bathroom? If the venue does not have a single-
use washroom or all-gender washrooms, are you able
to temporarily change the bathroom signs for the event?
A lack of all-gender washrooms can make your event
non-inclusive for trans and gender non-binary individuals.
Is there a wheelchair or scooter accessible washroom/
bathroom? Are the sinks reachable from a wheelchair?
Try to guarantee a scent-free environment, including
in the washrooms. To account for scent sensitivities, which
can cause nausea and headaches, ask participants in

Engage in Public Scholarship! 254

advance to refrain from using strong perfumes and soaps.
Inform participants about the location of all-gender and
wheelchair-accessible bathrooms.

For parents who are breastfeeding or pumping, lactation
rooms are a necessity. As University of Washington graduate
student Carrie Glenney explains, a lack of access to
lactation rooms is a widespread issue.[9] Insufficient access
to lactation rooms limits the ability for breastfeeding
parents to participate in events. While the legal requirements
for lactation rooms vary by location, lactation rooms should
be private spaces that have electrical outlets to plug in an
electric breast pump, have comfortable seating, have a small
refrigerator or cooler for women to store their milk, have a
sink with running water close by, and have cleaning supplies
such as paper towels and wipes to clean the space after use.

3   Location: Land Acknowledgements

Acknowledging the history of unceded territories on which
your event is taking place, as well as the history of the space,
is an important practice. Land or territory acknowledgements
occur at the beginning of public events. They are often concise

9   Carrie Glenney, "Why Lactation Rooms Matter," *Beacon Center Blog*,
October 14, 2014, https://www3.beaconcenter.org/blog/2014/10/14/
why-lactation-rooms-matter/.

Events   255

and follow a similar format: "I want to acknowledge that
we are on the traditional territory of [nation names]," though
they can be more comprehensive. It is important that
you know how to properly pronounce the name of the nation
or community. It is even better if you can learn the name
of the nation or community in its original language. Ideally a
member of the community on whose land your event takes
place will give the opening address. You need to financially
compensate this person and provide an honorarium gift.

The violence of the colonization of North America is not
relegated to the past. The ongoing impacts of colonization
shape our present society. Land acknowledgements raise
awareness about Indigenous presence and land rights. They
encourage settlers to recognize the history and political
reality of the United States and Canada, which is often omitted
from school curricula. Native Land Digital has created
invaluable resources to help people understand the histories
of the lands that we live and work on, including: a map that
indicates Indigenous territories, languages, and treaties; a
teacher's guide; and a list of further resources.[10]

There is some critique that land acknowledgements are
token gestures, especially when the people doing them
and the audience hearing them do not think about steps
beyond acknowledging the territory where the event
is taking place. This critique questions how there can be
reconciliation if there is not yet justice. In response, Chelsea

---

10   Native Land Digital, "Territory Acknowledgement," 2020, https://native-
     land.ca.

Vowel (âpihtawikosisân), a Métis writer and scholar from the Plains Cree-speaking community of Lac Ste. Anne, Alberta, writes: "If we think of territorial acknowledgments as sites of potential disruption, they can be transformative acts that to some extent undo Indigenous erasure. I believe this is true as long as these acknowledgments discomfit both those speaking and hearing the words. The fact of Indigenous presence should force non-Indigenous peoples to confront their own place on these lands."[11] Land acknowledgements are merely a starting place. They do not replace the necessary work of reconciliation. The Truth and Reconciliation Commission of Canada's calls to action provide a framework for this work.[12]

3.1 Acknowledging Other Forms of Violence Relating to the Space of the Event

The United States and Canada built their nations through the practice of enslaving African and Indigenous peoples. The violent legacy of slavery continues across society, ranging from racialized economic disparity, high rates of incarceration of people of colour, and lower life expectancies and less access to medical care for communities of colour. Profits made from colonial violence and slavery were used to found universities and other institutions in which you may hold

---

11 Chelsea Vowel, "Beyond Territorial Land Acknowledgments," âpihtawikosisân, September 23, 2016, https://apihtawikosisan.com/2016/09/beyond-territorial-acknowledgments/.
12 Truth and Reconciliation Commission, "Calls to Action," 2015, http://trc.ca/assets/pdf/Calls_to_Action_English2.pdf

Events 257

events. In addition to land acknowledgements of unceded territories, consider acknowledging these historical legacies. The histories of violence within our institutions continue to influence and impact the kinds of conversations that are had. I encourage you to think critically about the role of space in the events that you organize.

4 Catering

If the event includes food and drink, choices over catering can impact the accessibility of your event. Provide a variety of meal options and include items that are easy to eat. Include foods that do not require utensils or intricacy. Ensure catering staff are briefed and available to assist attendees with serving items where required. Check that food is clearly labelled (vegan, gluten free, kosher, halal, etc.) and mark common allergens. Depending on its preparation and certification, vegan food with some gluten-free options can often meet the needs of halal, kosher, and many other diets. However, food carries cultural significance. Depending on your event's objectives, you may make different choices surrounding food. Cost of food can impact accessibility for participation and is a class issue. However, cheap food usually means that the farm workers, the people working in the food-processing plants, the people cooking the food, and/or the people selling the food are not paid a living wage. This is a labour issue. This is also a feminist issue, as women disproportionately do the underpaid or unpaid work of preparing food. Furthermore, this labour is highly racialized

Engage in Public Scholarship! 258

and classed and is intertwined with immigration policies that criminalize workers. Cheap food comes at environmental costs under industrialized food systems that disregard biodiversity, use pesticides, and lead to the destruction of ecosystems. It is a difficult balance to make sure that food is priced so that every worker is properly compensated and that all participants can afford the food. There is rampant cruelty, exploitation, and injustice throughout the food chain, even when serving vegan food.[13] Offering food items available at a range of prices and sourcing food from local sources are possible ways to address these vast issues.

The decision to serve alcohol may limit the age of participants for the event. It can also impact who feels welcome to attend the event. People who wish to stay sober may refrain from attending. Have water available for free and encourage people to bring their reusable water bottles/containers. Restricting access to water can jeopardize the health of people attending the event. Depending on the venue, this may be more difficult due to the infrastructure of the facility. The choice to serve alcohol may also require a permit, and servers may require specialized training, as stipulated by the venue or local laws. Check far in advance, as liquor permits can be difficult to obtain depending on your venue and city.

Single-use plastic plates and utensils go straight to the landfill. Consider serving food options that do not require utensils. Can you avoid using single-use items? Can you serve food on compostable plates? Encourage participants to bring

---

13   Ketchum, "Cooking the Books."

Events 259

reusable cups and water bottles. Have some straws available for participants who may require them to eat or drink.[14] In addition to a trashcan, have recycling and compost bins to reduce the environmental impact from the event. Make sure these are well marked.

5   Language

Language impacts the inclusiveness of events showcasing public scholarship. As chapter three discussed, jargon-heavy lectures, speeches, or panel discussions limit access for participants. Audiences participating in a second language may face barriers. Participants who are Deaf or hard of hearing may require sign-language interpretation. Therefore, it is important to keep in mind the various types of language needs when planning your event.

Depending on the anticipated needs of participants, your event may require one or a combination of interpreters, translators, intervenors, or captioners. Interpreters work with spoken or signed words, conveying a message from one language to another, including sign languages. Translation deals with written texts. Intervenors work with people who are Deaf-Blind to provide adequate information

---

14   Crippled Scholar, "When Accessibility Gets Labeled as Wasteful," *Crippled Scholar Blog,* March 4, 2016, https://crippledscholar. com/2016/03/04/when-accessibility-gets-labeled-wasteful/.

Engage in Public Scholarship! 260

and communication, such that the person who is Deaf-Blind is aware of who and what is going on around them, can anticipate future events, travel safely within their environment, and make informed choices. Real-time captioners transcribe events, creating captions composed of text, which are used by people who are Deaf or hard of hearing to access content delivered by spoken words and sounds. Even when the event has materials and presentations in the most commonly spoken languages, speakers from other language groups can be excluded. The location of your event and your target audience will determine your interpretation and translation needs. Furthermore, on publicity materials, encourage participants to contact organizers in advance if there are specific interpretation requirements in addition to those already made. Make sure that sign language interpreters on a stage are well lit so that audience members can see them clearly. Try to connect with interpreters in advance in case there is specific vocabulary relating to the event's topic that they need to prepare.

There are international, national, and local resources for finding interpreters and translators. The International Association of Conference Interpreters provides a great tool to find certified professionals.[15] The Canadian Translators, Terminologists and Interpreters Council provides a database for certified professionals outside of Quebec,[16] and within

---

15   International Association of Conference Interpreters, "About," 2020, https://aiic.net.

16   Canadian Translators, Terminologists, and Interpreters Council, "Finding a Certified Translator or Interpreter," 2020, http://www.cttic.org/chercher. asp.

Quebec, see L'Ordre des traducteurs, terminologues et interprètes agréés du Québec.[17] If you are looking for a translator in the United States, you can also use the American Translators Association.[18] For intervenors and captioners, contact the Canadian Hearing Society[19] or the Association of Visual Language Interpreters of Canada.[20] They can direct you to local service providers and provide captions for virtual events. The Canadian Deafblind and Rubella Association (CDRA) can put you in touch with intervenors and has local chapters throughout the country.[21]

6   Audio-Visual Technology for In-person Events

Technology can expand accessibility. While chapters seven, eight, and ten explained the potential drawbacks of technological solutions in detail, certain technologies will enable your event to be more inclusive. It is likely that your event will require some kind of electronic equipment. For those with disabilities, technology becomes an even more important tool to create accessibility. Microphones can

---

17   L'Ordre des traducteurs, terminologues et intreprètes agréés du Québec, "About," 2021, https://ottiaq.org/.

18   American Translators Association, "About," 2020, https://www.atanet.org.

19   Canadian Hearing Services, "About," 2020, http://www.chs.ca.

20   Association of Visual Language Interpreters of Canada, "About," 2020, https://www.avlic.ca.

21   Canadian Deafblind Association, "About," 2020, http://www.cdbanational.com/.

improve sound quality if people are speaking. Maybe you will show a film. Perhaps a performance will include music, projection, or dance. People who are Blind or have limited vision may have difficulty reading slides. Participants who are Deaf or hard of hearing may have difficulty understanding presentations. Other cognitive conditions may require that participants require accompanying texts for audio presentations. Various technologies assist in this process.

Audio equipment serves multiple functions. Consideration of the acoustics is important for those who are hard of hearing. Limit unnecessary background noise. Check if the facility has a hearing loop (sometimes called an audio-induction loop). This is a special type of sound system for use by people with hearing aids. The hearing loop provides a magnetic, wireless signal that is picked up by the hearing aid. Ask presenters to use microphones and insist the audience pose their questions into a microphone (speaking loudly is not an adequate substitute), or request the presenter to repeat the question into their microphone. Microphones are important tools in and of themselves and also expand other kinds of accessibility, as they are required for auto-captioning and auto-translation tools.

If, for some reason, you cannot find interpreters or captioners for your event due to cost, timing, or other factors, auto-captioning and auto-translation technologies are useful tools. Rua M. Williams, who works on disability and technology, argues that while auto-captioning tools are not adequate substitutes for formal transcription and translation services,

Events

they can be very helpful for all audience members.[22] PowerPoint and Google Slides both offer auto-transcription tools. Microsoft offers an automated translation plug-in, which functions as an auto-captioning device when used to translate from the presenter's language to the same language, such as English to English. This tool also provides a short URL where participants can select their preferred language to follow along on their own devices.[23] These tools require a fast internet or wifi connection, and a good connection with the microphone. The results are imperfect but valuable.

Decisions around projections and graphics impact access. In addition to auto-captioning, if presenters use images encourage them to describe what is on the slides orally. This technique is beneficial for participants that have reduced vision or are Blind. It is also a useful practice if the event is being audio recorded. When playing videos, turn on closed captioning. If there is a projection, such as a PowerPoint or Prezi presentation, the font should contrast with the background. Avoiding too much text and using a large font makes slides easier to read. The UK Home Office has created a guide with tips for accessible graphic design.[24]

---

22 Rua M. Williams, "Delivering Accessible Presentations," personal website, September 9, 2019, http://www.ruam ae.com/disability-advocacy/delivering-accessible-presentations/.

23 Microsoft, "Download Presentation Translator," 2020, https://www.microsoft.com/enus/translator/apps/presentation-translator/.

24 UK Home Office, "Designing Accessible Services," 2019, https://ukhomeoffice.github.io/ accessibility-posters/?fbclid=IwAR0sV9gdcby8 fCB8Y9rKUiOUHOzhOFLc5wQIh-4AIBtdXw R9kFR-Ew0Fga.

Engage in Public Scholarship! 264

Consider asking speakers to submit materials in advance so that they can be forwarded to individuals who may not be able to view screens. Screen readers are not able to read slides when they are shown on teleconferencing software such as Zoom. In addition, making printed copies of the slides with a larger font size can be beneficial to participants who may need to read along. While "some people resist digital materials because they are worried about theft of scholarship," as Rua M. Williams argues, "by producing event archives, the origins of these ideas are actually more traceable."[25] Documentation enables citation practices. These kinds of considerations involve advance planning but make a significant impact.

If you are affiliated with a university, you will usually have access to an audio-visual service with free or inexpensive rentals, even if the event is not held at the university. This equipment can include microphones, digital and video cameras, and more. Public-lending libraries often offer different kinds of recording and projection equipment. If none of the above options work, or if you need a particular piece of gear, private rental companies exist. Decisions surrounding AV equipment can either radically expand or decrease accessibility. As a presenter, even if you are not in control of the event organization, using these tools can maximize the amount of content that attendees have access to.

Dissemination of media and materials from in-person events further promotes access. You may choose to film, record, or livestream the event so that people who cannot attend can still

---

25 Williams, "Delivering Accessible Presentations."

Events   265

access the event. The next section's discussion of cyber events also includes information that pertains to disseminating materials from in-person events.

7 Online Events and Dissemination

Virtual events (also referred to as cyber events) enable people from around the world to connect with public scholarship synchronistically and/or asynchronistically (people can watch or listen after the recording).[26] This section brings together information about virtual events and dissemination practices for in-person and hybrid events. (Hybrid events take place in-person and virtually, either simultaneously with the event or archived after the in-person component.) The concerns and tools applicable to cyber and hybrid events overlap, especially regarding issues of accessibility and sustainability. While disability-rights advocates have raised some of these issues for years, concerns were brought to the fore during the 2020 coronavirus pandemic.[27] This section is also useful for organizers of in-person events who wish to broadcast or document their event.

---

26 There is no distinction between the two terms. Cyber events harken to 1990s cyberculture. Both refer to essentially the same phenomenon and are used interchangeably in this chapter.
27 Riegel et al., "How to Run a Free Online Academic Conference: A Workbook (version 0.3)."

Engage in Public Scholarship! 266

7.1 Limitations to Tools

There are numerous types of software that enable online events. This section will mention various providers of software that are controlled by companies that may challenge your ethics or sense of justice. It can be a challenge to find tools, especially free tools, which are not created by companies that may sell your data and/or engage in unethical practices. It might be unfeasible to avoid using the software from these corporations when your audience is already using a social media platform or is comfortable with specific applications. This section provides various resources so you can decide what works for you. To be clear, I am not endorsing any of the services listed below. While digital tools expand accessibility in some senses, it is important to note that marginalized communities are more likely to experience the negative impacts of technologies and online harassment, including trolling and doxxing. Online spaces can be violent spaces. Chapters three and four expand on this discussion. No solution is perfect. Software is ever-changing. When choosing software and tools, it is important to consider cost, encryption, security, simplicity of the user interface, number of users allowed, and the ability to record.

7.2 Video-Chat Services

Video-chat services can be useful for events like book readings, lectures, and panels, in which you want the audience to be able to speak and ask questions. Some

Events

267

software allows you to record the video chat and share the footage after the event.

A popular format for online events (at least in 2020 during the COVID-19 pandemic) is the video-chat service Zoom. Zoom can host meetings, which is a service you can use for free up to a specified number of users, after which you have to buy a Zoom licence. Zoom webinars require a paid licence and are used to host a view-only platform where the attendees cannot see each other. If you are sharing a live musical performance via Zoom, use the strongest wifi available, leave the "automatically adjust microphone volume" box unchecked so that the software does not auto-adjust sound levels as it would for speaking voices, and make sure everyone else is on mute. With some Zoom licences, auto-captioning (exclusively available in English) is a feature that should be used when a professional captioner is not available (the preference should be to have a human captioner). As the meeting host, you must enable the captions; the software does not automatically activate them. Criticism has been made of Zoom's security and privacy. Security breaches have resulted in "zoombombings"—a phenomenon in which people use the platform to harass the presenter or participants. The Zoom webinar option can help reduce the chance of zoombombings, especially if the chat function is turned off. Harassing comments may still appear in the question and answer box on the platform. While Zoom is a popular option, it is not the only one. Jitsi is a free and open-source video conferencing tool.[28] Bluejeans is another option.

---

28   Jitsi, "About," 2020, https://jitsi.org/.

Engage in Public Scholarship! 268

Google Meetings enables auto-captioning without the meeting host needing to enable it. The Corona Virus Tech Handbook is a free resource that offers even more alternative options for online meetings.[29]

7.3   Livestreams

Livestreaming is a live transmission of an event over the internet. You can choose to livestream an event that is happening in-person with some people physically present, or you can livestream a single speaker or a group call. Popular livestream platforms include: YouTube (owned in 2021 by Google), Facebook Live, Instagram Stories (owned by Facebook), Twitch TV (traditionally used by videogamers), and Periscope (owned by Twitter). The benefit with these platforms is that all you need is a smartphone or computer and a free account. Most of these platforms also include a space where audiences can ask questions or post comments in real time. Platforms like YouTube also make it easy to save the video so that it is available after the event ends, allowing people to watch the event at a later time and making the event even more accessible. YouTube also auto-generates closed captioning for videos. These captions are imperfect but are useful for people who are hard of hearing, Deaf, or are participating in a second language.

29   Corona Virus Tech Handbook, 2020, https://coronavirustechhandbook. com/home.

Events 269

7.4 Online Video

With the consent of presenters and performers, it is possible to record video or audio at your in-person and hybrid events. The sound quality will be improved if the speaker uses a microphone. Services such as YouTube or Vimeo allow you to upload videos from events. You can create a channel to gather videos from related events that you host. Remember to enable auto-generated closed captioning. These services are useful for post-event dissemination. Self-hosting video content requires more technical expertise, a phenomenon discussed in chapter seven.

7.5 Audio vs Video Streams

Video streams require stable internet connections, which are unavailable to many people. Audio files require less data to download, which is easier for people with less stable internet connections. The lower bandwidth option will be more accessible to more folks. Audio-streaming services and internet radio enable these lower bandwidth audio streams.[30]

If you record audio from an event, you can release it as a podcast. Free, open-source editing software, such as Audacity, can enable you to edit your audio. You can release your podcast after generating an RSS feed, and then distribute it

---

30   Traci Ruether, "How to Create an Internet Radio Station," *Wowza Blog,* November 14, 2019, https://www.wowza.com/blog/create-internet-radio-station.

across podcast players that aggregate RSS feeds, such as Apple Podcasts. You may choose to release audio on music-sharing platforms such as Bandcamp. You can create a free account for a limited number of files. More information on podcasts is available in chapter eight. To increase accessibility, providing transcriptions of the audio can make events inclusive of people who are hard of hearing or Deaf. Services like otter.ai and SpeechTexter can assist in this work.

7.6   Website

Creating a website facilitates the embedding of videos and audio, sharing photos, or disseminating other materials from the event. Websites can also be useful for publicity. Website design can impact accessibility, particularly for people who use screen readers. The WCAG (Web Content Accessibility Guidelines) is the main international standard for web accessibility. Things to consider include: font-colour contrast, font size, not embedding essential information in graphic formats (as assistive technologies such as screen readers may not be able to process the text), written descriptions of images, and keyboard navigation.[31] If you choose to use pictures from in-person events on your website, inform participants about the use of photography or consider blurring photos. More information about website design is available in chapter eight.

---

31   W3C Accessibility Initiative, "W3C Accessibility Standards Overview," January 6, 2021, https:// www.w3.org/WAI/standards-guidelines/.

Events 271

8   For the Speakers

If your event involves artists, musicians, performers, speakers, or presenters, it is important to recognize that not paying for art and work is a class issue. Only people with financial flexibility and class privilege will be able to routinely work without pay, and this limits the kind of art, performance, and ideas that are displayed. As class in the United States and Canada is racialized and gendered, the voices, perspectives, and artworks of people of colour, Indigenous people, women, nonbinary, and trans individuals are less likely to be showcased. This is not to say that people will not volunteer their time and efforts to showcase their work, but if you are paying the venue and vendors, it is important that the artists, performers, and/or speakers are paid. Exposure does not pay the rent.

When first contacting potential lecturers, panelists, or performers, mention compensation in the initial email. As an organizer, you may have a limited budget. It is important to be honest and forthcoming about what you can pay the people that you are contacting. This way they can decide if the amount is acceptable to them. It is also important to think critically about the amounts you are offering various performers. Women, Indigenous people, and folks of colour continue to be paid at lower rates for their work. Be transparent with how you are paying folks.

Paying people promptly is important. Oftentimes people are asked to front the money for their own work and have to

Engage in Public Scholarship!

wait months to be reimbursed. Universities are notoriously slow to reimburse presenters. The best practice is to book the travel for presenters or have a cheque or form of payment for performers on the day of the event (though depending on your funding, this is not always possible).

9 Funding

Reserving a venue, renting AV equipment, hiring interpreters, and paying for speaker honorariums and travel requires funding. It is outside the scope of this book to go into detail about all available funding options from scholarly research councils, but the section below includes some resources.

Universities' departments and programs can be a great source of funding for events. Look outside of your own department and consider co-hosting the event with others. In addition to internal funding as a scholar, consider partnering with a student group, as students often have access to funds that professors do not.

Grants from research councils, foundations, and private institutions can vary in the kinds of application materials they require. Money may be available for the kind of work that you are trying to do. Most grants require some form of matching funding. Check if the grant accepts in-kind matching funding. If you plan to hold your event in donated

Events 273

space and document the show with donated camera and sound equipment, all of this counts as in-kind funding. A bit of money grows. Funding agencies are more likely to give money and support if they see that you have already received some form of funding and support.[32] Start small and you can build on this experience.

Municipal funding is another great option. It is likely that your town or city has some form of funding available for local-events programming. Does your event idea relate to any local community initiatives? Is there a festival, theme, or goal of your municipal government? State, provincial, territorial, and regional funding is a similar option. Many states and provinces offer grants. Consider potential limitations to receiving this type of funding, and how state and municipal control can limit the message or effectiveness of your event. National and international grants can be more complex but, depending on your project, can be another option. It is important to note that these kinds of grant applications can require hundreds of pages of paperwork and might not be worth completing for many kinds of events.

Tickets are one route to fund an event. Selling tickets in advance can help you have a better sense of your budget.

---

32 My most successful grant application for a speaker and workshop series resulted in a $23,455 CAD grant, which required 50 percent matching funding. I began by getting small contributions of $100. I could then leverage this funding into contributions of $200, and then $500, and then larger contributions. This process is time intensive and required me to write smaller grants to count towards the matching funding. I dedicated three months of my life to this work, on top of my primary employment.

Engage in Public Scholarship! 274

There are numerous online portals that can facilitate this process. However, many take a cut of the sale. Read the fine print. Selling tickets at the door is a low-tech way to handle sales, but not everyone carries cash. Tickets can also create barriers to access. One solution is to use a Pay What You Can (PWYC) model or a "Nobody Turned Away for Lack of Funds" policy. Sliding scales can be useful or consider tiered ticket prices, where students and elders pay a lower ticket price.

Sponsors can be another option. As an event organizer, you need to decide if you are comfortable accepting sponsorships. Likely this will entail that you advertise for the company, which might feel inappropriate depending on your event. Remember that you are in control of what kinds of companies and organizations you take money from. Maybe there is a local business that reflects your values and would sponsor your event? These partnerships can put your audience in connection with local businesses or channel corporate money towards a cause you believe in.

10   Publicity

In order for people to participate in your event, they need to know it exists. Your choices surrounding publicity will impact the inclusivity of your event. Make sure that your publicity includes important details such as time, place,

Events 275

cost, information about accessibility, and how to contact the event organizer about additional accommodations.

10.1 Physical Publicity and Radio

Posters are a classic option for publicity. Printing black-ink posters is one of the cheapest options. Posting on public cork bulletin boards and taping flyers to streetlights is a method of information distribution that can lead to passersby experiencing chance encounters and help people learn about events they never would have known about otherwise. However, be mindful of municipal regulations as unapproved flyering can result in fines. Using a large san-serif font with a high level of contrast against the background is useful for people with dyslexia and people with reduced vision. Signage, presentations, and written materials should also have sufficient contrast levels. Always use inclusive language.[33] Other forms of physical publicity include direct mail and advertisements in newspapers and magazines. You can also consider announcing the event on community or university radio stations!

---

33 Australian Network on Disability, "Event Accessibility Checklist," 2020, https://www.and.org.au/pages/event-checklist.html.

10.2 Online Publicity

Publicizing your event exclusively online may limit who will attend the event, as not everyone uses the internet. Social-media platforms are popular choices that can allow you to create an online event announcement and registration list, often for free. Many of these platforms use opaque algorithms that impact who sees your event, and you might not be able to control your listserv after the event. Posting information across platforms increases visibility. If you want to create subsequent events, consider generating an email listserv through which people can receive news about future dates.

11 Question and Answer Periods

Question and answer periods are common practice. During these Q and A periods, there is a tendency for people with more privilege to raise their hands first and dominate the microphone. It can be useful to remind people to be aware of the space that they are occupying in the room. Professor of Indigenous and critical race studies Eve Tuck believes in heavily mediated Q and A sessions and suggests that audience members first be asked to chat for a few minutes amongst themselves before opening up the question period.[34]

---

34 Eve Tuck, "Indigenous Feminist Approach to Facilitating Academic Question and Answer Periods," Twitter thread, June 19, 2019, 8:22 PM, https://twitter.com/tuckeve/status/1141501422611128320.

Events 277

She also suggests that someone who knows the audience better facilitates the Q and A period. If, as an organizer, you are the one choosing who gets to ask questions, think about the demographics of the people who are asking most of the questions. If you are worried about encountering the dreaded "this is more of a comment than a question" response, not receiving any questions from shy audience members, or the possibility of trolling and/or harassment at the event, it is possible to collect audience questions in advance or pass a hat to collect questions. This way you can filter some of the questions. If your event is happening in a digital space, it is similarly possible to filter questions by asking people to send their questions in advance, or through an online platform.

Q and A periods can be wonderful for audience members to connect with the speaker. It is important, however, to set a clear timeframe. Many of us have encountered a Q and A period that seems to go on and on and on. This can be hard on the audience and on the speaker. Check with your speaker in advance if an informal question period may continue after the event. If there is a merchandise (or "merch") table with the speaker's art, music, or books on it, audience questions will likely continue there.

For remote and virtual Q and A, a few tools are available. Google Meetings, Zoom, and YouTube each have live comment boxes that can be used for questions. Sli.do does not require an account to participate.

12 Conclusion

Inclusive public events can take a variety of forms. Cost, space, technology, and forms of dissemination are important to consider as all will impact who can attend. These events can act as an introduction to a scholar's work and may lead audiences to seek out other forms of one's work.

CHAPTER 12

Working with Journalists and Writing Op-Eds

Earlier chapters focused primarily on producing your own scholarly outputs. This chapter takes seriously the intellectual labour of working with journalists as a form of public-facing scholarship. Working with journalists is a great way to share research findings with the public and provide evidenced-based commentary on current events. Journalists are accustomed to amalgamating information from secondary sources and interviews. Radio, television, podcast, and newspaper interviews are options for communicating one's research to the public. This process is not without challenges. This chapter highlights what to expect, as well as the benefits and the drawbacks of doing this work. The end of the chapter discusses how universities can better support scholars in doing this work. The chapter finishes with advice on writing Op-Eds.

1 Benefits

Working with journalists can benefit scholars in a variety
of ways. From an intellectual standpoint, reporters
interviewing you will often ask very different kinds of
questions than audience members at academic conferences
or peer reviewers making comments on your article.
By having to answer these questions, your research may go
in a new direction. Reckoning with another perspective
may spark inspiration. Similarly, you might be used to
speaking about your research only to another set of experts.
Interviews with journalists force you to learn to describe
your work in new ways. You will have to avoid jargon and
technical terms. These skills can also be useful when
applying for grants and fellowships, as funding committees
can be comprised of readers from outside of your field.
Additionally, if you are writing a book you will often need
to translate certain jargon and information about your
field to larger audiences. Media work can improve your
scholarship.

Have you ever noticed that celebrities seem to appear on all
of the talk shows right before their movie comes out? You
may have noticed a similar pattern with your fellow scholars.
As part of promoting a new book or project, scholars might
become more visible in the media. While your expertise
may be critical for illuminating current events, working
with journalists may also help you promote a new book
or other work. Media work has the potential of helping your

Working with Journalists and Writing Op-Eds   281

research make a greater impact, benefiting your career, and improving your scholarship.

2   How to Be Interviewed

Have you ever wondered why certain scholars appear on the news or radio time and time again? While the field of research may be one reason that journalists repeatedly call upon a certain scholar for her expertise, the answer may often be even more simple: it is because a scholar has indicated that she is interested in being interviewed.

It is common for universities to have communications and public-relations offices. In Canada, almost every single university has one.[1] These offices have a variety of names: Media Relations, Newsroom, Media Relations Offices, Institutional Communications, and Communications. Despite the variety of names, they all serve a similar function: the offices are a university's central point of contact with the media. Representatives from the media can contact these offices to connect with a university's scholars. The office will often also work with journalists to promote newsworthy stories about a university's research and events, serving as a public-relations office. It is not uncommon that the Media Relations Office will also produce its own materials. For example, the McGill University media-relations office, The

---

1   I checked. My research team also contacted every single one in June 2020.

Engage in Public Scholarship!

Newsroom, will manage and promote news, events, and announcements via channels including the *McGill Reporter*, *McGill Dans la Ville*, and "What's New" e-newsletters, as well as via their social-media channels.[2] These offices often have procedures for scholars at their institutions to complete if they are interested in being interviewed by the media. It is likely that if you go to your university's media-relations office's website, you will be asked to fill out a form describing your research areas of expertise, comfort in speaking in certain languages, and your preferred form of contact. It is common for universities to keep a database of their scholars that are willing to speak about certain topics, so that they can provide this information to journalists when they are contacted. While graduate students are not always included in these databases, graduate students should not be dissuaded from reaching out to their university's media-relations office. After filling out the online form, the media-relations office may create a web page with information about your expertise, your contact information, and include an official photo (which you may or may not supply yourself). When there is a current event relating to a specific topic, the media-relations office may create a "channel" in which they direct journalists to the list of scholars who work on that topic. If you work in a bilingual or multilingual region, the media-relations office may create multiple versions of your information in those languages.[3] Before holidays or during certain current events, the

---

2   McGill Media Relations Office, "Who We Are," McGill Newsroom, 2020, https://www.mcgill.ca/newsroom/ contacts.

3   McGill Media Relations Office, "Expert Female Only Spaces," *McGill Newsroom,* December 17, 2019, https://www.mcgill.ca/newsroom/channels/news/expert-female-only-spaces-303512.

Working with Journalists and Writing Op-Eds   283

media-relations office may contact scholars within its database and ask them if they are interested in commenting about certain topics. From this information, they can make a contact page for journalists to access easily. If you are interested in doing media work, contact the people at your university's media-relations offices, as they can guide you through the processes at your specific institution.

Media-relations offices can facilitate connections with journalists but journalists may also contact you independently. When your media-relations office acts as a conduit between you and journalists, reporters write to the office and the office forwards you the information. Since journalists are frequently on tight deadlines, they will often reach out to you independently. You can always copy your media-relations office on any emails with journalists if you would like assistance in navigating the process of working with a reporter. Letting the media-relations office know about interviews can give the office a better sense of the media work you and other scholars at your institution are doing.

The question of deadlines will come up repeatedly in this chapter. While scholars in the humanities and social sciences may have become accustomed to the often frustratingly slow pace of academic journal articles, which take months or even years to come out, journalists often have only a few hours to turn in a story. The speed of your response to a phone call or email often determines whether or not you are interviewed

Engage in Public Scholarship! 284

by the journalist. As a genre, radio has a particularly fast turnaround—sometimes a matter of minutes.[4]

Once you do an interview, you are more likely to be asked for follow-up interviews. You have now established yourself as someone willing to be interviewed. As newsrooms shrink, it is also common to be asked by media source after media source about the same topic. Journalists may see your name in an interview about a certain subject and you will become the de facto person to contact.

You are completely free to decline any interview requests that you do not want to do. You might be tired of discussing a topic if you have done multiple interviews about it—that is okay. Consider recommending a colleague who would appreciate the opportunity for media work, especially if you are a more senior scholar. You might not want to do an interview with a particular journalist or publication. Certain newspapers and radio stations have the reputation of seeking out scholars in order to create conflict or drama. Whenever possible, research the paper or reporter by looking at their other work before committing to an interview. You might also feel that a topic is outside of your area of expertise. It is important to consider whether or not you are the appropriate person to comment on a topic or be interviewed.

---

4 I once emailed my affirmative response confirming I could do an interview twenty minutes after receiving the initial query email and they had already gone with another person.

Working with Journalists and Writing Op-Eds 285

At present, white male scholars are interviewed significantly more often than women, people of colour, and non-binary scholars. For instance, women only account for 29 percent of the experts cited in Canadian media and 38 percent in American media.[5] Organizations such as Les Femmes Expertes, Informed Opinions, Women Also Know History, and other organizations committed to changing the demographics of who is cited as an expert by the media, demonstrate that the discrepancy is because male scholars will often feel comfortable speaking to journalists about areas outside of their area of expertise.[6] There are other causes for these imbalances—particularly fear of trolling, doxxing, or harassment—that will be explored later in this chapter.

While developing a relationship with your university's media-relations office and saying yes to interviews often means you will be asked for more, ease of contact is another factor in determining whether or not you are invited to do media work.

3   Searchability

As a scholar, particularly one interested in doing public scholarship and media work, there is no reason that someone should spend more than thirty seconds searching

---

5   These statistics come from Informed Opinions and The Women's Media Centre's SheSource and the Global Media Monitoring Program, https://womensmediacenter.com/about/learn-moreabout-wmcwmc-shesource.

6   Femmes Expertes, "About," 2019, https://femmesexpertes.ca.

Engage in Public Scholarship!

for your email address or web contact form.[7] If you are affiliated with a university as a faculty member or graduate student, have your contact information on your faculty page or graduate student bio. If your university does not have a page like this, ask for one from your department or program administrator.

Creating a website with information about your scholarship is key. There will always be a narrative about you; control that narrative by creating a web page with information about your work. These websites may or may not be the same websites you use for your public scholarship. You do not need to know how to code to create a web page. As discussed in chapter eight, website builders such as Squarespace, Wix, Weebly, and Wordpress.com are options, but most of their plans require payment. If you do not want to pay hosting or plan fees, consider using a free platform such as Blogger to create your site. A variety of options exist at different price points. It is useful to include a list of past interviews on your web page. In addition to making an archive, it can demonstrate your willingness to do media work. You can include a line that says "Please do not hesitate to contact me for interviews" on your site. See Ruha Benjamin's page for an outstanding website of a scholar who does significant public media work, which includes contact forms, media information, and more.[8] Personalized websites are useful tools for public scholars.

---

7   There is an exception. You may need to temporarily remove your email address and contact information from the web if you are being doxxed.

8   Ruha Benjamin (Website), 2020, https://www.ruhabenjamin.com.

Working with Journalists and Writing Op-Eds 287

Names and branding can affect how searchable you are. In order to improve your searchability, think intentionally about the way you credit yourself and name your projects. Having a consistent name across platforms ensures that it is easier to find you. If your name is John Smith, it might be more difficult to ensure that your results appear at the top of a search. If your research or project sites have a name explicitly tied to what you research, however, journalists might learn about your work when they perform a basic search. (Poetic titles can come after a colon.) Paying for a domain name that matches the name you use professionally or the name of your project is useful for improving your search engine optimization, which is how high you appear in the search list due to search algorithms.[9] Search algorithms are not neutral; they are gendered, raced, and classed.[10] While the algorithms are opaque, by building consistency in the name you use professionally and the way you title your work, websites, and projects, you can improve your chances of optimizing the "all-encompassing and increasingly invisible information infrastructure" of search.[11] Even if you decide to use a website builder, buy your domain name independently so that you can continue to use it even if you decide to change platforms. The concept of "branding" may be off-putting, but for scholars it can be as simple as making clear your area of expertise and the kinds of public media you work with, who will then be interested in participating.

---

9   Google Search, "How Search Works," 2020, https://www.google.com/search/howsearchwo rks/?fg=1.
10   Noble, *Algorithms of Oppression*.
11   Haider and Sundin, *Invisible Search and Online Search Engines*.

Engage in Public Scholarship! 288

Professional social-networking sites are another option for increasing your visibility as a scholar. Platforms such as Academia.edu and the more science-oriented ResearchGate are commercial (American and European, respectively), social-networking platforms for researchers. While these sites are controversial, due in part to their commercial nature and the legal ambiguity surrounding the copyright of documents uploaded to their sites, search algorithms prioritize these websites so they appear higher in search engine results. If you have concerns about uploading your research, you can create a basic profile page, which just hosts your bio, contact information, and a copy of your CV. The Humanities Commons is a nonprofit, interdisciplinary, broad ranging alternative to commercial networks.[12] LinkedIn is an American business and employment-oriented online service that can function as a social-networking site. With a free, basic account you can include a CV and contact information.

Social-media platforms often have a feature for direct messaging. Depending on the privacy settings that you select on the platform, this feature allows people to write directly to you, which can facilitate contact with journalists for interviews. Twitter, Instagram, Facebook, and TikTok all have this feature. It is less orthodox for reporters to contact a scholar via their personal Facebook or Instagram accounts, but if you manage a Facebook Page or Instagram account oriented around your research interests you may receive queries through those channels.

---

12 Humanities Common, "Welcome," 2021, https://hcommons.org/core/.

Working with Journalists and Writing Op-Eds 289

Whether you create a website or professional social-networking page, use social media, or all of the above, make sure your email address is readily available if you want journalists to contact you. If you are concerned about security, you can embed a web contact form on your web page that will hide your actual email address but will still allow people to contact you.

3.1 Media Press Kits

Creating a press kit can be particularly valuable if you are trying to promote a certain project—a book, for example. If you are hoping to draw media attention to your latest monograph, you can upload a PDF of press materials to your website or social-media page. This press kit will include your contact information, bio, and the name of the book or project. The first page should show your press release, which is a one-page summary of everything else in the kit. Your promotional information should include a summary of the book, author photos, and images of and from the book. Include a section on interview resources with a list of sample interview questions and answers. These questions will allow you to showcase your project, your role as the author, and indicate what topics you might discuss in an interview. If you have endorsements (also called blurbs) from reviewers, include these pull quotes and media reactions. Include an excerpt of your book. Make sure to follow copyright law regarding how much of the book you can include. Select a section that speaks to the themes of your book and can stand on its own. While choosing the

Engage in Public Scholarship!

first chapter is a standard practice, you can use another chapter. In addition to creating a PDF version of the press kit, include some of these materials within the body of your website page itself.

4 Navigating Interviews: The Process

Speaking on camera or on the radio is a skill set. It requires speaking concisely and backing up your statements with evidence. University media-relations offices often offer training. If your university's office does not, consider asking them to make this training available. Independent organizations such as Femmes Expertes[13] and Informed Opinions[14] offer training sessions for women scholars that pay particular attention to gendered dynamics, as well. Regardless of the medium, remember to state important facts first and illustrate your key points. Using short anecdotes or metaphors can help illustrate your ideas.

Remember, sometimes stories and interviews don't get published, or they get shortened, or they are saved for a later date. Breaking-news stories may interrupt a planned interview. News media functions at a quick pace.

---

13   Femmes Expertes, "About," 2019, https://femmesexpertes.ca/.
14   Informed Opinions, "About," 2019, https://informedopinions.org/.

Working with Journalists and Writing Op-Eds

4.1 Newspaper and Magazine Interviews

Newspaper and magazine interviews vary in their length and the turnaround times for their publication. A journalist will contact you and set a time to speak. They might email and only ask for a quote. The benefit of providing a written quotation is that they are less likely to misquote you. These interviews may also happen through a video-conferencing application such as Skype, or by phone. Be prepared for the journalist to ask to record the conversation. When possible, ask if they might be able to provide their questions to you in advance so that you may prepare. You can also decline to answer questions. On occasion, unaffiliated freelance journalists may contact you for a story. They need to know that you will consent to a future interview before they pitch their story to an editor. Even if you agree to the interview, it may never happen or never be published.

Even though this chapter focuses primarily on working with professional journalists, you may work at a university that has student-run publications. Consider speaking with these student journalists as well. When students are in the early stages of honing their journalistic skills, they may commit errors, misquote you, and/or forget to follow up. Be generous and use this as a teaching opportunity to explain the mistake. Student publications tend to respond by publishing a correction in the next issue or updating the online publication.

4.2   Radio and Podcast Interviews

Radio interviews often happen live on the air but can be pre-recorded. Podcast interviews are pre-recorded and, as a result, may be edited. After emailing or speaking with a journalist or their production assistant, it is likely that you will do a pre-interview for radio. Usually someone on the production team will ask you the same or similar questions as the interview. Be warned, occasionally during a live, on-air interview, a journalist will ask completely different questions than those from the pre-interview. Some journalists will only include a perspective that they want to hear. It is not uncommon to do a one-hour long pre-interview and, because you did not agree with their take, the journalist may ultimately decide not to use any of the content.

If you are doing the interview by phone, you will receive a call from a production assistant a few minutes before the start of the scheduled interview. Through the phone you will hear the audio from the radio show. You will likely be asked to not have the phone on speaker phone, as it can warp the audio quality. When it is time for your interview to start the assistant will ask, "Are you there? Ready?" It is common that your interview will begin after an advertising break or a musical interlude. The interviews are often around eight minutes long, but can feel as if they are taking hours while simultaneously ending very quickly. After the interview, the production assistant will switch onto the line and say a quick "thanks." If you want a copy of the interview, try to record it independently, as not all radio shows will send copies.

Working with Journalists and Writing Op-Eds 293

Sometimes you will physically go to a studio to do radio interviews. During studio sessions, you will wear a headset and sit across from an interviewer. This can be a fun opportunity. While you will not be paid to do the interview, if you have an early call time the studio may pay for your taxi ride.

Podcasts tend to have a slower turnaround. Depending on the podcast, you may have the opportunity to speak at length about a topic. The benefit of the form is that you can go into detail about your research or opinions and do not have to worry about the ten-second soundbite that dominates other forms of media. The level of professionalism of podcasters varies widely. If you enjoy a particular podcast relating to your research, consider contacting the podcast host and expressing your interest in being on the air. Some podcasts function as radio shows and vice versa.

On occasion, radio interviews will simultaneously function as television interviews. Some radio-station studios have cameras that record the interviews, which are simultaneously or subsequently broadcast on television. In these instances, consider the information below relating to television interviews.

4.3 Television Interviews

The experience of television interviews can range widely depending on the program. Local (or public-access) television will be different than a major network show. The experience

Engage in Public Scholarship! 294

of being on a nationally or internationally broadcast late-night show is going to be entirely different than one at a local news station. Occasionally, you will go to a studio. You might get to go to hair and makeup, but it is likely that you will appear as you are. For television cameras, wear comfortable clothes in solid shades and minimize the amount of jewelry you wear (while still being true to your own style) or anything else that might distract the viewer's eye. Dark, solid colours are best. Avoid wearing thin strips and pin stripes as they cause moiré patterns, an optical illusion where the stripes appear to move on the screen.

There are a few common formats for television interviews. In-studio interviews are typically conducted while sitting on a studio couch, or behind a desk or a table. Scholars are often interviewed from home or from their office. Although the image of the academic speaking in front of her bookcase is so expected that a Twitter account, Bookcase Credibility, pokes fun at the selection of books and design of the cases,[15] if you do an interview in front of your bookshelf, consider placing copies of your own books behind your shoulders. Make sure to close the door and inform the people you live with to not interrupt you during the call. Another common format is the "walking and talking" set up, where you and the journalist are filmed as you walk. There is also the familiar format where the reporter holds a microphone to your face as you speak beside a landmark, or a place outside on the campus of your university. Knowing the format in

---

15 Bookcase Credibility, "Bookcase Credibility Twitter," 2020 https://twitter.com/bcredibilit y?lang=en.

Working with Journalists and Writing Op-Eds   295

advance can help you prepare your remarks and decide how to dress appropriately and comfortably.

5   Requests and Demands

When working with journalists, you are in a position in which you can make requests and demands. While making these requests does not guarantee that you will get what you desire, you can try. When possible, ask to be able to read the article in advance of publication, especially if the interview was long and they are only using one or two quotes. Sometimes journalists are on such tight deadlines that this is not possible. If the headlines are written by their editors, reporters often do not have any say over the title attached to their work, but you can make suggestions. Clearly state how you want to be referred to in the piece. If your official title is Dr. and it is important to you that the reporter states this, make sure that you tell the reporter your proper title. Some newspapers and magazines are inconsistent, in that they will refer to men as Dr. or Professor and women scholars as Mrs. or Ms. You are giving your time and labour by participating in their work. It is okay to ask that the reporter plugs your forthcoming book, website, or project. This is not just a capital exchange—consider making a request for the journalist to mention your projects if you want more people to fill out a research study, read an article, or more. Especially if you are doing an interview in your second language, ask for the questions in advance. If you are

Engage in Public Scholarship! 296

appearing on the show as a scholar, the reason you are asked is less likely to be so that reporters can ask you "gotcha" kinds of questions, but rather to seek your expertise. Of course, this depends on the kind of network with which you are working. Pre-interviews can help you prepare for the actual interview as well. Do not expect that journalists will send you a link to their published piece, so make sure to ask for a link.

6 Challenges

The challenges of media work range widely. There can be challenges regarding the actual interviews. Occasionally the interviewer will go off script while on the air. It is okay to politely decline to answer a question. Sometimes a reporter will misquote you. If this happens, you can try to contact the media outlet after the fact, and they may issue a clarification. If you are able to read the piece in advance of publication, this kind of error is less likely to occur. Media outlets have an extensive legacy of misquoting individuals, especially people of colour and Indigenous people, and/or framing stories in ways that extract and exploit their communities.[16] This legacy must be addressed,[17] as this phenomenon continues to impact the media-work experiences of scholars, especially scholars whose research stems from their lived experiences,

16   Kathy English, "Media Must Do Better on Aboriginal Issues," *The Star,* June 12, 2015.
17   Government of Canada, "Media and Reconciliation," 2019, https://www. rcaanc-cirnac.gc. ca/eng/1524505692599/1557513408573.

Working with Journalists and Writing Op-Eds 297

identities, family and/or community connections, or whose research focuses on these topics.[18] While a particular interview may end up being less than ideal, many challenges with media work happen before or after the interview.

6.1 The Politics of the Voice, the Politics of the Image

As a scholar engaging in media work, your voice and appearance affect how you are heard and understood. There are gender politics around the register and pitch of who is speaking. Chapter eight touched on the manner in which voices that are considered "masculine," or are lower pitched, are often considered the voice of authority. There is a particularly gendered policing of women's voices. Women's voices will receive criticism for being considered shrill or for having vocal fry.[19] It is vital to consider whose voices are listened to and who has the voice of power. In addition to being gendered, these power dynamics are further classed and racialized. Some accents are coded as educated, while others are deemed less intelligent or less worthy.

These power dynamics also occur according to the way that scholars appear visually. If you are doing media work

---

18 Bridgette Watson, "Journalists of Colour React to CBC Host Resigning Over Lack of Indigenous, Black Representation," *CBC News,* June 18, 2020.

19 Hannah McGregor (host), "Secret Feminist Agenda and Stacey Copeland: Producing Queer Media," *Secret Feminist Agenda* (podcast), May 15, 2020, https://secretfeministagenda.com/2020/05/15/episode-4-20producing-queer-media-with-stacey-copeland/.

Engage in Public Scholarship! 298

that includes visual representation of yourself, such as a television interview, some scholars will be sexualized or will have their intelligence undermined based on the way they appear, particularly relating to how their age, race, gender, and ability are interpreted. When the societal expectation of a scholar is that of an older, bearded white man with glasses and elbow patches, any scholar who presents differently may face pushback. It is important that scholars doing media work come from diverse backgrounds, as this enables a wider range of perspectives and also demonstrates to the public the possibilities of who can be a scholar. At the same time, marginalized scholars doing media work may encounter a greater amount of trolling, doxxing, or harassment if they engage in media work.

6.2   Trolling, Harassment, and the University

Universities often claim that they are committed to community engagement via publicly engaged scholarship and media work. Radio, television, podcast, and newspaper interviews are options for communicating one's research to the public, yet they are not without drawbacks.[20] As discussed in chapter four, the cost of doing work in public spheres is disproportionately paid by marginalized scholars. It is not rare for women academics and scholars of colour to face harassment, especially after doing media work.

---

20   Massanari, "Rethinking Research Ethics, Power, and the Risk of Visibility in the Era of the 'Alt-Right' Gaze."

Working with Journalists and Writing Op-Eds

Furthermore, even when harassment has not yet occurred, the fear of harassment can lead to self-silencing.

At present, universities do not do enough to support their scholars engaged in media work. In the summer of 2020, I sought out what information Canadian universities make available to scholars for dealing with trolling, doxxing (also known as doxing), and harassment when they do public-facing scholarship and media work. I investigated the availability of this information online (on media-relations offices' websites) as well as the information that media-relations offices provide to scholars that might not be on their website (i.e., plans, policies, advice). At that time, only one Canadian university had information posted on their website regarding trolling, doxxing, or harassment. As for university media-relations offices that had internal materials, protocols, or plans, the findings were quite underwhelming. From May to mid-July 2020, my research team contacted every Canadian university's media-relations office via email, using the same English or French script. We outlined our research project and inquired about materials the office had for scholars regarding the risks of trolling, doxxing, or harassment and what protocols the scholar should follow if she experienced any of these while doing public-facing scholarship. If offices did not respond within a few weeks to the first email, they were contacted a second time, leading to a response rate of 41 percent. For the media-relations offices that acknowledged the threat of trolling, doxxing, or harassment, most offices dealt with the issues on a case-by-case basis. The team found that only one media-relations office had explicit protocols or documents.

Engage in Public Scholarship! 300

Two media-relations offices had already incorporated discussions about trolling in workshops, and three wanted to begin including this material in future workshops.

The most optimistic finding from the research thus far is that, since this project began in May 2020, several universities have already begun to work on creating protocols, documents, or workshops relating to these topics.[21] On May 5, 2021, University of Massachusetts Amherst professor Jennifer Lundquist co-organized an event with Ed Blaguszewski of her media-relations office to discuss the strategies that faculty and administrators may use to prevent and respond to public harassment and to support faculty if and when it occurs.[22] My hope is that more universities commit to this important work.

If universities are truly dedicated to community engagement through publicly engaged scholarship and media work, there is much room to improve support for their scholars. I strongly encourage universities to put information regarding their protocols for supporting scholars who are harassed while doing media work in a readily accessible place on their media-relations offices' websites. Providing

21 Ketchum, "Report on the State of Resources Provided to Support Scholars Against Harassment, Trolling, and Doxxing While Doing Public Media Work and How University Media Relations Offices/ Newsrooms Can Provide Better Support," 2020, https://medium.com/@ alexandraketchum/report-on-the-state-ofresources-provided-to-support-scholars-against-harassment-trolling-and401bed8cfbf1.

22 UMass Amherst, "When Public Engagement Comes with Public Harassment How to Prevent, Respond, and Support Faculty," May 5, 2021, https://www.umass.edu/sbs/calendar/event/when-public-engagement-comes-public-harassment-how-prevent-respond-and-support?fbclid=Iw AR2Bvwo96hsoFsrLIBouQHI43MVZ-_eLmMVj_-nAijkJcJ2aTP76ii2ekxs.

Working with Journalists and Writing Op-Eds

tips and resources for scholars beginning this work can also help guide scholars in choosing the media work they do in the first place. No scholar deserves trolling or doxxing for deciding to do public media work, and scholars who experience this harassment are not to blame. However, knowing in advance what to do in the event of a troll storm (for instance, immediately making all your social-media accounts private) can help scholars avoid some suffering. Media-relations offices can offer to deal with large waves of attacking tweets and posts for their employees. These communications officers can also document the harassment by taking screenshots, in case legal action becomes necessary. Furthermore, scholars may enter into media work with more confidence and enthusiasm if they know that resources exist to support them if something goes wrong.

While conducting this research, we were buoyed to learn that while some media-relations offices had never considered creating protocols or assembling resources in case scholars experienced harassment, some have used this project as inspiration to create these resources on their own campuses. These practices must be robust, adopted by the Tri-Council in Canada and across universities globally, as well as be adapted for each university's particular context and for the needs of individual scholars.

6.3   What Already Exists

Outside of media-relations offices, resources exist for scholars interested in doing public-facing media work. At the University of British Columbia, Okanagan, the Public Humanities Hub (PHH) initiative coordinates and amplifies the work of humanities scholars on the Okanagan campus so that colleagues across the disciplines and citizens in the Southern Interior can see what they bring to the table. Their work focuses on public scholarship more broadly for the humanities. The PHH is a three-year pilot project established in 2019 at the University of British Columbia's Vancouver campus. This project was created to foster and support collaborative research at UBC-V, and to highlight and develop public-facing research in the humanities in arts, law, and education. They also host a speaker series.

The Public Humanities at Western University, housed within the Faculty of Arts and Humanities, is a program designed to promote innovative forms of public scholarship, experiential learning, and community collaboration. These programs are laudable, however, they are limited in their scope. They are directed primarily at scholars in the humanities, and do not address the concerns of scholars in the sciences, social sciences, and other faculties. Even if the topic of harassment is raised at a public-humanities event, these hubs are not responsible for scholars if they are trolled, doxxed, or harassed. Furthermore, media-relations offices do not necessarily know about these public-humanities hubs. When asked about support offered to scholars experiencing trolling, doxxing, or harassment while doing media work, a representative from the UBC Media Relations Office responded that they had no resources on their campus. It is not surprising: offices, programs, and departments within universities often exist within

Working with Journalists and Writing Op-Eds 303

siloes. Public scholarship, especially public media work, requires collaboration across the university—especially if universities want to actually support the scholars doing this work.

Outside of media-relations offices, there are other resources that are not directed specifically at scholars but can still be useful. Femtechnet provides resources for both survivors of this violence and employers who aim to support them.[23] Geek Feminism provides advice to survivors of trolling.[24] Crash Override provides additional support.[25] Although most advice is targeted at individuals, universities can assist scholars in undertaking necessary steps to mitigate these situations. While historically most scholars have faced this work alone, or with the help of a few peers, universities must assist their employees.

7 Op-Ed Writing

"Opposite of the editorial page" pieces, known more commonly as "op-eds," are short articles typically published by a newspaper or magazine, which express the opinions of authors unaffiliated with the publication's editorial board.

---

23 Femtechnet, "About," 2019, http://femtechnet.org/csov/.
24 Geek Feminism, "Mitigating Internet Trollstorms," 2019, https:// geekfeminism.wikia.org/ wiki/Mitigating internet trollstorms.
25 Crash Override Network, "About," 2019, http://www. crashoverridenetwork.com/contact. html.

Engage in Public Scholarship! 304

There is a lot of advice available about writing op-eds. Your university media-relations office or writing centre likely offers workshops on op-ed writing, or at least has a web page dedicated to the topic. As Duke University's communications office states, if you have an interesting opinion that you can share "persuasively in an op-ed article, you may reach millions of people, sway hearts, change minds and perhaps even reshape public policy. In the process, you may also earn recognition for yourself and your department, all for less effort than it takes to write a professional journal article."[26] DeWitt Scott echoes this sentiment, writing, "while scholarly publications are very valuable and necessary, the impact they have outside of the academy is questionable ... we owe it to society to find ways for our work to reach broader publics. One way to do this is to engage in op-ed writing."[27] Op-eds are a great opportunity to communicate with the public about a current event that relates to your research.

It is important to situate your op-ed with current events and the news cycle. If a space launch or an election is happening next week, submit your piece a few days in advance. Be aware of upcoming days in the calendar such as Black History Month, Pride Month, a national holiday, Indigenous Peoples' Day, and so forth. Is it the 200th anniversary of a piece of legislation passing or the publication of an important text? Tying your piece into a set date enables editors to plan the

---

26 Duke Communicator Toolkit, "Writing Effective Op-Eds," 2020, https://commskit.duke.edu/writing-media/writing-effective-op-eds/.
27 DeWitt Scott, "Op-Eds vs Scholarly Journals," *Inside Higher Ed,* November 8, 2015.

Working with Journalists and Writing Op-Eds 305

story in advance and does what is known as creating "a fresh news peg." In sum, think intentionally about the timing of your op-ed.

There are certain structural rules that you need to follow. Keep it under 750 words. Op-eds require you to make your arguments in a succinct manner. You need to hook your readers into the piece quickly, making your main point at the top. Avoid jargon and technical terms—you are targeting your piece at a wide readership. Reduce clutter. Concise and poignant sentences are key. Shorter paragraphs that pack a punch are critical. The newspaper will come up with its own headline to the piece, although you can suggest one. This suggestion may be ignored, but it is worth asking. Be prepared to offer images, illustrations, photos, or another graphic that might accompany the piece.

Look at the requirements of the place you are hoping to publish. While big name papers such as *The New York Times* receive hundreds of op-ed queries a week, your op-ed might make more sense in a local paper. Think about the audience that will benefit the most from hearing your argument. Just as when you look at a journal's requirements in advance of writing an academic journal article, there are benefits in knowing a newspaper's requirements ahead of time. Do not be discouraged if your first-choice paper is not interested in the piece. You might have to pitch it to multiple papers. However, all op-ed work should be submitted to a single news outlet at a time. Do not send the piece to another paper until you have been declined.

Engage in Public Scholarship! 306

An op-ed is not a descriptive news story, it is your opinion—usually stating a point of view about how to improve matters. It is your job to convince readers why they should care about the subject matter. The University of Waterloo's communications office suggests writing in a traditional three-point essay style. Begin with a news hook, explain your thesis succinctly, and set out your argument in three points.[28] Use stats and evidence as much as you can. Include consideration of an opposing viewpoint or opinion—this is known as the "to be sure" paragraph.[29] Writing a paragraph like this anticipates and preempts objections. Finish with a paragraph that acknowledges any flaws in your argument or obvious criticisms, and follow with a strong conclusion linking back to your lead. A letter to the editor may be a more effective format if you are interested in writing an in-depth rebuttal to another piece published by the newspaper.

A few final details can be the key to success. Harvard University's Kennedy School Communications Program offers a checklist of final things to consider before submitting the piece: check clarity; make sure that you have coherence and unity; check the level of simplicity; check voice and tone (most are conversational, while some require an authoritative voice); confirm direct quotations and paraphrasing for accuracy; make sure you properly credit

---

28 University of Waterloo, University Communications, "How to Write an Effective Op Ed," 2020, https://uwaterloo.ca/university-communications/media- relations/faculty-and-staff/speaking-media/op-eds.

29 McGill Media Relations Office, "Op-ed Writing Tips," *McGill Newsroom,* 2020, https://www.mcgill.ca/newsroom/faculty/op-ed.

Working with Journalists and Writing Op-Eds 307

all sources (though formal citations are not necessary); and confirm the consistency of your opinion throughout your op-ed or column.[30] The editing turnaround is going to be much, much faster than at an academic journal. Media outlets will often want to edit or condense your copy. Always include your full contact details—including a mobile phone number, if possible.

There is a lack of diversity in the op-ed opinions that are shared. The OpEd Project is a social venture founded to increase the range of voices and quality of ideas we hear in the world.[31] They focus primarily on increasing the number of women thought-leaders in key commentary forums, and offer helpful tips and guidance on op-ed writing. Consider writing op-eds, especially if you are an underrepresented voice in mainstream media. Your media-relations office will likely offer suggestions about where to submit the piece and may be willing to look at it in advance.

Op-eds are, of course, not the only kind of pieces that scholars write for newspapers and magazines. Writing for these publications provides many benefits but it is important to note that when scholars elect to write for outlets at below market rates or for free, they may unintentionally undercut journalists. Writer Tim Maughan tweeted, "Dear academic

---

30 Harvard Kennedy School Communications Program, "How to Write an Op-Ed," *Harvard Kennedy School,* 2020, https://projects.iq.harvard.edu/files/hks-communications-program/files/newseglinhowto write an oped125177.pdf.

31 The Op-Ed Project, "About the Op-Ed Project," 2020, https://www.theopedproject.org.

friends: I know I've been saying this for years, but PLEASE think hard before agreeing to write for far less money than your professional writer/journalist colleagues need and expect. Especially now, when outlets are sacking those writers and editors."[32] Scholars may be unaware of freelancer rates, and by accepting lower pay they may drive down the prices outlets will pay for writing.[33] To engage in accessible scholarship while working in solidarity with journalists, it is useful to research publications' piece rates. Before publishing with a particular outlet, consider first checking the website, Who Pays Writers?, which is an anonymous, crowd-sourced list of what various publications pay freelancers.[34]

8   Conclusion

Doing media work as a scholar has multiple benefits for your scholarship and for society, but there are challenges. Media informed by expertise can work to combat the epidemic of fake news. Doing media work translates research for the public. Media work requires a skill set that you will develop over time. Most of the challenges, such as trolling, doxxing, and harassment,

---

32   Tim Maughan (@timmaughn), "Dear academic friends," Twitter, March 31, 2021, 1:47 PM, https://twitter.com/ timmaughan/ status/1377316682474139654.
33   I am grateful to an anonymous peer reviewer for making this point.
34   Who Pays Writers?, "About," 2021, http://whopayswriters.com/#/about.

Working with Journalists and Writing Op-Eds   309

that can accompany this work are currently experienced on the individual level. If universities are serious about encouraging their scholars to do media work, they must develop internal policies and procedures to support scholars in this work and combat harassment.

CHAPTER 13
Conclusion

Guided by feminist, social-justice, and disability-justice studies, this book addresses the challenges of creating accessible scholarship and functions as a guidebook for engaging in public scholarship. While advocating for scholars to undertake public-facing work, this book confronts the oversimplified narratives surrounding this endeavour and provides practical strategies. Employing a feminist approach, this volume takes seriously the class, gender, racial, sexual orientation, and disability of scholars. Such consideration is necessary when so much research dissemination and analysis occurs online and through social media, where harassment and threats can be rampant. The kind of work produced by a scholar also impacts how their audience accesses it. As a result, this book examines the power dynamics that affect who is able to create certain kinds of academic work and for whom these outputs are accessible. The environmental, social, and economic conditions in which scholars are presently

Conclusion

working, marked by digital technologies and climate change, matter. This book is guided by the idea that "how we do the work IS the work."[1]

We have witnessed an increased interest in circulating the results of research in the social sciences and humanities more broadly throughout society. With an increase of platforms for communication, there have been appeals from universities and funding committees to engage more with the public. Researchers at Simon Fraser University have likewise shown that the public has a stated desire to access university knowledge, and to learn more from university researchers.[2] In the post-truth era, it is all the more important to hear from specialists with a depth of thought and substantiated arguments.

With funding committees placing a greater emphasis on public scholarship, scholars in the humanities and social sciences need resources on how to actually do public-facing work. This push for accessibility and public communication has been especially evident when considering publicly funded research, with mandates of public dissemination from the Social Science and Humanities Research Council of Canada and the Andrew W. Mellon Foundation. However, while dissemination of research sounds inherently good, we need to think more thoroughly about what this entails and what public

---

1   Azooz (@AzzaAlt), "This. My friend Dessa always says: how we do the work IS the work," Twitter, November 12, 2020, 8:02 AM, https://twitter.com/Azza Alt/status/ 1326873047836618752.

2   Fleerackers and Albrecht, "You-niversity?"

Engage in Public Scholarship! 312

communication truly looks like. This book has assembled these important issues into a single, open-access volume.

Public scholarship is important. It is also scholarship. Full stop. Conservative definitions of what counts as scholarship contribute to the sentiment that academia is irrelevant. Public scholarship and research communication outside of peer-reviewed scholarly journals is not additive but is vital and central to our work as scholars. If scholarship is truly about education, by undertaking feminist and accessible public scholarship we are positioned to meet our audiences and communities inside and outside of the university context.

There are many ways to engage in public scholarship and research communication, as explored throughout this book. These strategies range from creating websites, zines, podcasts, and books, to working with journalists and organizing events. Depending on the audiences you aim to reach, your decisions will vary. You do not have to employ all these methods at once. This book seeks to present a variety of techniques in order to inspire your research communication.

This book provides a framework, but it is only the beginning. Accessibility and inclusion are not merely checklists. As Sean Lee, director of programming at Tangled Art + Disability, argues, this work of promoting access will not end.[3] We must

---

3 Hannah McGregor (host), "Secret Feminist Agenda and Sean Lee: Disability Art is the Last Avant Garde," *Secret Feminist Agenda* (podcast), June 12, 2020, https://secretfeministagenda.com/2020/06/12/ episode-4-22-disability-art-is-the-last-avant-garde-with-sean-lee/.

Conclusion 313

continue to adapt to new circumstances, new technologies, and new community needs. While the underlying argument of this book will remain relevant, as digital technologies continue to evolve and as media changes, future tactics and forms of public scholarship may change.

The book demonstrates that (a) public scholarship is necessary and needed, (b) there are often unrecognized challenges, and (c) there are solutions to move forward and make public scholarship a more accessible endeavour for the public and scholars alike. This project provides the framework to allow us to rethink credentials and conventions and establish new adjudicative criteria for the success of newer forms of media, while remaining acutely aware of the risks that marginalized scholars experience while undertaking public engagement. When our commitments shift from the work institutions acknowledge as scholarship to the work we believe in, we become better scholars, researchers, and educators.

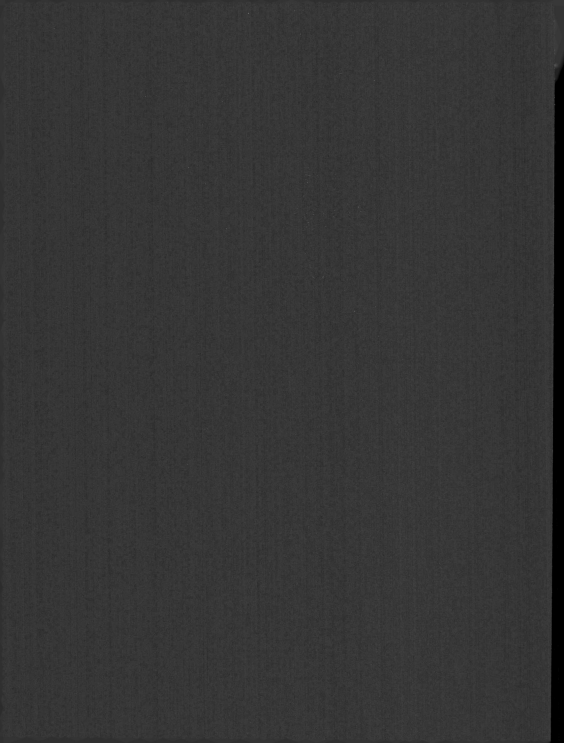

ACKNOWLEDGEMENTS

No acknowledgement section could fully encapsulate my gratitude for the people whose scholarship, art, activism, pedagogy, and ways of being in the world have inspired me. Thank you to everyone who made this book possible.

Everything that we do is tied to the land. I wrote most of this book while living in Tiohtià:ke (Montreal) on unceded Kanien'kehà:ka territory. These lands and waterways have also been a homeland and gathering place for many, including the Wendat, Abenaki, and Anishinaabeg peoples. I am grateful to the stewards of the land and waters from which I eat and drink. I also want to acknowledge and thank the people of the many lands that hold the servers enabling my research and writing, and the minerals that formed my technological devices.[1] I thank the Tongva and Kizh people of Southern California who are custodians of the lands on which I was born and raised. As this book seeks to draw attention to power relations that have been invisibilized, it is important to acknowledge both Canada's and the United States' long colonial histories and current political practices. Interwoven with this ongoing history of colonization is one of enslavement and racism. I wrote this book while employed

---

1   Thank you to Skawenatti and Jason Edward Lewis for sharing your "Thanksgiving Address: Greetings from a Technological World," in which you modelled how to thank our technological devices. (Skawenatti and Jason Edward Lewis, "Thanksgiving Address: Greetings to the Technological World," 2002, https://www.obxlabs.net/shows/thanksgivingaddress/.)

by McGill University, a university whose namesake, James McGill, enslaved Black and Indigenous peoples. It was in part from the money he acquired through these violent acts that McGill University was founded. These histories and continued injustices inform the conversations within this text. Let us strive for respectful relationships with all the peoples of this land so that we can work towards collective healing and true reconciliation.

I want to thank my editors, Ryan Van Huijstee and Meredith Carruthers. Your encouraging feedback throughout the process of creating this book has led to one of the most positive writing experiences that I have ever had. I admire and am grateful to have benefited from your collaborative editorial approach. Thank you to Geoffrey Little of Concordia University Press who first approached me with the idea to transform my work convening Disrupting Disruptions: The Feminist and Accessible Publishing, Communications, and Technologies Speaker and Workshop Series into a book.

Many of the ideas that inspired the creation of this book originated from Disrupting Disruptions. As of November 2021, the series has included forty-nine live and virtual events on a variety of topics relating to the themes named in the title. This series has been made possible by two generous Connection Grants from the Social Sciences and Humanities Research Council of Canada (#611-2018-0517 and #1003-2019-0516). I want to heartily thank all the speakers for your inspiring work and presentations. Thank you to (in order of appearance) Astra Taylor, Shawn Newman, Kristen Hogan, Suzanne Kite, Rumman Chowdhury, Mimi Onuoha, Sarah

Acknowledgements 317

Myers West, Hannah McGregor, Ashley Fortier, Oliver Fugler, Jenn Riley, Jessica Lange, Lauren Klein, Cait McKinney, Ruha Benjamin, Anna Sigrithur, Corina MacDonald, Meredith Whittaker, Yuan Stevens, Rackeb Tesfaye, Shalini Kantayaa, Jess McLean, Alice Wong, Meredith Broussard, Joy Lisi Rankin, Sasha Costanza-Chock, Deb Raji, Elinor Carmi, Caroline Sinders, Chancey Fleet, Ana Brandusescu, Keoni Mahelona, Peter-Lucas Jones, Morgan Klaus Scheuerman, Stephanie Dinkins, Rose Eveleth, Kate Crawford, Claire Evans, Moya Bailey, MC Forelle, Caroline Running Wolf, Michael Running Wolf, Alessandra Renzi, Diane DeChief, Julie Podmore, Elspeth Brown, Yuriko Furuhata, and Jennifer Lundquist. I also want to thank Amy Buckland, Stéphanie Dufresne, Zoe Wake Hyde, and Corina MacDonald for speaking at an event on publishing prior to the launch of this speaker series. Thank you to everyone who attended the events, asked questions, and learned with us.

In addition to the Social Sciences and Humanities Research Council of Canada and the funding for Digital Citizen Research, I am grateful to the other sponsors of the speaker series. Thank you to the Institute for Gender, Sexuality, and Feminist Studies of McGill, Milieux of Concordia University, the Initiative for Indigenous Futures, the Algorithmic Media Observatory and Machine Agencies, MILA of Université de Montréal, Cinema Politica, Réseau Québécois en Études Féministes, MUTEK IMG, McGill's Department of History and Classical Studies, the Black Feminist Futures Working Group, the Moving Image Research Laboratory, the Intersectionality Research Hub, McGill's Writing Centre, the Sustainability Projects Fund, Media@McGill,

L'Euguélionne: Montreal's Feminist Bookstore, Element AI, the William Dawson Scholar Fund, and the Digital Initiatives Department of the McGill University Library. Without your financial and in-kind support, I would have never been able to bring these speakers together.

This book was made possible through a Social Sciences and Humanities Research Council of Canada Insight Grant (#435-2020-0228) and the Tri-Council COVID-19 Fund. With this grant money I was able to employ a fantastic team of research assistants who have touched this project in numerous ways. Thank you to Sophie Ogilvie-Hanson, Kari Kuo, Amy Edward, Adi Sneg, Nina Morena, Meera Raman, Hana Darling-Wolf, Dominique Grégoire, Thai Hwang J, Charlene A. Lewis-Sutherland, Astrid Mohr, and Mohammed Odusanya. It has been wonderful to collaborate with all of you and build the Just Feminist Tech and Scholarship Lab.

My work would not be possible without the support of Kim Reany and Andrew Folco at the Institute for Gender, Sexuality, and Feminist Studies. Thank you both for all your help in processing paperwork, speaker fees, research assistant contracts, and so much more. Since 2018, I have been the Faculty Lecturer of the IGSF and have been the only full-time faculty member for the Gender, Sexuality, Feminist, and Social Justice Studies undergraduate program and the Women's and Gender Studies Graduate Option. In this contingent role, each year I have taught four courses in the fall semester and three courses in the winter semester. Writing this book with such a heavy teaching load would not have been possible without the administrative support

Acknowledgements

319

of Kim and Andrew. Thank you also to my fellow non-tenure-track colleagues at the IGSF: Dayna McLeod, Pascale Graham, Yolanda Muñoz, Vanessa Blais-Tremblay, Rachel Sandwell, and Suzanne Kite. It has been a pleasure to learn from you.

Thank you to Alanna Thain and Carrie Renschler of the IGSF for your continual support of my career and scholarship. Thank you to the interim IGSF directors Miranda Hickman and Natalie Stoljar for writing letters of support. Thank you to my former PhD supervisor Suzanne Morton and committee members Natalie Cooke and Jarrett Rudy. Thank you also to Stefanie Duguay and Shanon Fitzpatrick for your encouragement.

I appreciate the generous and constructive feedback of my peer reviewers. Thank you for taking the time to fully engage with my writing. Each time I returned to your reader reports while making my revisions, I was filled with gratitude and excitement. Thank you, Cheryl E. Ball, for your faith in what this book could become.

I am grateful for my invitation to participate in the Artist's Almanac Private Workshop on November 7, 2020, organized by the Feminist Media Studio, Alisha B. Wormsley, Suzanne Kite, Lindsay Nixon, and Lupe Pérez. Thank you to the co-participants Tomislav Medak, Valeria Graziano, Janelle Kasperski, Diane Roberts, Sebastian Aubin, Lucas Larochelle, Ladan Siad, Jesse Katabarwa, Venessa Appiah, Rudi Aker, Adrienne Huard, and Asinnajaq. Those conversations impacted my thinking about chapter eight.

Engage in Public Scholarship!   320

Thank you also to the Critical Archivists Group and Grant Hurley for inviting me to discuss my work. I appreciate the feedback you provided on digital-preservation practices.

Thank you to my collaborators on my public-scholarship projects. Our work together encouraged me to write this book. Thank you to Carolynn McNally for your suggestion in 2013 to make The Historical Cooking Project a website. Thank you also to Kathleen Gudmundsson and Emili Bellefleur for joining me on my first large online public-scholarship project and working to make food history more accessible. Thank you to the numerous archivists, librarians, and former owners and patrons of feminist restaurants whose generosity enabled my ability to create The Feminist Restaurant Project. Thank you to Maya Hey for your partnership on Food, Feminism, and Fermentation. Thank you, Microcosm Publishing, for publishing my work as zines/bookettes. My zine "How to Organize Inclusive Events" grew to become chapter eleven of this book. Thank you to the feminist and LGBTQ+ independent bookstores L'Euguélionne and Glad Day Books for inviting me to speak. Thank you to everyone who contributed, provided feedback, and/or interacted with these various projects.

Thank you to the authors of the books; the creators of the comics; the producers of the podcasts; the tweeters of tweets; and the teams behind the films, shows, and music that inspire me. You will find many of these names cited throughout this text.

Acknowledgements 321

Thank you to Pierre Faniel for your encouraging words and humour. Thank you to Mariel Rowe-Heupler and Taylor Hughes for your friendship. Thank you to my parents Norgene and Dan for fostering my love of books and to my late godparents Ann and Jim Denison for sharing your love of learning. To my dogs Bubbles and Sprout, thank you for reminding me what is important: walks and belly rubs.

It is because of you all that writing this book has been a joy.[2] Writing this acknowledgement section makes my heart feel full. I am so fortunate to benefit from such generous support, encouragement, and community.

2   Scholar and activist Angela Y. Davis once stated that "Outrage is not the only emotion that political people should experience. Joy is a political emotion ... If one is going to engage in this collective struggle over a period of years and decades, one must find ways to imagine a much more capacious political self" (Angela Davis and Tony Platt, "Interview with Angela Davis," p. 52).

BIBLIOGRAPHY

Alperin, Juan P., Carol Muñoz Nieves, Lesley A. Schimanski, Gustavo E. Fischman, Meredith T. Niles, and Erin C. McKiernan. "Meta-Research: How Significant Are the Public Dimensions of Faculty Work in Review, Promotion and Tenure Documents?" *ELife* 8 (2019): e42254.

Amrute, Sareeta. "Of Techno-Ethics and Techno-Affects." *Feminist Review* 123, no. 1 (2019): 56–73.

Anne, Kirk, Tara Carlisle, Quinn Dombrowski, Erin Glass, Tassie Gniady, Jason Jones, and J. Sipher. "Building Capacity for Digital Humanities: A Framework for Institutional Planning." Educause Center for Analysis and Research working group paper. Louisville, CO: ECAR (May 2017).

Ashok, Apurva, and Zoe Hyde. *The Rebus Guide to Publishing Open Textbooks (So Far).* Montreal: Rebus, 2020. https://press.rebus. community/the-rebus-guide-topublishing-open-textbooks/.

Avila, Ernie C, and Mary Kris S Lavadia. "Investigation of the Acceptability and Effectiveness of Academic Podcasts to College Students' Scholastic Performance in Science." *Indian Journal of Science and Technology* 12, no. 34 (2019): 1–8.

Bailey, Moya. "#transform(ing) DH Writing and Research: An Autoethnography of Digital Humanities and Feminist Ethics." *DHQ: Digital Humanities Quarterly* 9, no. 2 (2015).

Barker, Derek. "The Scholarship of Engagement: A Taxonomy of Five Emerging Practices." *Journal of Higher Education Outreach and Engagement* 9 no. 2 (2004): 123–137.

Barry, Lynda. *Making Comics.* Montréal: Drawn & Quarterly, 2020.

Barry, Lynda. *Syllabus: Notes from an Accidental Professor.* Montréal: Drawn & Quarterly, 2014.

Bath, Jon. "Artistic Research Creation for Publicly Engaged Scholarship." *KULA: Knowledge Creation, Dissemination, and Preservation Studies* 3 no. 1 (2019): 1–6.

Beer, David. "Productive Measures: Culture and Measurement in the Context of Everyday Neoliberalism." *Big Data & Society* 2 no. 1 (2015): 1–12.

Benjamin, Ruha, ed. *Captivating Technology: Race, Carceral Technoscience, and Liberatory Imagination in Everyday Life.* Durham: Duke University Press, 2019.

Benjamin, Ruha. *Race After Technology: Abolitionist Tools for the New Jim Code.* John Wiley & Sons, 2019.

Benkler, Yochai, Rob Faris, Hal Roberts, and Nikki Bourassa. "Understanding Media and Information Quality in an Age of Artificial Intelligence, Automation, Algorithms and Machine Learning." *Berkman Klein Center for Internet and Society at Harvard University,* July 12, 2018. https://cyber.harvard.edu/story/2018-07/understanding-media-and-information-quality-age-artificial-intelligence-automation.

Bennett, Cynthia L., and Os Keyes. "What Is the Point of Fairness? Disability, AI and the Complexity of Justice." In *ASSETS 2019 Workshop—AI Fairness for People with Disabilities.* Sig Access Newsletter, no. 125 (2019). http://www.sigaccess.org/newsletter/2019-10/bennet.html.

Bergstrom, Theodore C., Paul N. Courant, R. Preston McAfee, and Michael A. Williams. "Evaluating Big Deal Journal Bundles." *Proceedings of the National Academy of Sciences* 111, no. 26 (2014): 9425–9430.

Björk, Bo-Christer, and David Solomon. "How Research Funders Can Finance APCs in Full OA and Hybrid Journals." *Learned Publishing* 27, no. (2014): 93–103.

Boler, Megan, and Elizabeth Davis, eds. *Affective Politics of Digital Media: Propaganda by Other Means.* Abingdon: Routledge, 2020.

Bornmann, Lutz. "Do Altmetrics Point to the Broader Impact of Research? An Overview of Benefits and Disadvantages of Altmetrics." *Journal of Informetrics* 8 no. 4 (2014): 895–903.

Boyd, Danah M., and Nicole B. Ellison. "Social Network Sites: Definition, History, and Scholarship." *Journal of Computer-Mediated Communication* 13 no. 1 (2007): 210–230.

Bridger, Jeffrey C., and Theodore R. Alter. "The Engaged University, Community Development, and Public Scholarship." *Journal of Higher Education Outreach and Engagement* 11, no. 1 (2007): 163–178.

Brock Jr., André. *Distributed Blackness: African American Cybercultures.* NYU Press, 2020.

Brock Jr., André. "From the Blackhand Side: Twitter as a Cultural Conversation." *Journal of Broadcasting & Electronic Media* 56, no. 4 (2012): 529–549.

Broussard, Meredith. *Artificial Unintelligence: How Computers Misunderstand the World.* Cambridge: MIT Press, 2018.

Bibliography

Brown, Elspeth H., and Sara Davidmann. "'Queering the Trans Family Album': Elspeth H. Brown and Sara Davidmann, in Conversation." *Radical History Review* 122 (2015): 188–200.

Brown, Leslie Allison, and Susan Strega, eds. *Research as Resistance: Critical, Indigenous and Anti-Oppressive Approaches.* Canadian Scholars' Press, 2005.

Brown, Susan, Patricia Clements, Isobel Grundy, Stan Ruecker, Jeffery Antoniuk, and Sharon Balazs. "Published Yet Never Done: The Tension Between Projection and Completion in Digital Humanities Research." *Digital Humanities Quarterly* 3, no. 2 (2009).

Buchanan, Sarah A. "Curation as Public Scholarship: Museum Archaeology in a Seventeenth-Century Shipwreck Exhibit." *Museum Worlds* 4, no. 1 (2016): 155–166.

Buckland, Amy, Martin Paul Eve, Graham Steel, Jennifer Gardy, and Dorothea Salo. "On the Mark? Responses to a Sting." *Journal of Librarianship and Scholarly Communication* 2, no. 1 (2013): eP1116–1.

Carter, Angela M. "Teaching with Trauma: Trigger Warnings, Feminism, and Disability Pedagogy." *Disability Studies Quarterly* 35, no. 2 (2015): https://dsq-sds.org/article/view/4652/3935.

Carter, Jeff, and Mike Markel. "Web Accessibility for People with Disabilities: An Introduction for Web Developers." *IEEE Transactions on Professional Communication* 44, no. 4 (2001): 225–233.

Chakravartty, Paula, Rachel Kuo, Victoria Grubbs, and Charlton McIlwain. "#CommunicationSoWhite." *Journal of Communication* 68, no. 2 (2018): 254–266.

Chapman, Amy L., and Christine Greenhow. "Citizen-Scholars: Social Media and the Changing Nature of Scholarship." *Publications* 7, no. 1 (2019): 1–9.

Charlton, James I. *Nothing About Us Without Us: Disability Oppression and Empowerment.* Berkeley: University of California Press, 2000.

Chenier, Elise. "Reclaiming the Lesbian Archives." *The Oral History Review* 43, no. 1 (2016): 170–182.

Chun, Dorothy M., and Irene Thompson. "Issues in Publishing an Online, Open-Access CALL Journal." *The Modern Language Journal* 94, no. 4 (2010): 648–651.

Cifor, Marika, Michelle Caswell, Alda Allina Migoni, and Noah Geraci. "'What We Do Crosses Over to Activism': The Politics and Practice of Community Archives." *The Public Historian* 40, no. 2 (2018): 69–95.

Engage in Public Scholarship!

Cifor, Marika, and Stacy Wood. "Critical Feminism in the Archives." *Journal of Critical Library and Information Studies* 1, no. 2 (2017): 1–27.

Code, Lorraine. "Incredulity, Experientialism and the Politics of Knowledge." In *Just Methods: An Interdisciplinary Feminist Reader,* ed. Alison Jaggar, 290–302. Abingdon: Routledge, 2013.

Collins, Patricia Hill. *Black Feminist Thought: Knowledge, Consciousness, and the Politics of Empowerment.* Abingdon: Routledge, 2002.

Collins, Patricia Hill. "Learning from the Outsider Within: The Sociological Significance of Black Feminist Thought." *Social Problems* 33, no. 6 (1986): s14-s32.

Cook, Gary, and Jodie Van Horn. "How Dirty Is Your Data: A Look at the Energy Choices that Power Cloud Computing." Greenpeace Report, 2011. https://www.greenpeace.org/international/publication/7196/how-dirty-is-your-data/.

Cooper, Danielle. "Welcome Home: An Exploratory Ethnography of the Information Context at the Lesbian Herstory Archives." *Feminist and Queer Information Studies Reader* (2013): 526–541.

Copenheaver, Carolyn A., Kyrille Goldbeck, and Paolo Cherubini. "Lack of Gender Bias in Citation Rates of Publications by Dendrochronologists: What Is Unique About this Discipline?" *Tree-Ring Research* 66, no. 2 (2010): 127–133.

Costanza-Chock, Sasha. "Design Justice, AI, and Escape from the Matrix of Domination." *Journal of Design and Science* (2018). doi:10.21428/96c8d426.

Crane-Williams, Rachel. "Can You Picture This?" *Visual Arts Research* 38 no. 1 (2012): 87–98.

Crawford, Kate. *Atlas of AI.* New Haven: Yale University Press, 2021.

Crawford, Kate, and Vladan Joler. "Anatomy of an AI System: The Amazon Echo as an Anatomical Map of Human Labor, Data and Planetary Resources." *AI Now Institute and Share Lab 7* (2018). Accessed September 18, 2018, https://anatomyof.ai.

Cvetkovich, Ann. "The Queer Art of the Counterarchive." *ONE National Gay & Lesbian Archives (Hg.), Cruising the Archive: Queer Art and Culture in Los Angeles 1945–1980* (2011): 32–35.

Dahlberg, Lincoln. "The Corporate Colonization of Online Attention and the Marginalization of Critical Communication?" *Journal of Communication Inquiry* 29, no. 2 (2005): 160–180.

Bibliography

Daniels, Jessie, and Polly Thistlethwaite. *Being a Scholar in the Digital Era: Transforming Scholarly Practice for the Public Good.* Policy Press, 2016.

Davis, Angela, and Tony Platt. "Interview with Angela Davis." *Social Justice* 40, no. 1/2 (2014): 37–53.

D'Ignazio, Catherine, and Lauren Klein. *Data Feminism.* Cambridge: MIT Press, 2019.

Dobransky, Kerry, and Eszter Hargittai. "The Disability Divide in Internet Access and Use." *Information, Communication & Society* 9, no. 3 (2006): 313–334.

Duffy, Damian, Octavia E. Butler, and John Jennings. *Kindred: A Graphic Novel Adaptation.* New York: Abrams, 2017.

Edwards, Dustin W. "Digital Rhetoric on a Damaged Planet: Storying Digital Damage as Inventive Response to the Anthropocene." *Rhetoric Review* 39, no. 1 (2020): 59–72.

Eichhorn, Kate. *The Archival Turn in Feminism: Outrage in Order.* Philadelphia: Temple University Press, 2013.

Ellison, Julie and Timothy K. Eatman. "Scholarship in Public: Knowledge Creation and Tenure Policy in the Engage University." *Imagining America* 16 (2008): i–43.

Eubanks, Virginia. *Automating Inequality: How High-Tech Tools Profile, Police, and Punish the Poor.* New York: St. Martin's Press, 2018.

Eve, Martin Paul. *Open Access and the Humanities.* Cambridge: Cambridge University Press, 2014.

Faust, Jeremy S. "Sci-Hub: A Solution to the Problem of Paywalls, or Merely a Diagnosis of a Broken System?" *Annals of Emergency Medicine* 68, no. 1 (2016): 15A–17A.

Federici, Silvia. *Revolution at Point Zero: Housework, Reproduction, and Feminist Struggle.* Oakland: PM Press, 2012.

Finn, Jerry. "A Survey of Online Harassment at a University Campus." *Journal of Interpersonal Violence* 19, no. 4 (2004): 468–483.

Fleerackers, Alice, and Carina Albrecht. "You-niversity? Perceptions on the Public Effectiveness of University Knowledge Production." *Making Knowledge Public* 1 (2018). https://course-journals.lib.sfu.ca/index.php/pdc2018/article/ view/243.

Foley, Alan, and Beth A. Ferri. "Technology for People, Not Disabilities: Ensuring Access and Inclusion." *Journal of Research in Special Educational Needs* 12, no. 4 (2012): 192–200.

Friedman, Elisabeth J. *Interpreting the Internet: Feminist and Queer Counterpublics in Latin America.* Berkeley: University of California Press, 2017.

Friedman, Jane. *The Business of Being a Writer.* Chicago: University of Chicago Press, 2018.

Fuchs, Christian, and Marisol Sandoval. "The Diamond Model of Open Access Publishing: Why Policy Makers, Scholars, Universities, Libraries, Labour Unions and the Publishing World Need to Take Non-Commercial, Non-Profit Open Access Serious." *TripleC: Communication, Capitalism & Critique* 11, no. 2 (2013): 428–443.

Gagliardone, Iginio, Danit Gal, Thiago Alves, and Gabriela Martinez. *Countering Online Hate Speech.* Unesco Publishing, 2015.

Galloway, Laura. "Can Broadband Access Rescue the Rural Economy?" *Journal of Small Business and Enterprise Development* 14, no. 4 (2007): 641–653.

Germano, William. *Getting It Published: A Guide for Scholars and Anyone Else Serious about Serious Books.* Chicago: University of Chicago Press, 2016.

Gibson, William. *Neuromancer.* New York: Ace, 1984.

Goddard, Lisa, and Dean Seeman. "Building Digital Humanities Projects That Last." In *Doing More Digital Humanities: Open Approaches to Creation, Growth, and Development,* eds. Lisa Goddard and Dean Seeman, 38–57. London: Routledge: 2019.

Gold, Matthew K., and Lauren F. Klein, eds. *Debates in the Digital Humanities 2016.* Minneapolis: University of Minnesota Press, 2016.

Goodman, David, and Connie Foster. "Special Focus on Open Access: Issues, Ideas, and Impact." *Serials Review* 30, no. 4 (2004): 257.

Gray, Mary L., and Siddharth Suri. *Ghost Work: How to Stop Silicon Valley from Building a New Global Underclass.* Eamon Dolan Books, 2019.

Gribbins, Michele. "The Perceived Usefulness of Podcasting in Higher Education: A Survey of Students' Attitudes and Intention to Use." *MWAIS 2007 Proceedings* (2007): 1–8.

Groeneveld, Elizabeth. *Making Feminist Media: Third-wave Magazines on the Cusp of the Digital Age.* Waterloo: Wilfrid Laurier University Press, 2016.

Guédon, Jean-Claude. "In Oldenburg's Long Shadow: Librarians, Research Scientists, Publishers, and the Control of Scientific Publishing." In *Creating the Digital Future: Association of Research Libraries 138th Annual Meeting,* Toronto, Ontario (Canada), May 23–25, 2001.

Bibliography

Guha, Ramachandra. "Environmentalist of the Poor." *Economic and Political Weekly* 37, no. 3 (January 19–25, 2002): 204–207.

Guzmán, Rigoberto Lara, Sareeta Amrute, and Alexandra Mateescu. "How to Cite Like a Badass Tech Feminist of Color." *Data and Society: Points,* 2019. https://points.datasociety.net/how-to-cite-like-a-badass-tech-feminist-scholar-of-color-ebc839a3619c.

Haider, Jutta, and Olof Sundin. *Invisible Search and Online Search Engines: The Ubiquity of Search in Everyday Life.* Abingdon: Routledge, 2019.

Hamraie, Aimi. "Designing Collective Access: A Feminist Disability Theory of Universal Design." *Disability Studies Quarterly* 33, no. 4 (2013). https://dsq-sds.org/article/view/3871/3411.

Harmer, Emily, and Karen Lumsden. "Experiences of Online Abuse: Gendered Othering, Sexism and Misogyny." In *Online Othering: Exploring Digital Violence and Discrimination on the Web,* eds. Emily Harmer and Karen Lumsden, 117–120. New York: Springer, 2019.

Harnad, Stevan, Tim Brody, François Vallières, Les Carr, Steve Hitchcock, Yves Gingras, Charles Oppenheim, Chawki Hajjem, and Eberhard R Hilf. "The Access/Impact Problem and the Green and Gold Roads to Open Access: An Update." *Serials Review* 34, no. 1 (2008): 36–40.

Hartley, Gemma. *Fed Up: Emotional Labor, Women, and the Way Forward.* New York: Harper Collins, 2018.

Helbing, Dirk, Bruno S. Frey, Gerd Gigerenzer, Ernst Hafen, Michael Hagner, Yvonne Hofstetter, Jeroen Van Den Hoven, Roberto V. Zicari, and Andrej Zwitter. "Will Democracy Survive Big Data and Artificial Intelligence?" In *Towards Digital Enlightenment,* ed. Dirk Helbing, 73–98. New York: Springer, 2019.

Herr, Melody. *Writing and Publishing Your Book: A Guide for Experts in Every Field.* ABC-CLIO, 2017.

Hetland, Per. "Internet between Utopia and Dystopia: The Narratives of Control." *Nordicom Review* 33, no. 2 (2012): 3–15.

Hochschild, Arlie Russell. "Emotion Work, Feeling Rules, and Social Structure." *American Journal of Sociology* 85, no. 3 (1979): 551–575.

Hodson, Jaigris, Chandell Gosse, George Veletsianos, and Shandell Houlden. "I Get by with a Little Help from My Friends: The Ecological Model and Support for Women Scholars Experiencing Online Harassment." *First Monday* 23, no. 8 (2018): 1–16.

Hoffmann, Anna Lauren. "Terms of Inclusion: Data, Discourse, Violence." *New Media & Society* (September 2020). https://doi.org/10.1177/1461444820958725.

Engage in Public Scholarship!

Hofstader, Chris. "Internet Accessibility: Beyond Disability." *Computer* 37, no. 9 (2004): 103–105.

Hogan, Kristen. *The Feminist Bookstore Movement: Lesbian Antiracism and Feminist Accountability.* Durham: Duke University Press, 2016.

Hogan, Mél. "Data Flows and Water Woes: The Utah Data Center." *Big Data & Society* 2, no. 2 (2015): 2053951715592429.

Horton, Sarah, and Whitney Quesenbery. *A Web for Everyone: Designing Accessible User Experiences.* New York: Rosenfeld Media, 2014.

Imam, Talha H. "Response to the 'Open Issues with Open Access Publication.'" *The American Journal of Medicine* 126, no. 12 (2013): e43.

Jaggar, Alison M. *Just Methods: An Interdisciplinary Feminist Reader.* Abingdon: Routledge, 2015.

Joachim, Joana. "'Embodiment and Subjectivity': Intersectional Black Feminist Curatorial Practices in Canada." *RACAR: Revue d'Art Canadienne/Canadian Art Review* 43, no. 2 (2018): 34–47.

Jones, Nicola. "How to Stop Data Centres from Gobbling up the World's Electricity." *Nature* 561, no. 7722 (2018): 163–167.

Juhasz, Alexandra. "Video Remains: Nostalgia, Technology, and Queer Archive Activism." *GLQ: A Journal of Lesbian and Gay Studies* 12, no. 2 (2006): 319–328.

Kafer, Alison. *Feminist, Queer, Crip.* Bloomington: Indiana University Press, 2013.

Kempson, Michelle. "'My Version of Feminism': Subjectivity, DIY and the Feminist Zine." *Social Movement Studies* 14 no. 4 (2015): 459–472.

Ketchum, Alexandra. "Cooking the Books: Feminist Restaurant Owners' Relationships with Banks, Loans and Taxes." *Business History* (2019): 1–27. DOI: 10.1080/00076791.2019.1676233.

Ketchum, Alexandra. "Lost Spaces, Lost Technologies, and Lost People: Online History Projects Seek to Recover LGBTQ+ Spatial Histories." *DHQ: Digital Humanities Quarterly* 14, no. 3 (2020). http://www.digitalhumanities.org/dhq/vol/14/3/000483/ 000483.html.

Kite, Suzanne. "How to Build Anything Ethically." In *Indigenous Protocol and Artificial Position Paper,* ed. Jason Edward Lewis, 75–85 (2020). https://spectrum.library.concordia.ca/986506/7/Indigenous_Protocol_and_AI_2020.pdf.

Bibliography

Kuntsman, Adi, and Imogen Rattle. "Towards a Paradigmatic Shift in Sustainability Studies: A Systematic Review of Peer Reviewed Literature and Future Agenda Setting to Consider Environmental (Un) sustainability of Digital Communication." *Environmental Communication* 13, no. 5 (2019): 567–581.

Larivière, Vincent, Stefanie Haustein, and Philippe Mongeon. "The Oligopoly of Academic Publishers in the Digital Era." *PloS one* 10, no. 6 (2015): e0127502.

Lazar, Jonathan, and Paul Jaeger. "Reducing Barriers to Online Access for People with Disabilities." *Issues in Science and Technology* 27 no, 2 (2011): 69–83.

Leavy, Patricia. *Method Meets Art: Arts-Based Research Practice.* New York: Guilford Publications, 2020.

Leonard, Marion. "Exhibiting Popular Music: Museum Audiences, Inclusion and Social History." *Journal of New Music Research* 39, no. 2 (2010): 171–181.

Lewis, Jason Edward, ed. "Indigenous Protocol and Artificial Intelligence Position Paper." Honolulu, Hawai'i: The Indigenous Future and the Canadian Institution for Advanced Research (CIFAR) (2020). https://spectrum.library. concordia.ca/986506/.

Lewis, Jason Edward, Noelani Arista, Archer Pechawis, and Suzanne Kite. "Making Kin with the Machines." *Journal of Design and Science* (2018): https://doi.org/10.21428/ bfafd97b.

Lewis, Tamika, Seeta Peña Gangadharan, Mariella Saba, and Tawana Petty. *Digital Defense Playbook: Community Power Tools for Reclaiming Data.* Detroit: Our Data Bodies, 2018. https://detroitcommunitytech. org/?q=content/our-data-bodies-digital-defense-playbook.

Li, Xiaochang, and Mara Mills. "Vocal Features: From Voice Identification to Speech Recognition by Machine." *Technology and Culture* 60, no. 2 (2019): S129– S160.

Liboiron, Max, Justine Ammendolia, Katharine Winsor, Alex Zahara, Hillary Bradshaw, Jessica Melvin, Charles Mather, Natalya Dawe, Emily Wells, France Liboiron, et al. "Equity in Author Order: A Feminist Laboratory's Approach." *Catalyst: Feminism, Theory, Technoscience* 3, no. 2 (2017): 1–17.

Lorde, Audre. "Age, Race, Class, and Sex: Women Redefining Difference." In *Women in Culture: An Intersectional Anthology for Gender and Women's Studies*, ed. Bonnie Kime Scott, Susan E. Cayleff, Anne Donadey, and Irene Lara, 16–22. Hoboken: Wiley, 2014.

Luc, Jessica G.Y., Michael A. Archer, Rakesh C. Arora, Edward M. Bender, Arie Blitz, David T. Cooke, Tamara Ni Hlci, Biniam Kidane, Maral Ouzounian, Thomas K. Varghese Jr., et al. "Does Tweeting Improve Citations? One Year Results from the TSSMN Prospective Randomized Trial." *The Annals of Thoracic Surgery* 111, no. 1 (2012): 296–300.

Lund, Arwid, and Mariano Zukerfeld. "Profiting from Open Access Publishing." In *Corporate Capitalism's Use of Openness: Profit for Free?*, eds. Arwid Lund and Mariano Zukerfeld, 149–197. Basingstoke: Springer Nature, 2020.

Lupton, Deborah. *'Feeling Better Connected': Academics' Use of Social Media*. University of Canberra News Media Research Centre, 2014. https://www.canberra.edu.au/about-uc/faculties/ arts-design/ attachments2/pdf/n-and-mrc/ Feeling-Better-Connected-reportfinal.pdf.

Malakoff, David. "Opening the Books on Open Access." *Science* 302 (2003): 550–554.

Manca, Stefania, and Maria Ranieri. "Networked Scholarship and Motivations for Social Media Use in Scholarly Communication." *The International Review of Research in Open and Distributed Learning* 18, no. 2 (2017): 123–138.

Mantilla, Karla. "Gendertrolling: Misogyny Adapts to New Media." *Feminist Studies* 39, no. 2 (2013): 563–570.

Massanari, Adrienne L. "Rethinking Research Ethics, Power, and the Risk of Visibility in the Era of the 'Alt-Right' Gaze." *Social Media + Society* 4, no. 2 (2018): 2056305118768302.

Mateescu, Alexandra, and Madeleine Clare Elish. "AI in Cortext: The Labor of Integrating New Technologies." *New York: Data & Society Institute*, January 30, 2019. https:// datasociety.net/wp-content/ uploads/ 2019/01/DataandSociety AlinContext.pdf.

Matias, J. Amy Johnson, Whitney Erin Boesel, Brian Keegan, Jaclyn Friedman, and Charlie DeTar. "Reporting, Reviewing, and Responding to Harassment on Twitter." SSRN 2602018 (2015). http://womenactionmedia.org/twitter-report

Maum, Courtney. *Before and After the Book Deal: A Writer's Guide to Finishing, Publishing, Promoting, and Surviving Your First Book*. Berkeley: Catapult, 2020.

McCausland, Sigrid. "Archival Public Programming." In *Currents of Archival Thinking*, second edition, eds. Heather MacNeil and Terry Eastwood, 225–244. Santa Barbara and Denver: Libraries Unlimited, 2017.

Bibliography

McKinney, Cait. "Body, Sex, Interface: Reckoning with Images at the Lesbian Herstory Archives." *Radical History Review* no. 122 (2015): 115–128.

McKinney, Cait. "'Finding the Lines to My People': Media History and Queer Bibliographic Encounter." *GLQ: A Journal of Lesbian and Gay Studies* 24, no. 1 (2018): 55–83.

McKinney, Cait. "Printing the Network: AIDS Activism and Online Access in the 1980s." *Continuum* 32, no. 1 (2018): 7–17.

McLean, Jessica. *Changing Digital Geographies: Technologies, Environments and People.* London: Palgrave MacMillan, 2020.

McPherson, Tara. "US Operating Systems at Mid-Century: The Intertwining of Race and UNIX." In *Race after the Internet,* eds. Lisa Nakamura, Peter Chow White, 27–43. Abingdon: Routledge, 2013.

McRuer, Robert. *Crip Theory: Cultural Signs of Queerness and Disability.* New York: NYU Press, 2006.

Megarry, Jessica. "Online Incivility or Sexual Harassment? Conceptualising Women's Experiences in the Digital Age." *Women's Studies International Forum* 47 (2014): 46–55.

Mildenberger, Matto, Peter Howe, Erick Lachapelle, Leah Stokes, Jennifer Marlon, and Timothy Gravelle. "The Distribution of Climate Change Public Opinion in Canada." *PloS one* 11, no. 8 (2016): e0159774.

Mitchell, Katharyne. *Practising Public Scholarship: Experiences and Possibilities Beyond the Academy.* Hoboken: John Wiley & Sons, 2011.

Moreno, Lourdes, Paloma Martínez, and Belen Ruiz-Mezcua. "Disability Standards for Multimedia on the Web." *IEEE MultiMedia* 15, no. 4 (2008): 52–54.

Morozov, Evgeny. *The Net Delusion: How Not to Liberate the World.* London: Penguin UK, 2011.

Morris, Meredith Ringel, Jaime Teevan, and Katrina Panovich. "A Comparison of Information Seeking Using Search Engines and Social Networks." *Proceedings of Fourth International AAAI Conference on Weblogs and Social Media* 4, no. 1 (2010): 291–294.

Mountz, Alison, Anne Bonds, Becky Mansfield, Jenna Loyd, Jennifer Hyndman, Margaret Walton-Roberts, Ranu Basu, Risa Whitson, Roberta Hawkins, Trina Hamilton, et al. "For Slow Scholarship: A Feminist Politics of Resistance Through Collective Action in the Neoliberal University." *ACME: An International E-journal for Critical Geographies* 14, no. 4 (2015): 1235–1259.

Engage in Public Scholarship! 334

Mulcahy, Clare, Hannah McGregor, and Marcelle Kosman. "'Whoops I am a Lady on the Internet': Digital Feminist Counter-Publics." *Atlantis: Critical Studies in Gender, Culture & Social Justice* 38, no. 2 (2017): 134–136.

Nafus, Dawn. "'Patches Don't Have Gender': What Is Not Open in Open Source Software." *New Media & Society* 14, no. 4 (2012): 669–683.

Nafus, Dawn, James Leach, and Bernhard Krieger. "Gender: Integrated Report of Findings." Cambridge, 2006, file:///Users/alexketchum/Downloads/FLOSSPOLS-D16-Gender_Integrated_Report_of_Findings.pdf.

Newton, Hazel, Marin Dacos, Pierre Mounier, and Yrsa Neuman. "Snapshots of Three Open Access Business Models." *Insights* 27 (2014): 39–44.

Niles, Meredith T, Lesley A. Schimanski, Erin C. McKiernan, and Juan Pablo Alperin. "Why We Publish Where We Do: Faculty Publishing Values and Their Relationship to Review, Promotion and Tenure Expectations." *PloS one* 15, no. 3 (2020): e0228914.

Nixon, Rob. *Slow Violence and the Environmentalism of the Poor.* Cambridge: Harvard University Press, 2011.

Noble, Safiya Umoja. *Algorithms of Oppression: How Search Engines Reinforce Racism.* New York: NYU Press, 2018.

Norton, Penny, and Martin Hughes. *Public Consultation and Community Involvement in Planning: A Twenty-first Century Guide.* Taylor & Francis, 2017.

Novara, Elizabeth A., and Vincent J. Novara. "Exhibits as Scholarship: Strategies for Acceptance, Documentation, and Evaluation in Academic Libraries." *The American Archivist* 80, no. 2 (2017): 355–372.

O'Neil, Cathy. *Weapons of Math Destruction: How Dig Data Increases Inequality and Threatens Democracy.* New York: Broadway Books, 2017.

Onuoha, Mimi. "On Missing Datasets." In *International Workshop on Obfuscation: Science, Technology, and Theory,* 38–40. New York University, 2018. https://www.obfuscationworkshop.org/2017/10/on-missing-datasets/.

Overby, Lynnette Young. *Public Scholarship in Dance: Teaching, Choreography, Research, Service, and Assessment for Community Engagement.* Human Kinetics, 2015.

Bibliography

Panchanathan, Sethuraman, and Troy McDaniel. "Person-Centered Accessible Technologies and Computing Solutions through Interdisciplinary and Integrated Perspectives from Disability Research." *Universal Access in the Information Society* 14, no. 3 (2015): 415–426.

Parikka, Jussi, and Annika Richterich. "A Geology of Media and a New Materialism. Jussi Parikka in Conversation with Annika Richterich." *Digital Culture & Society* 1, no. 1 (2015): 213–226.

Pattabhiramaiah, Adithya, S. Sriram, and Puneet Manchanda. "Paywalls: Monetizing Online Content." *Journal of Marketing* 83, no. 2 (2019): 19–36.

Pellow, David N., and Lisa Sun-Hee Park. *The Silicon Valley of Dreams: Environmental Injustice, Immigrant Workers, and the High-tech Global Economy.* NYU Press, 2002.

Peoples, Brock, and Carol Tilley. "Podcasts as an Emerging Information Resource." *College & Undergraduate Libraries* 18, no. 1 (2011): 44–57.

Perez, Caroline Criado. *Invisible Women: Data Bias in a World Designed for Men.* New York: Abrams, 2019

Perfect, Erin, Atul Jaiswal, and T. Claire Davies. "Systematic Review: Investigating the Effectiveness of Assistive Technology to Enable Internet Access for Individuals with Deafblindness." *Assistive Technology* 31, no. 5 (2019): 276–285.

Perrin, Andrew. "Social Media Usage." *Pew Research Center* 125 (2015): 52–68. https://www.pewresearch.org/internet/2015/10/08/social-networking-usage-2005-2015/.

Pickens, Therí Alyce. *Black Madness :: Mad Blackness.* Durham: Duke University Press, 2019.

Piepzna-Samarasinha, Leah Lakshmi. *Care Work: Dreaming Disability Justice.* Vancouver: Arsenal Pulp Press, 2018.

Pinfield, Stephen. "Making Open Access Work: The 'State-of-the-Art' in Providing Open Access to Scholarly Literature." *Online Information Review* 39, no. 5 (2015): 604–636.

Pinfield, Stephen, Jennifer Salter, Peter A. Bath, Bill Hubbard, Peter Millington, Jane H.S. Anders, and Azhar Hussain. "Open-Access Repositories Worldwide, 2005–2012: Past Growth, Current Characteristics, and Future Possibilities." *Journal of the Association for Information Science and Technology* 65, no. 12 (2014): 2404–2421.

Engage in Public Scholarship!

Pinter, Frances. "Open Access for Scholarly Books?" *Publishing Research Quarterly* 28, no. 3 (2012): 183–191.

Podmore, Julie A. "Gone 'Underground'? Lesbian Visibility and the Consolidation of- Queer Space in Montréal." *Social & Cultural Geography* 7, no. 4 (2006): 595–625.

Poole, Alex H. "The Conceptual Ecology of Digital Humanities." *Journal of Documentation* 73, no. 1 (2017): 91–122.

Porter, Constance Elise, and Naveen Donthu. "Using the Technology Acceptance Model to Explain How Attitudes Determine Internet Usage: The Role of Perceived Access Barriers and Demographics." *Journal of Business Research* 59, no. 9 (2006): 999–1007.

Portwood-Stacer, Laura. *The Book Proposal Book: A Guide for Scholarly Authors.* Princeton: Princeton University Press, 2021.

Potts, Karen, and Leslie Brown. "Becoming an Anti-oppressive Researcher." In *Research as Resistance: Critical, Indigenous and Anti-oppressive Approaches,* eds Leslie Brown and Susan Strega, 255–286. Toronto: Canadian Scholars' Press/Women's Press, 2005.

Prieger, James E. "The Supply Side of the Digital Divide: Is There Equal Availability in the Broadband Internet Access Market?" *Economic Inquiry* 41, no. 2 (2003): 346–363.

Rabiner, Susan, and Alfred Fortunato. *Thinking Like Your Editor: How to Write Great Serious Nonfiction—And Get It Published.* New York: W.W. Norton & Company, 2002.

Rains, Stephen A. "Health at High Speed: Broadband Internet Access, Health Communication, and the Digital Divide." *Communication Research* 35, no. 3 (2008): 283–297.

Raji, Inioluwa Deborah, and Joy Buolamwini. "Actionable Auditing: Investigating the Impact of Publicly Naming Biased Performance Results of Commercial AI Products." In *Proceedings of the 2019 AAAI/ ACM Conference on AI, Ethics, and Society,* 429–435. Honolulu Hawai'i, January 27–28, 2019. https://doi.org/10.1145/3306618.3314244.

Rankin, Joy Lisi. *A People's History of Computing in the United States.* Cambridge: Harvard University Press, 2018.

Rhizome. *The Art Happens Here: Net Art Anthology.* Exhibition Catalogue, 2019.

Richardson, Rashida, Jason M. Schultz, and Kate Crawford. "Dirty Data, Bad Predictions: How Civil Rights Violations Impact Police Data, Predictive Policing Systems, and Justice." *NYU Law Review Online* 94 (2019): 15–55.

Roach, Audra K., and Jesse Gainer. "On Open Access to Research: The Green, the Gold, and the Public Good." *Journal of Adolescent & Adult Literacy* 56, no. 7 (2013): 530–534.

Bibliography

Rogowsky, Beth A., Barbara M. Calhoun, and Paula Tallal. "Does Modality Matter? The Effects of Reading, Listening, and Dual Modality on Comprehension." *SAGE Open* 6, no. 3 (2016): 2158244016669550.

Rouse, Julia, and Helen Woolnough. "Engaged or Activist Scholarship? Feminist Reflections on Philosophy, Accountability and Transformational Potential." *International Small Business Journal* 36, no. 4 (2018): 429–448.

Sarabipour, Sarvenaz, Humberto J. Debat, Edward Emmott, Steven J. Burgess, Benjamin Schwessinger, and Zach Hensel. "On the Value of Preprints: An Early Career Researcher Perspective." *PLoS biology* 17, no. 2 (2019): e3000151.

Sayer, Faye. *Public History: A Practical Guide.* London: Bloomsbury, 2019.

Scanlon, Eileen. "Scholarship in the Digital Age: Open Educational Resources, Publication and Public Engagement." *British Journal of Educational Technology* 45, no. 1 (2014): 12–23.

Scheuerman, Morgan Klaus, Jacob M. Paul, and Jed R. Brubaker. "How Computers See Gender: An Evaluation of Gender Classification in Commercial Facial Analysis Services." *Proceedings of the ACM on Human-Computer Interaction* 3, no. Conference on Computer-Supported Cooperative Work and Social Computing (CSCW, 2019): 1–33.

Scott, Ellen C. "Introduction: Black Images Matter: Contextualizing Images of Racialized Police Violence." *Black Camera* 9, no. 2 (2018): 76–81.

Scott, Joan W. "Experience." In *Feminists Theorize the Political,* eds. Judith Butler and Joan W. Scott, 40–58. New York: Routledge, 2013.

Shea, Neil, and Vinay Prasad. "Open Issues with Open Access Publication." *The American Journal of Medicine* 126, no. 7 (2013): 563–564.

Simplican, Stacy Clifford. "feminist disability studies as methodology: lifewriting and the abled/disabled binary." *Feminist Review* 115, no. 1 (2017): 46–60.

Sinnreich, Aram, Michelle C. Forelle, and Patricia Aufderheide. "Copyright Givers and Takers: Mutuality, Altruism and Instrumentalism in Open Licensing." *Communication Law and Policy* 23, no. 3 (2018): 197–220.

Smith, Kevin L. "Examining Publishing Practices: Moving beyond the Idea of Predatory Open Access." *Insights* 30, no. 3 (2017): 4–10.

Smithies, James, Carina Westling, Anna-Maria Sichani, Pam Mellen, and Arianna Ciula. "Managing 100 Digital Humanities Projects: Digital Scholarship and Archiving in King's Digital Lab." *Digital Humanities Quarterly* 13, no. 1 (2019): http://www.digitalhumanities.org/dhq/vol/13/1/000411/000411.html.

Sobieraj, Sarah. *Credible Threat: Attacks Against Women Online and the Future of Democracy.* Oxford: Oxford University Press, 2020.

Sommer, Bob, and John R. Maycroft. "Influencing Public Policy: An Analysis of Published Op-Eds by Academics." *Politics & Policy* 36, no. 4 (2008): 586–613.

Suber, Peter. *Open Access.* Cambridge, MA: MIT Press, 2012.

Suber, Peter. "Removing the Barriers to Research: An Introduction to Open Access for Librarians." *College & Research Libraries News* 64, no. 113 (2003): 92–94.

Sucharov, Mira. *Public Influence: A Guide to Op-Ed Writing and Social Media Engagement.* Toronto: University of Toronto Press, 2019.

Sullivan, John L. "Vincent Mosco, To the Cloud: Big Data in a Turbulent World." *International Journal of Communication* 8, no. 5 (2014): 2343–2347.

Swan, Alma, and Sheridan Brown. *Open Access Self-Archiving: An Author Study.* Technical report. UK FE and HE Funding Councils. Truro: Key Perspectives Limited, 2005.

Taylor, Astra. *Democracy May Not Exist, But We'll Miss It when It's Gone.* New York: Metropolitan Books, 2019.

Taylor, Astra. *The People's Platform: Taking Back Power and Culture in the Digital Age.* New York: Metropolitan Books, 2014.

Taylor, Linnet. "From Zero to Hero: How Zero-Rating Became a Debate about Human Rights." *IEEE Internet Computing* 20, no. 4 (2016): 79–83.

Terven, Juan R., Joaquín Salas, and Bogdan Raducanu. "New Opportunities for Computer Vision-Based Assistive Technology Systems for the Visually Impaired." *Computer* 47, no. 4 (2013): 52–58.

Tregenza, Tom. "Gender Bias in the Refereeing Process?" *Trends in Ecology & Evolution* 17, no. 8 (2002): 349–350.

Trubek, Anne. *So You Want to Publish a Book?* Cleveland: Belt Publishing, 2020.

Tuck, Eve. "Suspending Damage: A Letter to Communities." *Harvard Educational Review* 79, no. 3 (2009): 409–428.

Veletsianos, George, Nicole Johnson, and Olga Belikov. "Academics' Social Media Use Over Time Is Associated with Individual, Relational, Cultural and Political Factors." *British Journal of Educational Technology* 50, no. 4 (2019): 1713–1728.

Bibliography

Vinopal, Jennifer, and Monica McCormick. "Supporting Digital Scholarship in Research Libraries: Scalability and Sustainability." *Journal of Library Administration* 53, no. 1 (2013): 27–42.

Vinsel, Lee, and Andrew L. Russell. *The Innovation Delusion: How Our Obsession with the New Has Disrupted the Work That Matters Most.* Redfern: Currency, 2020.

Vlasschaert, Caitlyn, Joel Topf, and Swapnil Hiremath. "Proliferation of Papers and Preprints During the COVID-19 Pandemic: Progress or Problems with Peer Review?" *Advances in Chronic Kidney Disease* 27, no. 5 (2020): 418–425.

Vowel, Chelsea. "Beyond Territorial Acknowledgements." *âpihtawikosisân: law. language. culture* (blog), September 23, 2016. https://apihtawikosisan. com/2016/09/beyond-territorial-acknowledgments/

Waymer, Damion, and Robert L Heath. "Black Voter Dilution, American Exceptionalism, and Racial Gerrymandering: The Paradox of the Positive in Political Public Relations." *Journal of Black Studies* 47, no. 7 (2016): 635–658.

Weller, Martin. *The Digital Scholar: How Technology Is Transforming Scholarly Practice.* London: A&C Black, 2011.

Wernimont, Jacqueline, and Julia Flanders. "Feminism in the Age of Digital Archives: The Women Writers Project." *Tulsa Studies in Women's Literature* 29, no. 2 (2010): 425–435.

Westerman, David, Patric R. Spence, and Brandon Van Der Heide. "Social Media as Information Source: Recency of Updates and Credibility of Information." *Journal of Computer-Mediated Communication* 19, no. 2 (2014): 171–183.

Whicker, Marcia Lynn, Jennie Jacobs Kronenfeld, and Ruth Ann Strickland. *Getting Tenure.* Vol. 8. Sage, 1993.

Whitacre, Brian E., and Bradford F. Mills. "A Need for Speed? Rural Internet Connectivity and the No Access/Dial-up/High-speed Decision." *Applied Economics* 42, no. 15 (2010): 1889–1905.

Whittaker, Meredith, and Kate Crawford. *AI Now 2019 Report.* New York: AI Now Institute at New York University, 2019.

Whittaker, Meredith, and Kate Crawford, Roel Dobbe, Genevieve Fried, Elizabeth Kaziunas, Varoon Mathur, Sarah Mysers West, Rashida Richardson, Jason Schultz, and Oscar Schwartz. *AI Now 2018 Report.* New York: AI Now Institute at New York University, 2018.

Williams, Sherri. "Digital Defense: Black Feminists Resist Violence with Hashtag Activism." *Feminist Media Studies* 15, no. 2 (2015): 341–344.

Willinsky, John. *The Access Principle: The Case for Open Access to Research and Scholarship.* Cambridge: MIT Press, 2006.

Wilson-Hinds, R. "Affordability and Disability Access Technology." *International Congress Series* 1282 (2005): 1099–1102.

Wong, Alice. *Disability Visibility: First-Person Stories from the Twenty-First Century.* New York: Vintage, 2020.

Wood, Elizabeth H. "Open Access Publishing: Implications for Libraries." *Journal of Electronic Resources in Medical Libraries* 2, no. 2 (2005): 1–12.

Yates, Simeon, Elinor Carmi, Eleanor Lockley, Alicja Pawluczuk, Tom French, and Stephanie Vincent. "Who Are the Limited Users of Digital Systems and Media? An Examination of UK Evidence." *First Monday* 25, no. 7 (2020): https://firstmonday.org/ojs/index.php/fm/article/view/10847/9565.

Zhang, Ying, Shu Liu, and Emilee Mathews. "Convergence of Digital Humanities and Digital Libraries." *Library Management* 36, no. 4/5 (2015): 362–377.

Zuboff, Shoshana. *The Age of Surveillance Capitalism: The Fight for a Human Future at the New Frontier of Power.* London: Profile Books, 2019.

INDEX

abbreviations, 44. *See also* language and jargon

able-bodied privilege, 37, 48. *See also* disabled communities; power dynamics

abstracts, 102. *See also* journals, scholarly

Academia.edu, 109, 288

accents, 297. *See also* voice, politics of

accessibility: assistive technologies and, 45–49, 58; audiobooks and, 207–8; audio-visual technology and, 261–65; books and, 197; digital technologies and, 232–33; digital to physical media and, 211–12, 214–15; disability studies framework for, 38–42; events and, 243–44, 247–48, 249–54, 270, 274, 278; events online and, 245, 265, 268; financial barriers to, 25–28, 49–51, 70–73, 74; harassment online and, 55–57, 75–80; internet and, 51–55, 57; language and jargon and, 42–45, 259–61; limitations to, 37–38, 42; media outlets and, 73; monographs and, 201–2; open access and, 100–1, 116–18, 133–34; open source and, 119; overview, 4–7, 18–19, 35–37, 61; peer review and, 68–69; plain language and, 204–6; podcasts and, 188, 189–91, 193; preservation and, 223; privacy features and, 154; public scholarship and, 34, 310, 311, 312–13; for researchers, 62–63; skills of scholars and, 71–75; social media and, 74, 158–59; tenure and, 63–66, 69–70, 71; Twitter

and, 152–53; videos and, 170, 172, 177–78; websites and, 57–60, 166–67, 168–69

Accessibility for Ontarians with Disabilities Act, 249

Accessible Publishing Research Project (report), 208

Account for Labor Implications of Open Publishing, 128

acoustics, 253, 262

Affective Politics of Digital Media (Davis), 23

The Age of Surveillance Capitalism (Zuboff), 143

AI Now Institute, 7, 10, 51

algorithms: artistic works and, 210; citations and, 65; event publicity and, 276; open data and, 122; power dynamics and, 6, 13, 19, 126, 143–45, 146, 287; search engines and, 6, 287, 288

Allied Media Projects, 214–15

altmetrics, 66

alt-right groups, 76–77. *See also* post-truth era

alt-text, 158

Amazon, 142

Americans with Disabilities Act, 249. *See also* disabled communities

American Translators Association, 261. *See also* translation

Amplify Podcast Network, 179. *See also* podcasts

Amrute, Sareeta, 20, 147

Andrew W. Mellon Foundation, 88, 311

Anthrodish (podcast), 193

âpihtawikosisân (Chelsea Vowel), 255–56

Apple, 142, 239

Index

343

Apple Podcasts, 180, 187, 270
apps, 193–95
Archive-It, 229–30
Archive.org, 186
archives and archiving: digital dark ages and, 224–25; open access and, 89, 90, 94, 97, 99, 100, 103, 104; power dynamics and, 131–32, 230–32; preservation and, 219, 227, 228, 233–35; public scholarship and, 218; repositories and, 105, 106; websites and, 166
Are.na, 212
art, 64, 201–3, 209–11, 214, 228–29, 233, 271
Artbase, 168. *See also* open data
article processing charges, 89, 90, 95–96, 98–99. *See also* journals, scholarly
artificial intelligence (AI), 10, 12–13, 144–46, 210, 214. *See also* data and data sets
ASP.NET, 165
assistive technologies, 45–49, 58, 168, 270
Association of Canadian Publishers, 207–8
Association of Visual Language Interpreters of Canada, 261. *See also* interpreters
Audacity, 185, 269
audiences, 31–32, 34, 36–37, 138, 197, 312
audiobooks, 207–8
Audiobooks: Building Capacity (report), 208
audio editing, 180, 181, 183, 185–86. *See also* recording
audio streams, 269. *See also* events
audio-visual technologies, 173, 261–65
auto-translation, 262–63. *See also* translation
Azooz, 311

Bailey, Moya, 45, 116
Bandcamp, 187, 270

Barnard College Zine Library, 199
Barry, Lynda, 202
Bath, Jon, 16, 209
bathrooms, 253–54. *See also* events
Bello Collective, 190–91
Benjamin, Ruha, 42, 70, 146, 286
Berkmen Klein Center for Internet and Society, 145
Berners-Lee, Tim, 59
bibliometrics, 64–66. *See also* tenure and promotion
Big Data, 19, 121–22, 126, 146. *See also* data and data sets
Bindery.js, 212
Black communities, 30, 53, 125, 132, 150, 158. *See also* people of colour
Black Open Access, 110. *See also* openness and open access
Black Twitter, 30, 150
Blender, 174. *See also* videos
Blind communities: accessibility and, 43; assistive technologies and, 47–48; audiobooks and, 207; events and, 259–60, 261, 262, 263; internet access and, 58; public scholarship and, 4, 5, 45–46; social media and, 158; web design and, 168
Blogger, 163–64, 286
blogs, 163–64, 169
Bluejeans, 267–68. *See also* events
Blue Yeti Mic, 185. *See also* recording
Bookcase Credibility, 294
bookettes, 199–200
book processing charges, 113. *See also* article processing charges
The Book Proposal Book (Portwood-Stacer), 197
books and monographs, 111–14, 197–98, 201–2, 212, 233, 280
bookstores, 5, 245, 250
breastfeeding, 254
British Library, 225
broadband, 52–55, 180. *See also* internet

Engage in Public Scholarship! 344

Broad Science (Tesfaye), 31
Brock, André, 30, 150
Broussard, Meredith, 13, 50, 240
Brown, Leslie, 20, 33, 44–45
Brown, Lydia X.Z., 38, 42, 244
Brown, Susan, 218–19, 228
browsers, web, 108, 142, 164, 175, 176. *See also* websites
Budapest Open Access Initiative, 88–89, 99, 100. *See also* openness and open access

Canadian Academic Research Libraries (CARL), 105
Canadian Association of University Teachers, 106
Canadian Centre for Occupational Health and Safety (CCOHS), 78
Canadian Copyright Act, 176–77. *See also* copyright
Canadian Deafblind and Rubella Association (CDRA), 261
Canadian Hearing Society, 261
Canadian National Research Councils, 11, 14, 26, 87, 122–23, 248, 272, 311
Canadian Translators, Terminologists and Interpreters Council, 260
capitalism, 143, 237, 241
captioning, 172, 177–78, 260, 261, 262–63, 267, 268, 269
cartoons, 201–3, 214. *See also* art
Cascading Style Sheets (CSS), 164n6, 165, 212
cellular phones, 173, 180, 184
census data, 125. *See also* data and data sets
chains of access, 211, 212. *See also* accessibility
Chapman, Amy, 28, 29–30, 161
"Checklist for Planning Accessible Conferences," 246
childcare, 247, 248–49. *See also* events
chronological writing, 206. *See also* plain language

Chun, Dorothy, 101, 102, 103
citational practices, 20–21, 65, 190, 198, 264, 306–7
citizen-scholars, 28, 30
class: accessibility and, 17, 61, 62; data and, 146, 287; design justice and, 40, 41; digital technologies and, 12, 147, 237–38; events and, 257, 271; feminism and, 9; internet access and, 52–54, 55; journals and, 49–51; open access and, 132, 133; public scholarship and, 3, 18, 310; and voice, politics of, 297; websites and, 57–58
Cleveland Historical, 194
climate change. *See* environmental impact
coding, 120, 164, 165, 166, 167–68, 176, 195, 221
ColdFusion (CFML), 165. *See also* websitesColeman, Gabriella, 216
collaboration, 74, 161, 167, 168, 169–70, 202–3
Collective for Liberation, Ecology, and Technology (COLET), 132
Collins, Patricia Hill, 20, 32–33
colonization, 255–56. *See also* power dynamics
comics, 201–3, 214. *See also* art
Common Gateway Interface, 165
Communication Partnership for Science and the Sea (COMPASS), 15
communication strategies. *See* public scholarship toolkits
community archives, 230–32. *See also* archives and archiving
community centres, 245, 250
conferences. *See* events
content and trigger warnings, 139–41
Contois, Emily, 153, 169
conversion, file, 175–76
copyright: digital preservation and, 229; open access and, 88, 96–97, 101, 104, 106, 111; open data and, 121; podcasts and, 186; press

Index

kits and, 289; repositories and, 109; social media and, 149; social networking and, 288; videos and, 176–77

Cornell University, 224, 246–47

Corona Virus Tech Handbook, 268

Costanza-Chock, Sasha, 40, 41–42, 57

COVID-19 pandemic, 107, 182n35, 265

Crash Override, 79, 303. *See also* harassment, online

Crawford, Kate, 51, 239

crawling, 230, 234. *See also* archives and archiving

Creative Commons, 111, 114, 132, 186

crossover books, 197–98. *See also* books and monographs

cross-referencing, 103

crowdsourcing, 232. *See also* funding

Curatescape, 194

curation, 209

cyber events, 245, 265–70, 277. *See also* events

CyberFeminism Index, 167–68

damage, digital, 236–41. *See also* environmental impact

dance, 209, 210. *See also* art

Daniels, Jessie, 23–24, 77

dark ages, digital, 19, 219, 223–26

data and data sets: digital obsolescence and, 223–24; environmental impact of, 10, 238–39; power dynamics of, 6, 13, 19, 127–32, 143–46; tenure and, 64, 66, 68. *See also* open data

Data Feminism (Klein), 6, 68–69, 123

Data for Black Lives, 126

data lakes, 144

deadlines, 283–84

Deaf and hard of hearing communities: accessibility and, 37, 46; events and, 259–60, 261,

262; internet access and, 58; livestreams and, 268; podcasts and, 189, 191, 270; videos and, 171, 177

"A Declaration of the Independence of Cyberspace," 133

deportation, 127. *See also* data and data sets

design and design justice: accessibility and, 35, 40–42, 48, 247, 263; book publishing and, 197; digital technologies and, 5, 7, 47; events and, 252–53; journals and, 46; power dynamics and, 13, 40, 141, 142

websites and, 57–60, 162–63, 165, 167, 168–69, 270. *See also* accessibility

Detroit Community Tech, 213–14

dial-up internet, 53–54. *See also* internet

diamond open access, 90. *See also* openness and open access

digital citizenship, 17, 22–25

Digital Commons, 108

digital dark ages, 19, 219, 223–26

Digital Defense Playbook, 213–14

digital humanities, 226–27

digital technologies: accessibility and, 43–44, 45–49, 51–54; apps, 193–95; artistic works and, 210–11; audiobooks, 207–8; challenges of, 137; comics and, 202, 203; environmental impact of, 10, 54–55, 218, 235–41; events and, 245, 261–65, 265–70, 274, 276; financial considerations, 50; labour of, 147; maintenance and preservation of, 19, 219, 220–23, 227–30, 232–35; obsolescence and, 223–26; open access and, 18, 89–90, 103, 108–9; open source and, 119–20; paywalls and, 115; physical media and, 196, 211–16; podcasts, 179–93; in post-truth era, 23–24; power dynamics and,

7, 19, 48–49, 125–31, 141–48, 160; public scholarship and, 4, 6–7, 12–13, 17, 18–19, 21, 195; searchability and, 285–89; social media, 28–31; videos, 170–78; websites and, 57–60, 162–70

D'Ignazio, Catherine, 6, 68–69, 123, 143

direct messaging, 288

Directory of Open Access Repositories, 105

"Disability Standards for Multimedia on the Web," 58

disability studies, 35, 38–40

Disability Visibility (Wong), 39, 140, 205

disabled communities: accessibility and, 17, 37, 40, 43, 46, 50, 61; assistive technologies and, 45–49; books and, 207; comics and, 202; demographics, 38–39; events and, 244, 247, 249, 251–53, 259–64, 268; internet access and, 58; open access and, 101; open source and, 120; plain-language versions and, 204–6; podcasts and, 189, 191, 270; public scholarship and, 3, 4, 5, 37, 45–46, 310; social media and, 158; videos and, 171, 177; websites and, 41, 57–60, 168

Disrupting Disruptions (podcast), 190

dissemination of knowledge: accessibility and, 33, 37, 46, 48, 52, 116, 215, 310; assistive technologies and, 47; audiobooks and, 207, 208; books and, 197, 198; copyright and, 111; digital technologies and, 5, 48, 50–51, 60; events and, 243, 244–46, 264–65, 269–70; feminism and, 5; financial barriers to, 49; grants and, 11, 26, 87, 311; harassment and, 55; Indigenous communities and, 129–31; language choice and, 44–45, 205, 206, 214; media relations and, 14, 280, 308; open access

and, 89, 91, 93, 94, 95, 103, 118; open data, open source and, 119, 121; podcasts and, 183, 187–89; power dynamics and, 40, 66, 70; public scholarship and, 16, 17, 34, 45, 66, 115, 118; repositories and, 90, 107; social media and, 28, 137, 148, 151; zines and, 199–200. *See also* public scholarship

DIY, 184

DJ (artist), 214

The Documentary Media Society, 179

do it yourself (DIY), 184, 199

domain names, 74, 85, 110, 163, 219, 221, 222, 287. *See also* websites

doxxing. *See* harassment, online

drawing, 202. *See also* art

DSpace, 108. *See also* repositories

Duke University, 304

dynamic websites, 165. *See also* websites

editing software, 173–74, 180, 181, 183. *See also* recording

Edwards, Dustin, 236–37, 238

Elsevier, 85, 86–87, 97, 98, 109. *See also* journals, scholarly

email addresses, 286, 289

Emmett Till Memory Project, 194

emotional labour, 8, 9. *See also* labour

enslavement, 126, 256

environmental impact: AI development and, 10; digital technologies and, 50–51; events and, 258–59; food production and, 258; internet access and, 54; public scholarship and, 4, 5, 14–15, 19, 217–18, 235–41

Eprints, 108. *See also* openness and open access

Equitable Open Data Report, 213

European Commission, 83

events: audio-visual technology for, 261–65; catering and, 257–59; childcare at, 247, 248–49; cost of,

Index

347

249, 250; disseminating materials from, 264–65, 269–70; Facebook and, 154, 155–56; formats for, 244–47; funding for, 272–74; land acknowledgments and, 254–57; language and, 259–61; online, 265–70, 277; overview, 36, 243, 278; in-person, 249–54, 268; publicity for, 274–76; public scholarship and, 19; question and answer periods, 276–77; scheduling, 247–48; speakers, 271–72; Twitter and, 152–53

e-waste, 236, 238, 239. *See also* environmental impact

exhibitions, 209–11. *See also* events

Facebook: accessibility and, 158; direct messaging on, 288; livestreams on, 268; open access and, 111, 133–34; power dynamics and, 142, 143, 145; public scholarship and, 29, 74, 138, 154–56, 157, 159

facial recognition, 145–46

fair dealing, 176–77. *See also* copyright

favicons, 164

feminism and feminist theory, 4, 6–10, 18, 30, 32–33. *See also* public scholarship

Feminist Data Manifest-No, 124

Feminist Internet Project, 56

The Feminist Restaurant Project, 169

feminist scholarship. *See* feminism and feminist theory; public scholarship

Femmes Expertes, 73, 285, 290

Femtechnet, 79, 303

Ferri, Beth A., 48, 49, 59–60

52 Pick-Up, 174–75, 176. *See also* videos

file formats, 175, 219, 224, 229

films. *See* videos

Final Cut Pro, 174

Firefox, 175

Fleet, Chancey, 5, 47, 158–59, 168–69

floppy disks, 224. *See also* obsolescence, digital

Foley, Alan, 48, 49, 59–60

Fonds de Recherche du Québec (FRQ), 87–88

foodtimeline.org, 220–23

450 Movement, 98. *See also* openness and open access

freelancers, 308

FreeMusicArchive.org, 186

Freesound.org, 186

funding: bibliometrics and, 64, 65; book publishing and, 197; events and, 248, 272–73; open access and, 83–84, 87–88, 90, 91, 94–97, 111, 112–14; preservation and, 219, 225, 227, 228; public scholarship and, 25–26, 66, 68, 71, 74, 80–81, 84, 311

Garageband, 186

Geek Feminism, 79, 303

General Data Protection Regulation (GDPR), 122

GetTheResearch, 109

Getting It Published (Germano), 197

gold open access, 89, 92, 95, 96, 98, 113

Google: apps and, 194–95; events and, 251, 263, 268, 277; open access and, 97; podcasts and, 191; power dynamics and, 142; repositories and, 108; videos and, 178; websites and, 162, 163, 164

grants. *See* funding

graphic novels, 201–3, 214. *See also* art

Greenhow, Christine, 28, 29–30, 161

green open access, 90, 96–97, 99, 104, 105, 106, 109, 112–13

H.264 videos, 175

harassment, online: accessibility and, 55–57; events and, 266, 267; media relations and, 285, 298–

Engage in Public Scholarship! 348

301, 309; public scholarship and, 55–57, 75–80, 302–3; social media and, 153–54; websites and, 286n7

hard of hearing communities. *See* Deaf and hard of hearing communities

Harnad, Stevan, 100, 106, 107

hashtags, 30, 110–11, 158–59

hearing loops, 262. *See also* events

Hindenburg, 185. *See also* audio editing

Historical Cooking Project, 169–70

hosts, 182–83. *See also* podcasts

How to DiscoTech (zine), 213

HTML (Hypertext Markup Language), 164, 165, 166, 175, 212, 221

Humanities Commons, 288

hybrid events, 244–45, 265, 269

hybrid open access, 90, 98. *See also* openness and open access

Hypertext Markup Language (HTML), 164, 165, 166, 175, 212, 221

#ICanHazPDF, 111. *See also* openness and open access

idioms, 44. *See also* language and jargon

images: accessibility and, 4, 46, 59, 158; events and, 263; politics of, 131, 297–98; public scholarship and, 138, 202–3; social media and, 144, 151, 155, 156; trigger warnings and, 140n4; websites and, 165, 168

Imagining America, 64. *See also* tenure and promotion

immigrant communities, 77, 127, 132, 258. *See also* people of colour

iMovie, 174. *See also* videos

inclusivity. *See* accessibility

Indigenous communities, 53, 124, 129–31, 132, 255–56. *See also* people of colour

Indigenous Protocol and Artificial Intelligence Working Group, 130

Informed Opinions, 73, 285, 290

Initiative for Open Abstracts, 102

in-person events, 244–45, 249–54, 261–65, 268

Instagram, 143, 145, 156, 159, 268, 288

International Association of Conference Interpreters, 260

Internet: accessibility and, 4, 46–47, 51–55, 57, 223; digital dark ages and, 224–25; environmental impact of, 10, 236–37; events online and, 269; harassment on, 55–57, 75–80; labour of, 147; open access and, 89, 103, 133–34; to physical media, 211–12; podcasts and, 180; power dynamics and, 52–55, 141–42; public scholarship and, 5–7, 24; videos and, 175; web design and, 57–60

Internet Archive, 221, 224–25, 229–30, 233

interpreters, 32, 125, 171, 253, 259, 260–61. *See also* language and jargon

interviews, 280, 281–85, 286, 289, 290–95, 296–97

Intro to Feminist and Social Justice Studies Course Podcast, 182

iTunes, 187. *See also* Apple

jargon and language use, 42–45, 116–17, 204–6, 245, 259–61, 262–63, 280, 305

JavaScript, 164n6, 168

Java Server Pages (JSP), 165

Java Servlets, 165

Jitsi, 267. *See also* events

Joler, Vladan, 51, 239

journalism. *See* media and journalism

journals, scholarly: accessibility and, 117; author rights and, 104–6; open access and, 89–90, 92–96, 98–99, 101–3; paywalls and, 83, 84–88, 98; podcasts and, 188; shadow libraries and, 110

JSTOR, 112

Index

349

Kennedy School Communications Program, 306

keywords, 158, 162, 178, 189. *See also* search engines

Kite, Suzanne, 130–31, 239–40

Klein, Lauren, 6, 68–69, 123, 143

labour: audiobooks and, 208; digital technologies and, 147, 239; events and, 271–72; food preparation and, 257–58; institutional support for, 80; maintenance and, 219; media relations and, 279; open access and, 89, 91, 97, 99, 114, 118, 132–33; open source and, 120–21; preservation and, 233–34; public scholarship and, 8, 9, 18, 19, 21, 63, 66–67, 97, 147; sustainability and, 217–18; zines and, 200

lactation rooms, 254. *See also* events

Lakota epistemology, 240

land acknowledgments, 254–57. *See also* events

Lange, Jessica, 93, 105

language and jargon, 42–45, 116–17, 204–6, 245, 259–61, 262–63, 280, 305

Latinx communities, 53. *See also* people of colour

leaflets, 199–200

lectures. *See* events

Lesbian Herstory Archives (LHA), 231

letters to the editor, 306. *See also* opinion editorials

LGBTQ2S+ communities: archives and, 230–31, 232; citational practices and, 20; data and, 6, 127, 131–32, 146; events and, 271; harassment online and, 55, 75; media relations and, 285; open access and, 82; open source and, 120; podcasts and, 184; washroom access and, 253

libraries: events and, 218, 250, 264; open access and, 94, 99–100, 102, 108, 112; paywalls and, 83, 84;

podcasts and, 189; preservation and, 221, 225, 226–27, 230, 234; repositories and, 107; shadow, 109–10; zines and, 200

Libsyn, 187. *See also* podcasts

LinkedIn, 288

listservs, 276

literacy, 23, 24, 43, 45

Little Brain Comics, 201. *See also* art

livestreams, 264, 268

live tweeting, 152–53. *See also* events

Logic Pro X, 186. *See also* audio editing

longevity. *See* maintenance and preservation

L'Ordre des traducteurs, terminologues et interprètes agréés du Québec, 261

machine learning (ML), 144–46. *See also* algorithms

magazines, 291, 295. *See also* media and journalism

Maintainers (listserv), 120

maintenance and preservation: challenges of, 219, 235; digital obsolescence and, 223–26; environmental impact of, 235–41; food timeline case study, 220–23; overview, 218–19; podcasts and, 184; public scholarship and, 5, 218, 242; strategies for, 226–34; websites and, 165–68

Manifold, 112. *See also* openness and open access

marginalized communities: accessibility and, 17, 37, 40, 43, 44, 46, 50, 61, 62; archives and, 230–31, 232; assistive technologies and, 45–49; audiobooks and, 207; citations and, 20–21; comics and, 202; data and, 6, 12, 124, 125, 127, 129–32, 143–46, 287; digital technologies and, 12, 50, 55, 147, 237–38; events and, 244, 247,

Engage in Public Scholarship!

249, 251–53, 257–58, 259–64, 268, 271–72; feminism and, 9; harassment online and, 55, 75–80, 142, 150, 298; internet access and, 52–54, 55, 56, 58; journals and, 49–51; land acknowledgments and, 255–56; media relations and, 73, 285, 296, 297, 298–301; op-eds and, 307; open access and, 82–83, 100–101, 132, 133; open data and, 125–32; open source and, 120–21; plain language and, 204–6; podcasts and, 184, 189, 191, 270; project maintenance and, 230–32; public scholarship and, 3, 4, 5, 18, 21, 37, 45–46, 147, 310, 313; research practices and, 44–45; slow violence and, 237–38; social media and, 30, 150, 158, 266; tenure and, 65–66; trigger warnings and, 139; videos and, 171, 177; and voice, politics of, 192, 297; websites and, 40, 41, 57–60, 168; zines and, 199, 200
marketing, 144–45. *See also* data and data sets
McGregor, Hannah, 9, 12n20, 45, 63, 116, 179
McKinney, Cait, 7, 211, 231
McLean, Jessica, 10, 236
McLeod, Dayna, 174, 176
media and journalism: benefits of, 280–81, 308; challenges of, 296–97, 308–9; harassment and, 285, 298–301; interviews, 281–85, 289; interviews, navigation of, 290–95; op-ed writing, 27–28, 68, 279, 303–8; paywalls and, 115; press kits and, 289–90; public scholarship and, 19, 66–67, 73, 117–18, 279; requests and demands of, 295–96; resources for, 301–3; searchability and, 285–89; voice and image, politics of, 296–97
Métis in Space (podcast), 182–83

microphones, 184–85, 261–62, 263, 269
Microsoft, 142, 263
Milner, Yeshimabeit, 126, 132
mining, 240. *See also* environmental impact
Minnesota Environments, 193–94
Missing Datasets (Onuoha), 6, 127
Mixcloud, 187. *See also* podcasts
mobile devices, 173, 180, 184
monographs and books, 111–14, 197–98, 201–2, 212, 233, 280
Mozilla, 169
MP3 files, 179, 183
MP4 files, 175
music, 209–11. *See also* podcasts

names and naming, 287
Native Land Digital, 255
natural language processing (NLP), 10, 144. *See also* data and data sets
neoliberalism, 17, 67
Netflix, 142
Netscape Navigator, 228–29. *See also* maintenance and preservation
New Books Network, 193
Newman, Shawn, 5, 46
newspapers. *See* media and journalism
New York Times, 115, 305
Noble, Safiya Umoja, 6, 143–44

OAISter, 103. *See also* openness and open access
Obama administration, 122
obsolescence, digital, 223–26, 228–29. *See also* digital technologies
Ogg, 175. *See also* videos
Ologies Podcast (Ward), 181
Omeka, 194. *See also* apps
O'Neil Cathy, 6, 143
online events, 245, 265–70, 277. *See also* events
Onuoha, Mimi, 6, 126–27, 132, 146, 214

Index

351

OpEd Project, 307

op-eds, 27–28, 68, 279, 303–8. *See also* media and journalism

open access. *See* openness and open access

Open Archives Initiative Protocol for Metadata Harvesting (OAIPMH), 103

open data: accessibility and, 134; benefits of, 123; limitations for, 124–25, 126, 127–32; overview, 14, 18, 119, 121–23; power dynamics and, 121–22, 123–24, 125–32. *See also* data and data sets

Open Data Directive, 122

open educational resources (OER), 114

Opening Data (zine), 213

openness and open access: accessibility and, 100–101, 116–18, 133–34; alternative and informal models of, 99–100, 109–11; author rights and, 104–6; benefits of, 101–3; definition and models of, 88–92, 98–99; financial challenges, 95–99, 106–7; labour of, 97, 132–33; meanings of, 31; for monographs, 111–14; myths about, 92–93; overview, 18, 82–83; paywalls and, 83–86, 86–88, 115; power dynamics in, 82, 100–101, 128, 132; promotion and perceptions of, 93, 94; repositories and, 104–9; social media and, 29; for textbooks, 114

Open Publishing Fest, 128

Openshot, 174. *See also* videos

open source, 119–21, 132, 134, 194, 195

opinion editorials (op-eds), 27–28, 68, 279, 303–8. *See also* media and journalism

otter.ai, 190, 270. *See also* transcription

pamphlets, 199–200, 227, 233

panels. *See* events

paywalls: academic research and, 26, 68, 83–86; accessibility and, 4, 49–51; for non-academic resources, 115; open access and, 82, 90; podcasts and, 180; profits from, 97–98; public scholarship and, 7, 26, 67; resistance to, 86–88, 110–11

Pay What You Can (PWYC), 274

PDFs, 111, 212

pedagogy, 189

peer review: accessibility and, 83, 84, 117; critiques of, 20; open access and, 87, 92–93, 94, 98, 99; podcasts and, 12n20, 68; public scholarship and, 36–37, 68–69; repositories and, 107; social media and, 29; tenure and, 63, 65, 68, 71

people of colour: citational practices and, 20; data and, 6, 12, 124, 125, 127, 129–31, 132, 144, 146; design justice and, 41; digital technologies and, 50, 55; events and, 257–58, 271; harassment online and, 55, 75, 76, 77, 142, 150; internet access and, 53; land acknowledgments and, 255–56; media relations and, 285, 296, 297; open access and, 82, 133; open source and, 120; public scholarship and, 3, 18, 147, 310; social media and, 30, 150, 158; trigger warnings and, 139; and voice, politics of, 192

A People's Guide to AI, 214

The People's Platform (Taylor), 23, 133

performance, 209–11. *See also* art

Periscope, 268. *See also* Twitter

Perl, 165. *See also* coding

PHP, 165. *See also* coding

physical media, self-produced: audiobooks and, 207–8; books, 197–98, 212; comics, cartoons, and graphic novels, 201–3; digital technologies and, 196, 211–16;

Engage in Public Scholarship! 352

environmental impact of, 235–36; exhibitions, art, music, and performance, 209–11; overview, 196; plain-language versions, 204–6; policy briefs and reports, 203–4; preservation of, 233; zines, bookettes, and pamphlets, 199–200

Pirate Care Syllabus, 166

pirating, 109–10

plain language, 204–6. *See also* language and jargon

Plan S, 87. *See also* openness and open access

platinum open access, 90, 95, 99, 113

plug-ins, 142, 166, 168, 263

PodBean, 180, 187

podcasts: accessibility and, 46, 74, 188, 191, 193; captions and, 178; editing, 185–86; gender politics of, 191–92; genres of, 180–82; hosting, 180, 181; interviews for, 292, 293; online events and, 269–70; overview, 179–80; peer review and, 12n20, 68; preservation of, 233; production of, 180, 181, 183; as public scholarship, 13, 187–88, 193; recording, 183–85; releasing and sharing, 186–87; remote teaching and, 182n35; roles and tasks, 182–83; as teaching tools, 189; tenure and, 64; transcription of, 189–91, 192

policy briefs, 203–4

policy making, 26–28

pop screens or filters, 185. *See also* recording

posters, 227, 233, 275

post-prints, 105, 107, 108. *See also* repositories

post-truth era, 17, 22–25, 28, 68, 311

Potts, Karen, 20, 33, 44–45

power dynamics: accessibility and, 17–18, 37, 61, 62–63, 70–71; algorithms and, 6, 13, 19, 126, 143–45, 146, 287; citational

practices and, 20–21, 65; data and, 6, 13, 19, 121–22, 123–24, 125–32, 143–46; design and, 13, 40, 141, 142; digital technologies and, 7, 19, 48–49, 125–31, 141–48, 160; events and, 257–58, 271–72, 276–77; financial barriers and, 50; harassment online and, 55–56, 77, 298; internet access and, 52–55, 141–42; knowledge and, 32–33; land acknowledgments and, 255–56; language and, 44–45; media and, 285, 296–301; op-eds and, 307; open access and, 82, 100–101, 128, 132; open source and, 120–21; podcasts and, 191–92; preservation and, 230–32; public scholarship and, 3–4, 8–9, 34, 69–70, 141–48, 160, 310–11, 313; publishing and, 5, 12; slow violence and, 237–38; tenure and, 64–66

PowerPoint, 172, 263

pre-prints, 105, 107–8. *See also* repositories

preservation. *See* maintenance and preservation

Preserve This Podcast, 233–34

presses, university, 24–25, 68, 112, 197

press kits, 289–90. *See also* media and journalism

Prezi, 172, 263

printing, 212

Prison Industrial Complex, 126

privacy and privacy settings: data and, 122, 124; social media and, 151, 153, 154, 155, 288; Zoom and, 173, 267

processing charges, 89, 90, 95–96, 98–99, 113. *See also* journals, scholarly

production, digital, 173, 180, 181, 183, 199, 208

production, material, 50, 239. *See also* environmental impact

productivity, 65, 70

Index

programming, 120, 164, 165, 166, 167–68, 176, 195, 221

Project MUSE, 112. *See also* journals, scholarly

promotion. *See* tenure and promotion

public, definition of, 36–37

Public Humanities (Western), 302

Public Humanities Hub (PHH), 302

publicity, 274–76. *See also* media and journalism

Public Library of Science, 96. *See also* libraries

public scholarship: accessibility and, 34, 35–61, 310, 311, 312–13; accessibility for scholars and, 62–81; anti-oppressive framework for, 32–33; assistive technologies and, 45–49, 58; benefits of, 22–34; challenges of, 11–13, 19, 310; compensation and, 70–73, 74, 81, 97–98, 242; from disability studies framework, 38–42; environmental impact of, 4, 5, 10, 14–15, 19, 217–18, 235–41; feminism and, 7–10; financial barriers to, 49–51; harassment online and, 55–57, 75–80, 302–3; importance of, 14–15, 66, 67–68, 312, 313; internet access and, 51–55; labour of, 8, 9, 18, 19, 21, 63, 66–67, 97, 147; language and jargon and, 42–45; limitations to, 37–38, 42; media relations and, 19, 66–67, 73, 117–18, 279; open access and, 82–118, 132–34; open data and, 119, 121–34, 141–48; open source and, 119–21, 133–34; overview, 3–4, 13–18, 21; peer review and, 68–69; power dynamics of, 3–4, 8–9, 34, 69–70, 141–48, 160, 310–11, 313; praxis of, 11–12; preservation and, 5, 218, 242; and public, definition of, 36–37; skills and, 71–75; tenure and, 34, 62–66, 69–71, 72; university support for, 72–73, 80–81, 311; web design and, 57–60

public scholarship toolkits: apps, 193–95; audiobooks, 207–8; books, 197–98, 212; choosing the medium, 137–39; comics, cartoons, and graphic novels, 201–3; digital and physical media, 211–16; events, 243–78; exhibitions, art, music, and performance, 209–11; interviews, 281–85, 290–95; maintenance and preservation, 217–42; maintenance and preservation strategies, 226–35; media and journalism, 279–80, 301–3, 309; media press kits, 289–90; op-ed writing, 303–8; overview, 18–19, 135, 137, 161–62, 195, 196; plain-language versions, 204–6; podcasts, 179–93; policy briefs and reports, 203–4; for repositories, 108; searchability and, 285–89; social media, 29–30, 148–60; trigger and content warnings, 139–41; videos, 170–78; websites and blogs, 58–59, 162–70; zines, bookettes, and pamphlets, 199–200

public transit, 251

publishers: of academic papers, 85; accessibility and, 207, 208; how to choose, 197; open access and, 89, 90, 92, 96–97, 104, 105; paywalls and, 84, 100; power dynamics and, 5; repositories and, 106, 110; university, 24–25, 68, 112, 197; zines and, 200

Punk Scholars Network, 155

Python, 165, 168. *See also* coding

"Queer Archive Activism," 231

queer communities. *See* LGBTQ2S+ communities

question and answer periods, 276–77. *See also* events

radio stations, 275, 284, 292–93. *See also* media and journalism

Engage in Public Scholarship!   354

Raji, Deborah, 125, 145
readings. *See* events
Really Simple Syndication (RSS), 179, 180, 183, 187, 269–70
recording: articles, 188; audiobooks, 208; events and, 263, 264, 267, 269; interviews and, 291, 292, 293; podcasts, 74, 181, 183–85; videos, 172–73, 178; remote teaching, 182n35
reports, 203–4. *See also* physical media, self-produced
repositories: accessibility and, 116; author rights and, 105–6; content quality and, 107–8; financial challenges and, 106–7; funding and, 87; growth of, 104–5; informal models, 109–10; open access and, 90, 97, 99, 100, 104; open data and, 124; searches in, 108–9
research, scholarly. *See* public scholarship
ResearchGate, 109, 288. *See also* journals, scholarly
resolution, video, 175
Rhizome organization, 168, 228–29
right to repair, 10, 19, 220, 224. *See also* environmental impact
Riley, Jenn, 93, 105
Rode Smart Lav, 184. *See also* microphones
RSS feeds, 179, 180, 183, 187, 269–70
Ruby, 165. *See also* coding

Safari, 175. *See also* websites
SAGE Publications, 85. *See also* journals, scholarly
Sagittarian Matters (Georges), 184
Sandvine, 142. *See also* internet
scent-free environments, 253–54
scheduling, 247–48
Scholars Portal, 234
Scholars Portal Dataverse, 230
Sci-Hub, 109, 110. *See also* openness and open access

Scopus, 109. *See also* search engines
screen readers, 43, 46, 59, 158, 168, 264, 270
screen sharing, 172
sea levels, 54. *See also* environmental impact
search engine optimization (SEO), 162
search engines, 6–7, 108–9, 143–44, 158, 162, 189–90, 285–89
Secret Feminist Agenda (McGregor), 63, 68, 179, 191
self-archiving, 89, 90, 94, 97, 99, 100, 104, 106. *See also* archives and archiving
self-silencing, 77, 149, 299. *See also* power dynamics
servers: environmental impact of, 10, 51, 216, 238, 240; public scholarship and, 148; repositories and, 107; websites and, 163, 164, 176
Seu, Mindy, 167–68, 212
shadow libraries, 109–10. *See also* repositories
SHERPA/ROMEO, 104. *See also* openness and open access
SheSource, 73
shortcode, 176. *See also* coding
sign languages, 171, 253, 259, 260. *See also* language and jargon
Simon Fraser University, 179, 311
SimpleCast, 191. *See also* podcasts
slavery, 126, 256
sliding scales, 249, 250, 274
Sli.do, 277. *See also* events
slow violence, 237, 240. *See also* environmental impact
Smartify, 194. *See also* apps
social media: accessibility and, 11, 158–59; benefits and limitations, 149–50; choosing the medium, 150–51, 159; data extraction and, 144–45; event publicity and, 276; Facebook, overview, 154–56;

Index

harassment online and, 75, 76–77, 149–50, 266, 301; Instagram, overview, 156; open access and, 103; to physical media, 212; power dynamics of, 143; preservation and, 222; privacy features on, 154; public scholarship and, 28–31, 67, 74, 148–49; searchability and, 288; sharing across platforms, 157; tenure and, 66; TikTok, overview, 156–57; Twitter, overview, 151–54. *See also specific platforms*

social scholarship, 28, 29–30. *See also* public scholarship

Social Sciences and Humanities Research Council of Canada, 11, 26, 87, 248, 311. *See also* funding

solar power, 176

Soundcloud, 187

sound repositories, 186. *See also* repositories

sovereignty, data, 130, 146. *See also* data and data sets

SPARC Canadian Author Addendum, 105

SpeechTexter, 190, 270

speech-to-text, 177

Spoken Word (podcast), 179

sponsorship, 274. *See also* funding

Spotify, 180, 187

Springer, 85, 97. *See also* journals, scholarly

Squarespace, 163, 286. *See also* websites

static websites, 165

stewardship, data, 130, 131. *See also* data and data sets

Stitcher, 187. *See also* podcasts

STQRY, 194. *See also* apps

student groups, 272

student journalism, 291

Suber, Peter, 89, 133

subscriptions: accessibility and, 50; for digital content, 115; digital preservation and, 229, 232; journals and, 83–84, 85; open

access and, 95, 98, 99, 101, 102; shadow libraries and, 110; videos and, 172; websites and, 166

sunsetting, 19, 218, 219, 220, 226, 228, 232

supply chains, 19, 239. *See also* environmental impact

sustainability. *See* environmental impact; maintenance and preservation

Tarnoff, Ben, 121–22, 124

Tascam DR100 mkii, 185. *See also* recording

taxes, 26, 84, 94, 96

Taylor, Astra, 23, 133, 240–41

Taylor Francis, 85, 97. *See also* journals, scholarly

techno-utopianism, 18, 133, 240

television interviews, 293–95, 298. *See also* media and journalism

tenure and promotion: book publishing and, 197; open access and, 93, 94–95, 97; public scholarship and, 34, 62–66, 69–71, 72; universities and, 79, 80

territorial acknowledgments, 254–57. *See also* events

textbooks, 114. *See also* openness and open access

theme-song music, 186. *See also* podcasts

Thompson, Irene, 101, 102, 103

tickets, 249, 273–74. *See also* events

TikTok, 156–57, 288

toolkits. *See* public scholarship toolkits

trade books, 197–98. *See also* physical media, self-produced

transcription: audio files and, 182n35, 270; events and, 262–63; podcasts and, 37, 183, 189–91; power dynamics and, 192; social media and, 158; videos and, 172, 178

Transistor, 187. *See also* podcasts

translation, 43, 205, 259–61, 262–63

Engage in Public Scholarship!

Tri-Agency Open Access Policy on Publications, 101–2
trigger and content warnings, 139–41
trolling. *See* harassment, online
Truth and Reconciliation Commission of Canada, 256
Twitch TV, 268
Twitter: accessibility and, 158; citations and, 148; direct messaging on, 288; maintenance and, 222; open access and, 110–11; to physical media, 212; power dynamics and, 143; for public scholarship, 29–30, 74, 151–54, 159; resistance on, 30, 70, 150; sharing across platforms, 157; tenure and, 66

"UC Access Now Demandifesto," 247
UK Home Office, 263
universal design (UD), 40, 247. *See also* design and design justice
universal resource locators (URLs), 163. *See also* websites
universities: accessibility for scholars and, 62–63; audio-visual technologies and, 173, 264; events and, 246–47, 272–73; media relations and, 281–83, 286, 290, 302, 304, 306, 309; media resources and, 301–3; monographs and, 112; online harassment and, 78–80, 298–301, 302; open access and, 93, 94, 96, 99–100; paywalls and, 83–85, 86, 87–88; podcasts and, 179; in post-truth era, 24–25; preservation of scholarship and, 230, 231; public accountability and, 25–28; public scholarship and, 72–73, 80–81, 311; repositories and, 105, 106; tenure and, 63–65, 69–71, 80
University of British Columbia, 96, 246, 302
Unpaywall, 108–9. *See also* journals, scholarly

UpperGoer6, 206. *See also* plain language
URLs, 163. *See also* websites
USB microphones, 184–85
utopianism, 18, 133, 240

venues, 245, 248, 249–54, 258, 262
versioning, 103. *See also* openness and open access
video chat and conferencing, 172–73, 266–68
videos: accessibility and, 55, 74, 172; captioning and, 59, 158, 177–78; copyright law and, 176–77; creation, strategies for, 172–73; data extraction and, 144; editing, 173–74; events and, 263; formats for, 170–72; hosting and uploading, 174–76; online events and, 269; podcasts vs., 179; as public scholarship, 170; social media and, 148, 151, 156–57; trigger warnings and, 140n4; websites and, 165, 169
Vimeo, 174, 178, 269
violence, online. *See* harassment, online
virtual events, 245, 265–70, 277. *See also* events
visual impairments. *See* Blind communities
voice, politics of, 191–92, 297–98. *See also* power dynamics

W3C Publishing Working Group, 207
washrooms, 253–54. *See also* events
Wayback Machine, 221, 225, 234, 235. *See also* archives and archiving
Weapons of Math Destruction (O'Neil), 6, 143. *See also* algorithms
webcomics, 203. *See also* art
Web Content Accessibility Guidelines (WCAG), 168, 270
web design, 57–60, 162–63, 165, 167, 168–69, 270. *See also* design and design justice; websites

Index

357

WebM, 175. *See also* videos

Web of Science, 109. *See also* journals, scholarly

websites: accessibility and, 168–69, 270; apps and, 194; builders for, 162–64, 165–66; comics and, 203; digital dark ages and, 224–25; events and, 270; physical media and, 212, 233; press kits and, 289–90; as public scholarship, 162, 169–70; searchability and, 286, 289; sustainability and longevity of, 165–68, 219–23, 229–30, 234–35; types and categorization, 164–65; videos and, 175

Weebly, 163, 286. *See also* websites

wheelchair users, 251–53. *See also* disabled communities

Who Pays Writers? (website), 308. *See also* media and journalism

Wiley-Blackwell, 85, 97. *See also* journals, scholarly

Wilfrid Laurier University Press, 68, 179

Williams, Sherri, 30, 150

Wix, 163, 286. *See also* websites

Women Also Know History, 285. *See also* interviews

Wong, Alice, 39, 140–41, 205–6

Wordpress, 163, 286. *See also* websites

World Wide Web Consortium (W3C), 58, 59

Writing and Publishing Your Book (Herr), 197

"Writing Policy Briefs and Reports" (McIvor), 203–4

YouTube, 171, 174, 176, 177–78, 190, 268, 269, 277

Zencastr, 181. *See also* recording

zines, 199–200, 213, 227, 233

Zoom, 172, 173, 178, 190, 264, 267, 277

Zuckerberg, Mark, 133–34